T DIVINE ARCHITECT

THE ART OF LIVING AND BEYOND

Robert Perala

WITH

Tony Stubbs

Gretchen,
Your Spirit Shines Bright
And Lights The Way
For Many....
Blessings of Light
Robert Perala
2013

THE DIVINE ARCHITECT

THE ART OF LIVING AND BEYOND

ROBERT PERALA

Author of *The Divine Blueprint*

with

TONY STUBBS

Author of *An Ascension Handbook*

UNITED LIGHT PUBLISHING
SCOTTS VALLEY, CA

The Divine Architect: The Art of Living and Beyond
by
Robert Perala
with Tony Stubbs

Copyright © 2002   Robert Perala
First printing: Spring 2002
Second Printing: Spring 2006

ISBN 0-9663130-9-7

05 04 03 02   0 9 8 7 6 5 4 3 2

Published by
UNITED LIGHT PUBLISHING
PO BOX 66918
SCOTTS VALLEY, CA 95067
PHINE: (831) 345-0825
FAX: (831) 440-0445
E-MAIL: robert@unitedlight.com
INTERNET: www.unitedlight.com

Cover design by Norman Paul and Glen Wexler Studios

Author's cover photo by Tim Coleman

Printed in the USA

Contents

Dedication

This book is dedicated to my darling Dr. Joanne Lyon, whose love, light and wisdom have touched my soul. I am forever grateful for you being my biggest support.

Acknowledgments

I would like to thank those Divine Architects of our time who have inspired me with their timeless wisdom, insight and contributions in the fields of spirituality and personal growth.

To Tony Stubbs for his invaluable insight, wisdom, and contribution, for without him, this book would not have been the same. If you are looking for assistance in writing and publishing, you can contact him through the publisher.

To Dannion Brinkley, whose wonderful ongoing support has touched me so deeply.

To Tony Robbins, whose passionate wisdom has been a constant inspiration to my life and goals.

Special thanks go to Gregg Braden, John Edward, Deepak Chopra, Elisabeth Kübler-Ross, Bill and Judy Guggenheim, Marge Cuddeback, Drunvalo Melchizedek, George Harrison and his sister Louise, Dr. Diane Thorson, Shanta Shenoy, Dr. Jennifer Lendl, Nancy Stillings, Richard Boylan, Marge Rieder, Serena Wright, Robert Gerard, John Broeck, Deborah Welsh, Tricia McCannon, Tom and Walda Woods, Dr. Joel Whitton, George Anderson, Shirley MacLaine, and His Holiness the Dalai Lama.

Many thanks and blessings to my family and son, Christian.

To my spirit guides, whose tireless efforts astound and amaze me.

To my mother and father in heaven. Till we meet again …

Thank you, God.

Foreword by Dannion Brinkley

When you sense your own divinity, you feel many things, especially your true nature and the creator God. You are a particular point of the Creator itself. You and the Creator are one and the same. To think that you are in any way separate is only an illusion that you agreed to hold, backed up by the misinformation handed down to you by those who thought they knew life's universal truths. What you deliberately agreed to forget at birth was the intimate knowledge that you and God are one together. Letting go of this illusion now would allow you to walk in so much more joy and harmony, knowing that you are truly living your Divine Blueprint within the Creator.

Your blueprint, or the game-plan you mapped out for this life, is becoming increasingly evident to you as well as to others, due largely to the energies that are now coming into the planet. And those people with interlocking blueprints are coming together to form teams, for be in no doubt, ascension is a team effort. No one person can "do it all." We all have pieces of the whole puzzle, and to be effective, those pieces must be joined together, just as in a jigsaw puzzle.

You carry a very special piece of the Divine Blueprint. The question is what are you going to do with all this knowledge? As a way-shower, you have one of the greatest opportunities in the course of human evolution—the chance to step forward with some of the most significant information this planet has ever known. All your experiences, the books you've read, and the lectures and workshops you've attended add up to a huge body of wisdom. How well you own and use that wisdom is up to you.

We are alive at the most exciting time in human history, standing at a crossroads. One road leads to a fear-based paradigm of materialism, greed, and fear of death. The other road leads to a love-based world of spirituality, service, miracles, and the loss of fear.

Many fine books today point the way to the love-based road, and one of them is in your hands right now. We are mighty and powerful beings but often get distracted by the world around us, and act in ways that harm ourselves and others—something that we must deal with once we arrive on the other side.

Most people wait until their panoramic life review after death to examine sometimes the joy and sometimes the harm they've caused. I endorse the recommendation in this book to conduct a life review *before* you cross over. Examine every relationship, past and present, and gauge how loving and how supportive you are. Try to see yourself through the other person's eyes and to see ways to avoid causing pain. As you read this book, keep in mind the religious phrases, "Love thy neighbor as thyself," or, "Do unto others as they would do unto you." You will discover this is the true nature of the panoramic life review. It's all just really you.

Hopefully, by the time you've finished the book, you too will see, as do I that life is a wonderful learning experience. "Death" is just another opportunity to excel and grow—a true cause for celebration.

— Dannion Brinkley

Preface

The Divine Architect. Why such a grand title? Because of the grand subject matter, namely you, the reader. Yes, this book is about you and what you do. You may not know this, but you create reality. You do it by virtue of what you think, every second of every day. If you consistently have fearful thoughts, the chances are that you're creating a pretty scary reality for yourself. If you consistently have loving thoughts, you are probably a lot more comfortable with what comes your way. From the enormous range of all possible outcomes available to you in any given situation, your thoughts select what you will experience. It's that simple. You get to choose.

You have been choosing all your life, of course, probably without knowing it. Centuries ago, religions hid that little fact from humanity, and we've been running on autopilot ever since. Well, this book is about reclaiming your conscious reality creation skills and putting them to good use—the conscious evolution of our species. You are a vital player in this grand scheme, and this book shows you how to be a conscious player. *That* deserves a grand title.

There is more to the story, of course, for there's more to you than you ever thought possible. You're much more magnificent than the person you see in the mirror or on your driver's license. Your primary identity is soul, and you've been around a long time. Forever actually. And you'll be around for a lot longer yet. You guessed it. Forever. You're on one of your periodic field trips down to the physical plane, which is why you don't remember too much about yourself. Forgetting who you *really* are is a condition of playing the game, for knowing that would spoil everything, like having the answers to a test ahead of time. Where's the fun in that? No surprises. No challenges. No growth. Boring.

My life seems to consist of one paranormal event after another—apparitions, celestial visitations and messages from the other side. Truth be known, everyone's life is filled with these phenomena but, in my case, I consciously look out for them. For example, a synchronous event is just coincidence until you see the miracle and magic behind it. Unfortunately, parents, schools and religions rob most children of the magic, so their young lives soon become devoid of the Great Mystery.

A major force that propelled me on to the spiritual path was an intense curiosity about how the universe works. Going after the answers I sought actually opened up my innate psychic abilities even further. Things are rarely what they seem on the surface. I recommend going through life with your eyes wide open, questioning everything for its inner significance. Your life can only be as rich as your belief system will allow, and your spirit guides can help you only as much as you will let them. Hopefully, this book will encourage you to open up your belief systems and let the miracles in.

Some of the extraordinary material in this book has been given to me by my guides during their nocturnal visitations, encounters that invariably leave me feeling humbled, blessed and greatly loved. I'm amused when researchers scan the heavens looking for intelligent life when, in fact, it's all around and inside us. The world is teeming with life that exists just above physical plane frequencies. Guides, angels, elementals, devas, the deceased, and some ET species abound at every turn, usually just going about their business and often paying us little heed. They're just on the other channels of the "celestial TV set."

You also exist on many of these other channels. So how can you integrate your various component selves—body, emotions, mind, spirit, and soul? If you surf the World Wide Web on the Internet, you link from site to site, following your interests. The more you surf, the more extensive your familiarity of a topic becomes. So, as with any subject, the more branches you explore, the wider your knowledge becomes and the more a part of your life it becomes. Ideally, you can immerse yourself totally, reading widely and meeting other like-minded people for the exchange of ideas. Once you begin to have conscious conversations with your guides, you open up to a whole new dimension of input.

Introduction

It is said that Leonardo da Vinci was the last person on Earth who knew everything. Since the days of that gifted scholar, artist, and inventor, human knowledge has burgeoned in every direction, and no one can claim to know "everything." In putting together such an ambitious book as this, Tony and I are the first to admit that we, too, do not. For this reason, we have reported on the work of several specialists in their field and bring you what we think of as "the best of the best" for the most comprehensive coverage of this enormous subject. All books mentioned are listed at the end.

In this book, we weave together the fine work of motivational speakers, mystics, paranormal researchers, psychic mediums, and even a few speakers from the other side. After all, who better to describe the afterlife than those already enjoying it? So, our gift to you, dear reader, is a smorgasbord that begins when the soul prepares to undertake an Earth plane life, and ends when it returns to resume its "interlife" activities. But Tony and I are more than just reporters, for you will find much more hidden among the brilliant work of those we cover. You will discover two Divine Architects who, like you, are trying to put the puzzle pieces of the Great Mystery together.

It happens every five seconds or so on planet Earth. A soul incarnates in a new body and begins a new human life, an experience that will last from a few seconds to maybe a century. Only the soul and its spiritual advisors know for sure what that life will accomplish and, even then, only the *probable* outcome.

Seconds after birth, even the soul begins to lose touch with home base, its point of departure and ultimate return, as this Divine Architect squeezes into the tiny body that will be its home and partner for the duration. That partnership could result in a brilliant mind that saves countless lives or one that takes them. Or it could be snuffed out after a few days as the body succumbs to disease or hunger. Only the higher self knows.

This book explores the experiences of these Divine Architects, those brave souls who leave the warm, loving soul plane and undertake what souls agree is the most arduous venture that any soul can tackle—a life on planet Earth, acknowledged as *the* densest environment for learning and growth *anywhere*.

Chapter 1 picks up the story as a soul begins its journey, defining its goals and choosing the circumstances of its next life. We examine the factors that it must consider, the myriad decisions it must make and its preparations for the trip ahead.

In Chapter 2, we follow the soul once it has taken up residence in its new home and watch as it "falls asleep" under the countless daily influences that shape who we become. We examine probably the greatest influence on who we think we are—organized religion—and explore the spiritually based institutions that they could be.

All souls have the potential for greatness and a life of joy and happiness, but how many of us achieve them? In Chapter 3, we look at a few shining stars who have risen above the herd and share their secrets. But many of us fall asleep at the wheel of life and live on "autopilot" so that one day we can hopefully wake up. Chapter 4 explores some of the countless ways in which souls wake egos up to the truth of who they *really* are.

For 6 – 8 hours a day, our conscious mind rests, leaving the soul and subconscious mind in charge. When we reawaken and review the apparent chaos of our dreams, we can often discover nuggets of information and insight into who we really are and changes that we need to make in our lives. Chapter 5 looks at the wonderful world of dreams and who the dreamer really is.

As brave new souls come to the Earth plane every few seconds, eager to learn and grow, souls who have completed their life mission head back home. Inevitably, one or more of those will be people we love, and we will experience the pain of loss in our lives. From their perspective, they have just "slipped into the next room" to wait for us and are still actively engaged in learning and growth, even though most of us cannot see or hear them. Chapter 6 explores the fascinating world of psychic mediums, those gifted people who serve as "two-way radios" to the other side, and bring us messages of love and reassurance from across the veil. And Chapter 7 introduces you to your own sixth sense and shows you how you can hone it and contact the soul plane directly.

Chapter 8 deals with the grief of losing physical contact with our loved ones when they cross over and opens us up to new levels of compassion for ourselves and others. Before we take a deeper look at life on the other side, Chapters 9 and 10 take a brief detour into some fascinating ancient wisdom that has been largely lost to us today.

Chapter 11 prepares us for the fact that one day our own sojourn on Earth will be over when, as a soul, we will decide, "It's a wrap," and slip out of our body.

What can we expect of our new life, free of many limitations of the Earth plane? A soul's return home is cause for great joy and celebration on the other side, and thousands may attend our "welcome home" party. Then, after a period of healing and reorientation, you (the soul) reviews your most recent life and rejoins your soul group. To those who stayed on the soul plane, only moments have passed, and you resume whatever you were studying and researching exactly where you left off.

The best way to avoid an uncomfortable life review once you arrive on that side is not to do anything on this side for which you are ashamed. Chapter 12 offers guidance on acting spiritually so that we can avoid generating karma with anyone, including ourselves. It also talks about the new Indigo Children currently incarnating and the changes that our DNA is going through.

So sit back and join us for a wild ride as we explore the Divine Architect's greatest creation so far—the life you are leading at the moment. By the end of this book, you will know *much* more about the magnificent being you truly are. Gone will be the days when you can look in the mirror without being in awe of your own reflection, for you, too, are a Divine Architect engaged in manifesting your own piece of the Divine Blueprint.

Chapter 1

Before You Were Born

THE WHOLE PURPOSE of this Earth game is for you, as part of the Creator Source, to learn *everything* about yourself. That's why you need all those lifetimes and not just one. And you can do that *only* if you don't know you are part of Source. It's easy to be loving in a loving environment. So, to really test your understanding of love, you've got to go where love is in short supply. Therefore, you come down here, put on a disguise, forget your true identity and play your part. In the midst of all the hatred and fear on the Earth plane, how does your love stand up? Can you walk your talk?

As a soul, you've done it hundreds of times—slip into a new body, live out a life full of experiences on the physical plane and return home to digest those experiences.

Why go to all the trouble? Why not just "play it out" on the soul plane? Simple. Because you would know two crucial things: 1) that you *are* just playing a game, and 2) that the goal of the game is to express unconditional love in every situation. Knowing this, where's the challenge and growth? Just like an actor who "dies" in Act III, you would get up, wash off the fake blood and go home, having learned nothing.

The physical plane is a brilliant plan when you think about it. You-the-soul deals a hand for a lifetime, and you-the-soul and you-the-ego together play that hand, usually taking it oh-so-seriously.

Who are the other players in your game of life? Usually, other souls from your *soul group* (of maybe a thousand souls) incarnate to be supporting actors on the stage of your life, just as you are a supporting actor in their life play. You normally draw the more intimate players, such as your parents and lovers, from your *soul family*, a band of maybe a dozen souls whom you get to know really well over countless incarnations. You also hang out with your soul family members between lifetimes.

Complicating matters in your life plays is the fact that every actor is reading from a different script, as if one is doing *General Hospital* and the other *All My Children*. In the resulting confusion, missed cues and fluffed lines are inevitable, so it's really amazing that we communicate at all, let alone so well.

A famous teacher used to teach by telling stories—he called them parables—because stories allow you to couch truth more softly and in ways that people can relate to. In the same vein, I'm going to tell a story about you-the-soul and a lifetime you could easily have led if you'd so chosen. (Because souls don't "do" time, please forgive me if I don't begin with "Once upon a time …")

Imagine this scenario … You're a soul entity on the soul plane, busy playing with advanced mathematical formulas when your spirit guide appears. Because you're both telepathic, you know that he's come to tell you that it's time for you to reincarnate once again. You protest that you have a lot of projects underway. Your soul family is working on a huge peace project for the Balkans that will take at least ten Earth years, but your guide insists because it's been over fifty years since you were down on the Earth plane.

You grudgingly admit the truth of that and ask your guide what options it and the advisors on the Reincarnation Committee have come up with. It tells you that the last two lifetimes were high profile lives in which you showed the trait of arrogance so they think a humble birth would limit the potential for that to happen again. Also, your guide tells you that, since you have already developed a music aptitude in many previous lifetimes, the advisors will let you take those skills with you into the new life.

You agree to preview the options the advisors have selected for you. So you both set your intent on being with them and are instantly before them. Because of their elder status, they may appear initially as sparkling indigo balls of light and then slowly manifest their preferred appearance of wise, aged counselors. In fact, the advisors are such wise, old souls that they've long since stopped incarnating.

They tell you that they have two possibilities for you. The first is a female, born of poor parents with good, sturdy genetics. The musical abilities you will take down with you will win you a scholarship to a top music school, and you'll end up playing with a world-famous orchestra. They tell you that the agreements with the souls of parents and music teachers are already in place for that to happen. All are members of your larger soul group. The body of the baby would be available in 1910 in London, England.

The second possible lifetime is as a male born in San Francisco during 1970. Your parents will be from your soul group and will be with a non-profit organization working to combat inner city drug addiction, so they won't be able to pay for your tuition. However, another soul from your soul group owes you a favor and will become your mentor. He will own a music recording company and will sign up the rock group that you will form. A member of your smaller, more intimate soul family has already agreed to be your principal soul mate.

The advisors ask if you're ready to preview the lifetimes and, on your agreement, a lifelike, three-dimensional hologram materializes before you. Like a movie on fast-forward, you watch the birth of a little girl in a drab London row house and follow her life as she grows up from being schoolgirl to a world-class concert pianist. She begins giving small concerts at the age of fourteen, wins scholarships, attends music school, and joins the London Philharmonic, ultimately becoming their piano soloist. Slowly, the hologram fades.

After a moment, a different scenario appears, and you watch your parents-to-be working in San Francisco's Haight-Ashbury district. In 1970, they have a son but, because they are so busy, the growing boy has few boundaries, spending much of his early teenage years skipping school to play keyboard with a rock group. His brilliance is recognized by a retired recording company owner, and his band makes an album that achieves platinum sales in its first week. His parents die when he's 17, he gets involved in drugs and is rescued by his mentor. Under this benign influence, he cleans up his life and attends the nearby Institute of Performing Arts, all the time his music becoming more proficient. As the old man dies and leaves his huge fortune to his protégé, the hologram fades.

When the advisors ask which life you prefer, you reflect briefly and announce telepathically that you choose the second option. Your spirit guide agrees and tells you that you next need to work on designing the personality for the incarnation. You both return to the area frequented by your soul family and select the personality trait overlays you think you'll need.

Next, you greet the two souls who will be your parents and discuss how you will be raised. Then, with another soul family member, you discuss the mate agreement the two of you will share, and the body types you will choose so that you're attractive to each other. The souls who will be your parents are ready to leave for the Earth plane to be born in 1952 so, after settling a few last minute details with you, they leave with their guides.

Your guide telepaths to you that it's time to meet with the Council of Elders. Instantly, you're transported to them, and they tell you of their great hopes and expectations for your lifetime. With their words ringing in your fields, you split off part of your energy from you-the-soul, grab your personality overlays and find yourself spiraling down a tunnel that ends in the body of the baby now growing inside your mother-to-be.

Over the next few months, you spend several hours a day in the baby's body to synchronize your energy with its brain chemistry and neural activity. When you're not in the body or hovering around your mother, you hang out with your soul mate's soul, planning your future life as a couple. Once the baby is born, your out-of-body sojourns are limited to when the body sleeps.

Your life goes exactly as the preview showed, and by age seven, you're emulating rock and roll keyboard artists. At ten, you're composing your own songs and form a rock group when you're 17. A recording company signs you up, and you meet and fall in love with your soul mate. She manages to curb your tendency towards arrogance, but can't prevent you from getting into drugs. When the retired owner of the recording company hears of your self-destructive spiral into drug use, he becomes your mentor, and the two of you form an almost father-son bond. Five years later, you inherit his vast fortune, move to Hawaii, build a state-of-the-art recording studio, and produce a steady stream of exquisitely synthesized "celestial symphonies" that enrich millions of lives. After long and worthwhile lives, you and your soul mate die together in your sleep and return to the soul plane, just a heartbeat after you left.

Does this little scenario sound far-fetched? Not at all. Every detail has been reported by hypnotherapy subjects regressed to the interval between lifetimes. My extensive contact with the other side has allowed me to personally validate it.

Before we go any further, suppose I take a boat trip up the Amazon and encounter a tribe of primitive rain forest Indians. I pull out my laptop computer and put it through its paces. Imagine their alternating surprise and disbelief as the images flash by. How would they explain what they see? Gods? Spirits? Demons? And how could I even begin to describe the technological marvels inside the gray box? Next, suppose I pull out my satellite uplink and tap into the Internet. More confusion for my baffled hosts. How can I convey to these people, whose idea of high-tech is the blowpipe, the notion of satellites in geo-synch orbit 25,000 miles up in the sky and wireless communication? As Arthur C. Clarke says, "Any sufficiently advanced technology is indistinguishable from magic."

I propose that the truth about our larger selves, the Divine Architects, is as far ahead of our conscious awareness as I was ahead of the rain forest Indians, technically speaking, of course. Similarly, I believe that what you are about to read of the soul plane is as real and tangible to you at the soul level as the technology that I demonstrated is to my conscious mind. Of course, the technology was incomprehensible to the Indians, just as life on the soul plane may be currently incomprehensible to our poor brains. However, that shouldn't stop us from taking a peek inside the box and seeing what goes on.

In our fascination with what happens during our lives or what has happened in past lives, the period between lives is often ignored. Most sources report that the number of incarnations in a soul cycle lies between 50 and 400. If the typical life lasts an average of, say, 50 years, that only accounts for between 2,500 and 20,000 years. Our souls have been around infinitely longer than that—millions, even billions of years. So, if Earth lives account for only a tiny fraction of our total existence, the obvious question is, "What do we do when we're not running around down here?" We'll revisit this fascinating topic in later chapters, but for now, let's explore the reality behind our story.

Souls Can Be Reluctant to Incarnate

Life between lives is a blast. There, we are limitless and unlimited, free to exercise our full creativity, but eventually the time comes to incarnate once more. Often prompted by your guide, you-the-soul must face the fact that incarnation is a tool to expand your capabilities and potentials and to actualize your soul identity. Or, as the recruiting posters put it, "To be all that you can be." After all, souls are created expressly to gather experience on behalf of Source during the long journey back to full merger with Source. This in turn creates fulfillment for Source, enriching its diverse expressions. And getting "down and dirty physical" is the only way to know *about* things instead of just knowing *of* them. So the day comes (not that souls care much about days) when you-the-soul must face it: it's time again to leave the warm, loving environment of the soul plane, and test your learning by going down to the Earth plane and walking your talk. It all looks so easy from the soul plane, at least until you hit the constricting vibration of the Earth plane. Ouch!

The Interlife Has No Fixed Duration

We are indebted to hypnotherapists who specialize in regression, not to childhood or past lives, but to the period between lives and in their sessions obtain fascinating information. One such pioneer is Dr. Joel Whitton, who with Joe Fisher, authored *Life Between Lives* (see Reading List).

According to Dr. Whitton, the duration of the interlife (a term he coined) varies from a few months to several centuries but averages 40 years. However, that average is coming down since, historically, life didn't change much from one century to the next, and the static cultures didn't offer much variety in challenges. However, recent scientific progress and cultural change make incarnating sooner more attractive. Also, today's weapons of mass destruction offer new ways of dying that used to be the sole province of epidemics such as the Black Death that once wiped out a third of Europe. And the soaring population provides more host bodies for souls.

After living a life on the Earth plane, you return to the soul plane exactly where you left off. In fact, the other members of your soul group may not even have missed you.

Life Purpose or Theme and Soul Age

The soul works through a number of ages during its Earth cycle, each age bringing its own understanding and insight. By virtue of wider experience and increasing wisdom, the older soul comes to view the world with greater compassion, more flexible belief systems and a larger philosophy as the influence of personality diminishes, allowing the true nature of the soul to manifest.

One of the best accounts of what goes into how a soul crafts a personality comes from the Michael entity, a group of 1040 souls. Over several years, the group, which prefers going by the name of Michael, has dictated an enormous body of knowledge known simply as the "Michael Teachings" through many different psychic mediums (see Resources).

The material presents probably the most useful model of personality, which Michael describes as being made up of various "overleaves." Overleaves are the fabric from which a personality is formed, and the soul chooses new combinations for each incarnation so that it can achieve the full range of experiences, viewpoints, and reactions. One overleaf the soul can't really choose is Soul Age, which is a function of its experience. According to Michael, the soul ages are:

Infant Souls, born into primitive situations and easily frightened by new challenges. They react to stimulus without thought, and distinguish clearly between "me/not-me," seeing "not-me" as hostile. Intimacy is alien; personal relationships are based on want and lust. According to Michael, few if any new infant souls are coming on to the Earth plane nowadays.

Baby Souls. Due to lack of soul experience, they are highly "programmable" and may develop early unshakeable beliefs, especially religious or racial, from those around them. They are normally agreeable until they encounter an opposing view, when they may react with hostility and possibly violence. They may be fiercely fundamental with a strongly personified concept of a god, and believe in evil as a reality. They may be uneasy about their own sexuality, possibly feeling it to be shameful, which may prevent enjoying sensual pleasure. They are often immaculate and antiseptically clean. Their lack of soul growth shows in their eyes, which look blank.

Young Souls have developed more discrimination and awareness of the world's subtleties, and their eyes may show more unrest and activity. They see "me/you," with "you" not as a threat but as a target to be won over. They are the "movers and shakers' of the physical plane, and can be idealists but, being still of limited perception, may still be dazzled by their own personalities and not question their motivations.

They can be religiously orthodox or nonconformist, and can be zealously for or against anything. They are physically attached to the plane and to the body, often failing to learn a lesson and incarnating soon after death. They can experience love but may often see it as erotic.

They can be socially polished and poised, externally tidy for appearances sake, and seek jobs and housing for status rather than comfort and convenience.

Mature Soul lives are among the most difficult and demanding because the mature soul begins to see and experience other people from the others' point of view, so social interaction is usually more complex and considerate. The soul uses these lifetimes to explore emotional issues, and may set up lives of drama. They seek understanding and begin to look inward for the answers. Towards the end of the series of mature age lives, they begin to open up to psychic contact. However, being still surrounded by physical plane illusion and influenced by outward appearances, their behavior may be artificial and stylized. They yearn for the higher perspective but do not yet have the old soul's spiritual confidence, so oscillate between personality and spirit. Because they are searching in earnest but don't always know what they seek, the resulting stress may require therapy, possibly from a bottle.

Old Soul lives are devoted to the quest of understanding the ultimate secrets of the cosmos. Old souls see self and others as part of a whole, and realize that most if not all human problems stem from ego acting in self-defense. In general, they are able to avoid such problems by drawing on the soul's insight, wisdom and perception and by anticipating the outcome of their choices, for which they take full responsibility. Their wisdom and understanding show in their direct, penetrating gaze and, as children, their eyes seem "to know too much."

Drawing on vast experience and expertise, old souls can master anything they turn their attention to but tend to focus on spiritual pursuits, eschewing status symbols since they realize the futility of material gain. They seek work and personal situations that offer freedom and lack of interference rather than status and control.

Towards the end of an old soul's cycle of lives, they can switch easily between personality and soul perspectives, allowing them consciously to use personality as a tool of the soul. The skills and memories of other incarnations of their soul bleed through, giving old souls access to knowledge and wisdom far beyond the current life's experience, i.e., they know without learning. Many old souls are "laid back" but, if a soul has some challenges it needs to face before it leaves the Earth plane for good, it may set up a difficult life, offering dramatic growth.

Old souls' religious views tend to be expansive and unorthodox, free of dogma. They may be casual about sex because of the small part it plays in the spiritual quest, but they can be intensely sensual and enjoy physical contact. Old souls confuse young souls because the former can do anything but prefer not to, and they confuse mature souls because of the lack of emotional drama in their lives.

While a soul progresses linearly through its soul ages, its actual incarnations can be all over the timeline according to the growth opportunities offered. For example, one young soul life may be set in current times, where the person sets up a successful "dotcom" company, with the next as a great military commander in the Imperial Roman Army. One of the soul's mature age lives may that of an artist in Italy at the height of the Renaissance, followed by old soul lives as a New Age promoter and then a high priestess in ancient Egypt.

Before anyone protests, "How can that be? The past has already happened," remember that from the soul perspective, the whole timeline of history is still happening and wide open to inserting incarnations.

In addition to the main theme, the soul incarnates to experience the consequences of its actions, otherwise known as "karma." Karma is one of the most misunderstood concepts of all time. Most people see it as punishment, but this is a gross simplification since *no one* is really in a position to punish anyone else. *And God especially is not interesting in judging us.* In fact, Source learns an incredible amount from the stunts we humans pull on each other, not that that in any way justifies or condones *any* departure from the Golden Rule: "Do unto others as you would have them do unto you." (To me, the Golden Rule stands far above and underpins all other Divine Laws.)

The soul knows that the only reason for existing is growth, and growth in any situation involves the fullest possible experience of it. So, if a soul's incarnation harms another, the soul itself eagerly seeks out situations in which it can experience being on the receiving end of what it gave. It's not as simple as "an eye for an eye." So a life as a rapist doesn't automatically mean being raped in another, but the soul must experience a comparable life as someone who is powerless and taken advantage of. Again, no one forces the soul to do this. It just wants and needs to experience both sides of the equation. At the soul level, we don't "cop out."

To me, karma occurs whenever one person does anything to limit the expression of another. Obviously, killing someone does that, but it also happens in subtle ways, such as being an overbearing husband who "forbids" his wife to change her hair color or have a girls' night out. Whether an act is karmic or not depends on *intent*, so obviously, parents teaching their kids boundaries are exempt, but the writing is on the wall: if you infringe on another's freedom of action or expression, your soul must experience it from the other side.

Some people say, "Well, that's going to fall to some other poor incarnation of my soul so, in *my* life, I'm going to generate karma as if there was no tomorrow." If that's how you think then, by the time you've finished this book, I hope you'll see things differently. Beginning to look at your life from your soul's perspective is probably the greatest growth I can recommend.

When and Where?

The "big" questions facing the reincarnating soul include:
1. What do I want to learn and can I handle it all in one lifetime?
2. Where should I best go, and to when?
3. Who should I be to best achieve that learning?

You-the-soul, your guides, and a council of wise elders gauge your readiness. As to what to learn, souls are all too well aware of the gaps in their experience, and know what issues they need to work on. The only question is in what order to fill those gaps and in how many lifetimes. It is up to the soul whether it tackles only a few challenges in a lifetime or jams in a number of major challenges—say, a disability coupled with poverty and abuse—so as to grow quickly.

According to the Michael entity, a soul may occasionally arrange a "rest life" but the soul knows that challenges promote growth. Easy lives don't promote as much soul growth as having to deal with, say, a tragedy or physical disability.

In terms of when and where to incarnate, the maze of interlocking issues involves such choices as:
- *Historical period.* From the soul's perspective, it can jump any-where on the timeline of this (or another) planet. If it wants to explore courage and bravery, it might choose a major war or a dispute between two countries or one of the many civil wars throughout history. In our story, all the souls left almost together, your parents destined for 1952 and you for 1970. But you could easily have headed off to ancient Egypt to help build the pyramids.

- *Cultural conditions.* If it wants to explore artistic expression, then the Renaissance is obviously a better choice than the Dark Ages. Experiencing a matriarchal society might involve going back into ancient history, but to the soul, the entire timeline is accessible and still going on. You might ask, "Isn't that lifetime already over and finished?" From our perspective, yes, but how do you know that it wasn't your soul that incarnated as a Roman senator or a soldier in Genghis Khan's army? That might be your soul's next incarnation. (Don't you love time paradoxes?)

- *Gender.* Most souls have a preference for male or female lives, but the inexorable laws of existence demand that we "do it all," which means that we must play on the both sides of the street. For karmic reasons, if a soul's incarnation explores cruelty to women, obviously that soul must incarnate as a woman to know how it feels to be on the receiving end. Cruelty to animals, however, doesn't mean that you must reincarnate as an abused dog. As a human being, you can experience cruelty in lots of ways. We are very resourceful in coming up with them.

- *Race.* Obviously, throughout history, the status that each race has enjoyed varies widely, from being a privileged ruling class to being a slave class by virtue of skin color, country of origin, etc. In order to have a wide variety of experiences, a soul will incarnate across the board.

- *Social standing.* Again, from king to pauper, a soul must experience it all. It is important to remember that a soul incarnating as royalty is not in the least bit better than a soul who chooses to experience poverty. In fact, the latter may achieve much more soul growth due to the challenges that must be overcome.

- *Astrology.* Often-overlooked aspects of a soul's timing are the astrological influences at work. Once the newborn leaves the womb and enters the world in its own right, it is immediately subject to a complex field in which each planet contributes its own energy: the Sun, Mars, Venus, the Moon and so on. Each adds its unique influence, and interacts with all the other influences. Many people think that a soul "puts up" with whatever astrological forces happen to be at play at birth, but more progressive astrologers believe that the soul knows *exactly* what it's doing in choosing planetary influences. So, if a newborn's delivery happens quickly or puts the poor mother through 18 hours of painful labor, chances are that the soul is waiting for just the right planetary configuration.

How Shall I Die?

The soul and its spirit guide even predetermine the timing and means of death. This is best exemplified in the book *Conversations with Tom* by the husband-and-wife writing team, Tom and Walda Woods. After 25 years of blissful marriage, Tom died in 1996 and now speaks through Walda to relay information back from the higher dimensions. Following a massive heart attack, Tom hovered over his body in ICU and pleaded with his guide to let him go back so that he could say his goodbyes. The guide told Tom, "The chest pains over the preceding month should have warned you to do just that."

We asked Tom, "If you had heeded the warnings, could you have staved off that heart attack?" He replied, "No. As soul, I cast the date and means in concrete, but at least my personality could have been prepared. As it was, my poor ego was stunned." (Later chapters will feature more of Tom's fascinating insights about the interlife, still fresh from his recent transition.)

This also raises the question of why a soul would choose an early death for an incarnation. The loss of a child is hard but in dealing with it lies the growth for those left behind. Grief is something we all must go through in at least one lifetime, and parents' grief for a child is as hard as it gets. All the children who speak through the psychic mediums we'll meet in Chapter 6 say the same thing:

1. On the other side, they're whole, healthy and happy.
2. They are well cared for, often by deceased relatives, and look forward to reuniting with Mommy and Daddy.
3. In cases of accidental death, the parents (or whomever) should *not* feel guilty for any perceived carelessness that led to the death. Everything was orchestrated, and they were just playing their part.

Who Shall I Be?

The question of "who" is enormous. A soul may choose a body type with a temperament that blends with soul temperament for a smooth soul/body relationship so that the soul can get on with its mission without any "internal friction." Or the soul may deliberately set up inner conflict for its own learning and growth in dealing with the challenge. Because it is certain that we are all destined at some point to be spirit guides to younger souls, the soul must understand better than any psychologist the process by which souls interact with the body, mind, and emotions of their incarnations.

In addition to Soul Age, the Michael entity identifies the other overleaves as:

a. *Goal*—the primary reason for incarnating, the main insights and lessons a soul seeks. The most common goal is *Growth* or the search for new experiences. When combined with other supportive overleaves, this goal leads to a life of clarity and challenges overcome. The next most popular goal is *Acceptance*, which leads to a desire to accept life's situations and deal with them as best one can.

b. *Mode*—how the soul expresses in its incarnation, the style adopted by the personality, the means by which it strives for its goals, the "how" behind the "what." The most popular is *Observation*, or watching as a way of learning. Next come *Power*, which projects strongly onto the world, exuding flair and style, and then *Passion*, where the personality "splashes" energy around with gusto.

c. *Attitude*—how the personality views the world and what it notices, which determines how it expends its energy on the way to goal achievement. The most popular choices are *Idealist* and *Realist*. The Idealist is full of "should" and "ought to" and can end up disappointed if things don't match expectations. The Realist, however, sees things with clarity and simplicity. The next most popular is the *Pragmatic*, who rarely "takes the scenic route" but just gets on with life without frills. Other attitudes include Stoic, Skeptic, and Cynic.

d. *Centering*—how the physical, emotional and mental channels are blended and transmit the workings of mind, emotions and will from the inner to the outer worlds. In any given situation, the personality will react through action to resolve a situation, with feelings about the situation or by thinking about the situation. Of course, all three channels operate in us all the time, but one will predominate. For example, my primary response to situations is emotional, whereas Tony will stop and think before acting.

e. *Density*—the soul also chooses how "dense" the personality will be and how tightly it will engage with its incarnation. Imagine that the above overleaves (or personality traits) are sheets of plastic of different colors. If all the colors are pale except one that is rich and full, when the pure white light of the soul shines through the stack of plastic sheets, the light that gets through will take on the hue of the densest color. Turbulent emotions or strong beliefs, for example, literally shout over the soul's "still, small voice" and drown other personality traits.

If all the sheets are dense colors, then little or no soul light will even get through, and the personality "drowns out" the soul completely. How many people do you know who are so "full of personality" that their soul doesn't get a word in edgewise? On the other hand, if the soul goes easy on personality traits, the plastic sheets will all be faintly colored, and the pure light of the soul can flood out into the world.

In a highly evolved lifetime, the sheets are almost perfectly clear, which allows the full light of the soul to shine forth. Since the "fabric" of our souls is pure, unconditional love, this is what such people exude to all around them.

The Michael model is just something to help us analyze and understand the personality, and Michael isn't saying that souls use it *per se*. However, it offers a wonderful way for us to look at the complexities of designing a personality. And yes, they are designed. Personality never "just happens," although it can be conditioned by life experiences. But, of course, the soul anticipates even that.

Anyone Care to Join Me?

It should come as no surprise that souls incarnate as groups to avoid the "getting to know you" phase when two incarnations encounter each other for the first time. This means that when you meet someone who will be significant in your life, you can immediately get on with your pre-life agreement, which accounts for love or hate at first sight. Chances are that you've interacted with that soul in many different roles before. It also means that you do not have just one soulmate but several, one or two of which may turn into a romantic encounter, with the rest playing other important roles, such as a kindly mentor or a cruel tormentor. Yes, even our worst enemies are our "soul buddies."

One of the most fascinating stories of group reincarnation is told in Marge Rieder's *Mission to Millboro* and *Return to Millboro*. Marge, a hypnotherapist, was regressing Maureen, a client, who flashed back to a life as Becky in Millboro, VA, during the Civil War. Becky told the story that she had married John, a Union spy operating behind Confederate lines. Due to John's long absences from home, Becky had an affair, and the whole thing got pretty ugly. Under Marge's adroit questioning, Becky gave her the full "who's who" of Millboro during the Civil War.

When Maureen came out of trance, she told Marge that many of the Millboro townspeople were her friends and relatives today. When Marge regressed them also, the correlations between their stories were breathtaking. When *Mission* was published in 1993, many readers contacted Marge claiming that they, too, had been there and were eager to add their personal accounts. Marge was able to enlarge the picture of interlocking detail about such things as the network of secret tunnels under Millboro that formed the "underground railroad," which allowed runaway slaves and Union soldiers to get back behind Union lines. All told, Marge regressed 28 people all connected with Millboro, half of whom "by coincidence" now live in the small town of Lake Elsinore, California.

When Marge and a group of her subjects visited Millboro in the mid-nineties, the group went into trance and revealed the locations of long-forgotten tunnels and bricked up cellars that had been used to hide soldiers and slaves.

No more compelling evidence for reincarnation can be found, but I was curious about why they all reincarnated together 130 years later. So we contacted the author. She referred to the Theosophist concept of "life waves" in which a whole group of souls periodically incarnates together for specific purposes. She told us that they'd done the same thing at least once before as a band of about 40 Celtic Druids in Connemara on the west coast of Ireland during the time of the Roman invasion of the British Isles. Contrary to the history books, the Romans did, in fact, invade Ireland about 350 AD and sought to stamp out the Druidic tradition as being antithetical to Christianity. Secrecy was vital to their survival, and it's ironic that 1,500 years later, secrecy would once again be important—as Union sympathizers in a Confederate-held state.

Many regression therapists have identified remarkable correlations between a subject's current life and past lives in skills such as language fluency, musical talent and interests. When I see groups of enthusiasts reliving Civil War battles, I can draw only one conclusion. This is not the first time they've fought in the Civil War, only this time, they'll just get muddy, not bloody.

Final Departure

Theosophist teachings explain in great detail how the soul actually descends to the physical plane. Basically, the soul oversees fertilization to guide the genetic blend, and then forms a mental body, with which it embraces the fetus that will become its new home. Next, it forms an emotional body, and then an etheric body, all the while coming in closer to the Earth plane. As the fetus develops, the soul builds the structure of chakras and meridians for energy circulation in parallel with the blood circulation system the the fetus forms.

When the etheric body is ready, the soul partitions off that part of itself which will incarnate, and drops its frequency to match its new etheric home. Because of the inherent limitations of its mental, emotional and etheric bodies, much of the soul's connection with the soul plane is lost, hence the automatic "amnesia" we all undergo at birth (although the so-called Indigo Children seem to retain more connection than those born before the 1980s).

Thanks to the diligent work of researchers such as Drs. Whitton and Rieder, we have a clearer idea of the life between lives and what goes on to get down here. They present a picture of extraordinary purpose and order behind existence. We live in an imperfect world to allow us to strive for perfection and to appreciate the importance of giving and receiving love. We engineer painful situations in our lives so that we can transcend them by becoming our own heroes. And we bounce between the physical plane and the soul plane to grow as souls, to achieve mastery and ultimately to guide human destiny as advanced souls ourselves.

And the purpose of all this? So that the Supreme Architect can learn everything there is to know about Itself.

Chapter 2

Oops! Now What?

*"What you are is God's gift to you.
What you do with yourself is your gift to God."*

— Unknown

F ORGING THE LINK between itself and the new body is one of the most difficult tasks an incoming soul will ever face. Adjusting its extremely high frequency to the relatively low frequency of its new home's nervous system will demand the soul's full attention for many months due to the relative complexity of the human system. Let's take a look at what's involved.

So This Is Home ...

Without actually taking up residence in the tiny body that will be your new home, it's vital that you, the soul, acclimate yourself. For maybe a few hours a day, you practice engaging with your new body, probing the brain activity and literally making new connections. You must learn how the brain recognizes and translates input from its environment and how you can assist with the process. In a biological miracle, an estimated 100 trillion neurons—tiny nerve strands that would reach to the moon and back if stretched end-to-end—connect to 1,000 others, communicating via a combination of chemicals and electrical charges.

Via the spinal cord, different areas of the brain are connected to various parts of the body from which sensations are received and pro-cessed by other parts of the brain, resulting in impulses that cause muscles to contract. The frontal lobes are responsible for higher functions such as thinking, memory, self-awareness, association, and projection into the future. Quite a handful for the soul to get a handle on.

When you take a break from getting to know your new body, you visit with other souls who are also doing the same thing, and you may interact with your parents-to-be in their dream state. You-the-soul monitors your body from wherever you happen to be and can jump back in a heartbeat if you detect an abnormality. You also use this "quiet time" to reflect on and plan for the upcoming lifetime and reaffirm your goals.

When do you formally move into your new residence? Regressed subjects report that it varies from a day or so before birth to just a few minutes afterwards, which explains why some babies seem to be "present" at birth while others appear "spacey." It all depends on the degree to which the soul is in the body and engaged. At this stage, the baby's consciousness is fully aware of the presence of you, the indwelling soul, but obviously can't discuss it with anyone.

As we saw in Chapter 1, you-the-soul manages the actual timing of your own birth to make sure the astrology is exactly right. (Hopefully, you won't be one of those souls who makes your poor mother endure prolonged labor while you wait for just the right Ascendant or planetary configuration.)

When you're ready, you get your body to release a certain hormone that prompts your mother's body to begin contractions … and you're on the way.

The Emerging Human

Once born, you've a lot to learn. The parts of your body best supported by your brain are your hands and mouth, so whatever moves goes into your mouth. Next, you learn to coordinate the images coming via your eyes and the sounds coming via your ears and organize it into a picture of your environment. You also learn to respond to your environment, such as withdrawing from pain. Next come motor and balance skills, and you learn to sit, crawl and walk.

At the same time, you begin to see the external world as "not you," and the influence that you-the-soul has on your mental and emotional processes begins to recede except when you're dreaming. (When you're asleep, you-the-personality pretty much shuts down, leaving you-the-soul to run the show. See Chapter 5 for more on dreaming.)

One of the phases in human growth that researchers such as myself find particularly fascinating comes after you've learned to talk but before you-the-ego forces you-the-soul "underground." During this time, you may say the darndest things, such as, "I've been here before, but I was older then than I am now." This is good proof of reincarnation. However, over the next few years, you-the-personality grows to dominate the partnership with you-the-soul, and memories of early intimate soul contact fade. Once getting on the cheerleading team or scoring with girls become all-consuming, your soul is relegated to the realms of make-believe, along with your imaginary friends (who, in fact, weren't imaginary at all).

What are often termed childhood "imaginary friends" are not imaginary at all but are guides and discarnate souls who like to hang out around the child for whatever reason. Maybe an elemental (nature spirit) just enjoys your energy or perhaps you-the-soul projects a form that only you-the-personality can see in order to keep you company or provide special coaching. Rather than issue a blanket, "Oh, it's just your imagination," hopefully your parents will ask you what kinds of things your friends tell you, and then judge whether it's a benign influence or not.

I chose my mother wisely because, normally, once speech opens up communication with those around you, that's when the damage begins. You reason that your survival depends on the continued approval on the part of other people. So you pay attention to what they tell you even if it doesn't make much sense. You figure that because of their apparent experience of the world, their beliefs must be the way it is. If they tell you that God is a vengeful man in the sky who watches and judges naughty children, then it must be true, right? Or if they say the world is a hostile place, with lurking evil just waiting to get you, then you should cower in fear of nameless monsters, shouldn't you? Of course, you should. Adults know about these things, don't they?

The indoctrination begins even earlier than that, however. Thoughts are electromagnetic patterns, and beliefs are merely thoughts that are repeated over and over as they are passed from person to person like a virus. Before your emerging mind is even aware of itself, you're swimming in the "belief soup" of your culture, and laying down background beliefs when you have the least discernment to question them. So, the next time you feel worried about something, ask yourself if it really belongs to you or the consensus belief field around you.

Not only do you inherit the beliefs of your primary imprinters, you also get them from those who imprint your peers. Many young minds have been led astray by a friend saying, "My older brother told me …." Now, beliefs involving Santa Claus and the tooth fairy are harmless fictions, but great harm is done by such beliefs as "The world is inherently dangerous," "Humans are basically flawed" and "God is just waiting for you to offend Him so he can slap you down."

The human mind is amazing, however, in that you can turn it inward to explore its own contents by asking, "Does this belief serve me?" Unfortunately, that's something we adults all too rarely do, and something that children simply cannot do.

Let's face it, what happened to you as you were learning about the world was nothing short of indoctrination, in which those in authority (parents, teachers, religious leaders, etc.) crammed your young mind full of their beliefs, usually backed up with punishment if you resisted. So who would? The payoff for those who brainwashed you was that they created someone else who thought as they did, and that made them feel better. Of course, they didn't realize the harm in this, for they truly believed that they were right. They were doing you a service.

As you bought into these assumptions of "the way things are," you didn't question them, and they became your view of the world, or picture of reality. Can you now ask yourself, "What if everything I believe is a lie?" Because I assure you that most of what we believe is. We simply cannot express truth in the English language, or any other language, because everything we know is an illusion.

Once on the soul plane and free of our limited thinking brain, we get much closer to truth, but why wait until then? Why not, right now, open your mind (like a parachute, it only works when it's open), and say, "Spirit, show me what is true. From now on, I want to know your truth."

You can ask about a particular situation or about life in general, but you must ask—and frequently. Make it you-the-personality's goal to strive to think as you-the-soul does, and I guarantee that the world will never look the same.

This doesn't necessarily mean that you'll get a cosmic "mind-dump," but new books and people will begin to show up in your life. Take what they have to offer, thank them, and move on, staying open and flexible. And finally, never believe anything for, once you do, you stop asking questions and your parachute closes. Oops!

Another reason why we don't examine our beliefs once we "lock them in" is that, in the ultimate paradox, experience seems to back them up, to reinforce them, so they must be true. Why is this? Because beliefs act as filters, screening out whatever doesn't conform to them and allowing in whatever does conform. If you believe that everyone of a certain race is _____, then every time you see a behavior that conforms to your belief, a part of you says, "There, I was right. They *are* all the same." You simply won't notice when someone of that race does not conform to your belief.

We all project thoughts like radio transmitters, and so we all live in an "energy soup" of other people's transmissions. As a child, your mind was a relatively clean slate and you were eager for "input." Like a sponge, you simply inhaled the ideas of those around you, usually without discernment, in your attempts to form a coherent picture of the world "out there." Unfortunately, once you form that picture, it tends to stick. After several years of investing in a belief system, as child, adolescent and young adult, you are understandably reluctant to tear it all up, throw away the pieces, and start over. But that is *exactly* what you *must* do in order to transcend the indoctrination you inherited from well-meaning friends, relatives, schoolteachers, and other imprinters.

The problem with beliefs is that once you believe something, you stop asking questions. If you believe that everything in the Bible is true, then it's a *fact* that the Earth is 6,000 years old. So nothing can exist before that date. You cannot ask questions to which the answer could exceed 6,000 years, which rules out a career as a geologist or paleontologist.

If I tell Fundamentalists that the Sphinx is at least 12,500 years old, they must either throw out their precious beliefs (unlikely) or throw me out (more likely). This is one of the reasons why the Egyptian authorities will not listen to arguments about the pyramids and Sphinx having been built much earlier than 2750 BC.

Taking the Bible as "God's literal word" means that you buy into an "off-the-shelf" belief system, and never have to figure out for yourself what is true. I happen to believe that the Bible is one of the most important books on the planet, but what if there *are* a few cracks? It's easier than starting over, thinking through everything, and coming up with your own belief system from scratch, isn't it?

If you believe what most other people believe, there's safety in numbers. Running with the herd is always safer than carving out a personal belief system that can set you up for ridicule and even persecution. History is full of people like poor Copernicus who was imprisoned for saying that the Earth revolved around the Sun or, before him, Columbus who was laughed at for saying the world was round.

What Is The Problem?

Because your beliefs determine what your brain notices and lets in, they create your day-to-day reality. If you believe in a random, hostile universe, you will give high priority to news reports of disasters, both natural and manmade, since these "sit right with you" and confirm that you're correct. If I came along and told you that the world was a safe, benign place, you'd ask which planet I was from.

Far more pernicious than just noticing only fragments of the world around you is the fact that when it comes to energy, like attracts like. Suppose you believe that the Queen of England is a shape-shifting, flesh-eating reptile disguised as a person (and believe me, many people do), then you can only hang out with like-thinkers, who will confirm your beliefs. And neither will you be open to an opposing belief.

Similarly, suppose you're walking along a dark street one night, sure that the world is safe and benign. A minute later, someone else walks down the same street, convinced that the world is hostile and dangerous. Now, a mugger hiding in an alley is waiting for his next victim. At the visceral level, he can sense the energy of both of you. Who will he choose? Whose energy will he best resonate with?

Psychological testing has shown that victims of a recent crime are far more likely to have been prior victims than pure chance would suggest. So the term "victim mentality" does have a basis in fact. The law of resonance is inexorable, for better or worse. It behooves us to learn about it and create the kind of reality we wish to experience rather than the reality we don't want. (More about this in Chapter 4.)

Erroneous Zones

Let's look at a few areas in which our culture tries to foist a bum deal off onto us and rob us of our birthright—peace of mind. To me, the biggies are with religion and health.

Organized religion institutionalizes what should be a personal search for one's own truth about our relationship with life and whatever we perceive as its source. In order to be accepted into whatever religious "club" it is, you must buy into whatever system of beliefs they're selling (unless, of course, like Tony, you just went to church to meet girls.)

A religion is useful to you only if it supports your personal search but, in order to even be a religion, it must espouse a certain set of beliefs that automatically excludes other beliefs. And this set of beliefs may change over time. An obvious example of this is how in the 4th and 5th centuries, assemblies of Christian bishops eliminated reincarnation from the Christian belief system because it ate into their income stream (see *The Divine Blueprint*). Within a century, we went from, "Let's not talk about reincarnation" to "Let's burn anyone who does."

Why do we even have religions? If the self you are aware of is only a tiny part of the much larger Self that you really are, and you are unaware of the enormity of that Self but hanker to connect with your true magnificence, then it's only human nature to project it as being "out there" rather than "in here."

Once upon a time, we humans didn't see ourselves separate from Nature but as an intrinsic part of it. However, in order to study ourselves, we took a species-wide decision to divorce ourselves from it and give up the birthright of natural grace enjoyed by the Animal Kingdom. In order to study our own divinity, did we project our soul—the "god-in-here"— to become the "god-out-there"? Maybe slowly, over countless millennia, we forgot all about the god-within and focused solely on the gods-out-there, assigning to them super-human qualities.

Ancient cultures conceived of the notion of external gods, fashioned in their culture's ideals. Warrior cultures invented fierce gods such as Thor and Woden, and matriarchal cultures invented female gods. One group in the Middle East coalesced all its gods-out-there into one, which they called Yahweh, alternately kind and compassionate on good days and ruthlessly smiting everyone in sight on bad days. The group's leaders ended up using this god-out-there concept to keep the group's membership on a short leash, as we see in the Ten Commandments, which are really just rules for social stability.

Some researchers speculate that, after thousands of years, the god-out-there was wearing thin and coming under fire, so an ascended master named Sananda incarnated to refresh and reinforce it—hence the story of Jesus. And it worked. A new religion sprang up around the teachings of Sananda, a blend of Middle East, Egyptian and Indian wisdom.

Returning to why we have religions, the term stems from *re* and *ligere*, meaning "to tie back," referring to our innate drive to forge the link between our mundane, everyday self and our exalted, divine Self. However, it's human nature to want to institutionalize everything for "safety in numbers," including our personal search for who we really are. And it's also human nature to use the resulting institutions to control other people and make a buck or two on the side. All of which, alas, brings us to today's organized religions.

Another erroneous zone is the "health" industry, which is actually the illness and disease industry. Doctors are not taught about the body's natural healing ability so they regard us as walking disease-carriers and treat our symptoms rather than the true causes of illness. We, too, fall into the same trap, so when they deliver their prognosis for our condition, we hypnotize ourselves into compliance.

Our bodies would be self-healing if, as children, we and our parents had not bought into the belief that they weren't. Now we are trapped, having turned our own healing abilities over to a medical school certificate. If you believe that your body is vulnerable, you are denying its innate ability to heal itself. Fortunately, the explosion in alternative health modalities and the proliferation of health food stores offer us choices, choices that the AMA and FDA are desperate to take away.

Fears and Phobias

We may not like it, but separation from who we *really* are allows for the phenomenon of fear. Because fear underpins much of our experience on the physical plane, it deserves a thorough examination.

Fears come from three sources: events of the current life, events of a past life, and placed by the soul as something to be overcome. Suppose you as a baby are in your crib, happy and gurgling away, and your parents begin a screaming match with each other just as a spider crawls across your pillow. Thirty years later, you've forgotten that incident, and all you-the-adult knows is that you're terrified of spiders to the point of getting someone else to go into a room first to check for them.

For an example of past life events, we turn to Marge Cuddeback, psychic medium, who specializes in working with clients' past lives and deceased loved ones. I've known Marge for many years, and we feature her work in Chapter 7. In the Introduction to her book, *Vanishing Veil*, she writes:

A client of mine used to go literally hundreds of miles out of his way rather than cross a bridge. He was a salesman in an area where, to be efficient, he needed to cross a multitude of bridges, and so this proved to be a tremendous hardship for him. After psychically ascertaining that this fear had not come from this life, I regressed him to a past life. He saw that he was driving across a bridge in a past life with his two very young children, became distracted, and drove off the bridge into relatively deep water. He drowned trying desperately to rescue his two young children, who also drowned. One of his young ones in that life is his wife in this life, and she also refuses to go near water in this life. Simply taking him back to the "cause" and having him see that his fear of bridges is from the past and not a premonition of pending doom allowed him to conquer his fear.

During a reading with another client, I flashed back to a past life where she died in a fire. After the reading, she told me, "My fear of fire is so overpowering that I can't even strike a match long enough to light a candle." When I regressed her, she discovered that she has died from fire in five lives, including one in which she was buried alive in hot lava from a volcano. No wonder she couldn't light a match. After the regression, she can now light matches.

The Human Fear "Biggies"

I've often heard people say that FEAR is:

"**F**alse **E**vidence **A**ppearing **R**eal."

As with all clichés, there's much truth to it. "But," you may argue, "if I'm late on my rent and my car payment, I'll be homeless and without a car. That will be very real."

Well yes, the bills are real, but the true issue is the state of mind that got you in that mess in the first place. What in your belief system attracted that scenario? Now, the way out is to remember the other meaning of FEAR:

"**F**orgetting **E**very **A**vailable **R**esource."

If things get rough, just remember to call on the wonderful entourage you carry with you at all times—guides, angels and your own spirit. Let them know in no uncertain terms that you need help with two things. First, you need help in getting out of the situation you're in, and second, help in changing your beliefs so that it doesn't happen again.

Now for a look at half a dozen of the biggies that seem inherent in just being physical.

Fear of Abandonment

This fear is actually an echo of the separation we originally felt when we left the interlife to incarnate. We left a magnificent experience on the soul plane to squeeze into a tiny body on the densest plane known in Creation, and were ejected into a cold, harsh world where separation is the norm. Of course, we feel abandoned.

As adults, part of us may even harbor the belief that we've been sent here as a punishment for some crime we committed as spirit or in another lifetime. I've met many people who believe that they were "kicked out of heaven" for some imagined reason. I suggest to these folks, "Look, you chose to leave, and you carefully planned every detail of your life. So take responsibility, and stop feeling sorry for yourself."

The way to heal this gaping wound is to learn all you can about your legacy as a "soul having a human experience" and the courageous decision you made to come here. Also, keep in touch with your guides and loved ones in the interlife.

Another factor contributing to a sense of abandonment in many is if their basic needs for food and attention were not met during their first year of life … which serves as a "heads up" to busy parents.

Fear of Failure

According to the Michael entity, the number one root fear assailing most humans is the fear of "not being good enough." Now, we all come here with a life plan, which by definition, we are following. We have no choice but to follow that plan, for our soul and guides set things up so that it's inevitable. The only variable is how easy or hard we make it on ourselves and those around us. If you have a string of failed marriages or businesses in your wake, maybe your soul planned it that way because of something it's researching this lifetime. And how can research ever fail? If after a painful divorce, you say, "Ouch, I won't do that again," look at how much you've learned. And we must go through the experience. Just mentally projecting ourselves there isn't enough.

This line of thinking also prevents us from judging another. What do you *really* know of the life mission of the homeless people living under the bridge or in doorways? Do what you can to help, of course, but without judgment, for they, too, are Divine Architects.

Fear of Success

People fear success and its fruits because they're scared that it can all be taken away in a heartbeat. Of course, that's true, but it's your spirit that decides if, when and how, so there's no point in worrying about it. In a financially lean part of his life, Tony's guides told him, "There is not a single penny you have ever earned or will ever earn that was not arranged and orchestrated by your spirit, and so don't worry because there's nothing you can do. You don't have any money right now because your spirit wants it that way in order to focus you."

Tony realized that he was being taught a lesson in control, and once he learned to "Let Go and Let God," the situation turned itself around from being $14,000 in debt to having $8,000 in the bank within days. Today, as a freelance writer, he can come to the end of a major project with no future prospects in sight but, inevitably, the phone rings with just the right client, eager to pay a hefty retainer for his services.

It all depends on what we mean by success. Fortunes can come and go but, if our lives are built on spiritual principles, how can it be anything other than successful? What would happen if you were financially wiped out and your uninsured house burnt down, so that you were left with only the clothes on your back? Could you pick yourself up and start over, or would you look for the nearest window ledge to jump from? Being resiliant is one of the greatest human attributes.

It's a sad commentary that in our culture, a "successful" writer or artist means that their work sells for a ton of money. To me, "success" means that you touch hearts and minds for the better and improve the quality of life for the rest of us.

Fear of Illness

As with poverty, if at the soul level, you have written illness into your life script, then it's going to happen, and it's up to you to use it as an opportunity to grow mentally, emotionally, and spiritually. And let those around you enjoy the opportunity to care for you. Most of us are far more comfortable with being the caregiver than the care-receiver, so stretch a little and let others baby you for a while.

Fear of Loss

Grief is the pain of no longer having someone we love in our daily lives. The passing of beloved friends and relatives is inevitable, and there are two approaches we can use to minimize or alleviate the pain. The first is to keep everyone at arms' length so that if they leave, you're not really attached and it doesn't hurt. This, of course, defeats the whole purpose of relationships.

In the second approach, you keep your relationships squeaky clean— no untreated wounds, no open abrasions, no unspoken words of love, regret or apology. Guilt and lack of closure can weigh heavy, especially when it's too late to make amends. If you are truly walking your spiritual talk, all your relationships are healthy and wholesome, so if one of you "buys the farm" tomorrow, at least your grief will be clean.

Fear of Death

Some souls write an early death into their scripts for their own purposes, but the average human lifespan continues to rise steadily. This, of course, opens the way for more degenerative diseases, providing more opportunities for loved ones and caregivers to practice unconditional love, the ultimate purpose of the game of life and death.

After reading Chapter 1, you know enough about your immortal soul to know that *it* at least will be okay. But what about your ego? Does that live on? It certainly does, and any negativity it may have picked up during life determines, through resonance, its level in the soul plane. So the energy of an unrepentent, heinous criminal will naturally gravitate to those of similar energy, where it will stay until healed.

How about the means of death? Again, that's a detail the soul works out. In fact, it may plan more than one possible death and, if we've completed all the tasks in our mission plan, we can choose to take the next exit … or not.

We may never know whether or not we have dodged a bullet. Some are obvious, such as walking away from a bad car wreck in which you "should" have died, or a miraculous recovery from a terminal illness. But when your car didn't start one morning, did you avoid being killed by a runaway truck on your way to work? You'll never know.

Typical is the story of Shari Peterson. On February 24, 1985, she was flying from Denver to New Zealand and was sitting next to the starboard window in row 13 of a Boeing 747. As the plane left Honolulu after a refueling stop, she loosened her seatbelt and settled down for the long flight. What no one knew was that a malfunction in the cargo bay door just below her was about to cause it to open.

Shari heard a clear urgent voice say, "Tighten your seatbelt." Odd advice, especially as there was no apparent source. Anyway, she complied, and seconds later, the cargo door flew off. The seats and passengers in rows 8 through 12 simply vanished. If she had not been tightly secured, the howling vacuum would have sucked her out, too. A guardian angel at work? An aborted possible death? She'll never know.

Gregg Braden's Three Universal Fears

A wonderful commentator on the subject of fear is Gregg Braden who wrote *Walking Between the Worlds*. He estimates that 98 percent of the fears that plague us are not even ours, while the remaining 2 percent is our ally that triggers a fight-or-flight response when we're in immediate danger. If most fear isn't even ours, whose is it?

Fears such as low self-esteem and the inability to trust exist within planetary grids.* When we are born, we simply absorb them and accept them as part of who we were. In other words, we adopt them and let them run our lives so surreptitiously that we don't notice. But once we know this, we can choose otherwise. We can turn the autopilot off and take the controls. Each second, we can choose to stay plugged into fear or decide to plug into love.

Gregg identifies the three universal fears that underpin our earthly experience so pervasively that we have institutionalized them into our collective mind and created acceptable social masks to disguise them and hide the pain. For example, note how frequently the media uses the word "victim." The three universal fears are:

1. *Fear of Abandonment or Separation* or the feeling that we are separate from Creation and have just been dumped down here and forgotten. This may manifest in the form of seeking relationships that cannot possibly work so that we can outpicture this fear, or leaving a perfectly good relationship before the other person leaves us.
2. *Low Self-worth* or the fear of not being good enough, something that is drummed into most of us from day 1. For example, Tony was brought up in the Church of England in which the Creed has followers recite: "We are not worthy so much as to gather up the

---

* Many energy grids encircle and penetrate the planet for a variety of purposes. Some provide geological stability, some support telepathic communication, and yet others allow for shared emotional states that influence the weather.

crumbs under Thy table." What a self-esteem boost! This fear leads us to settle for relationships or jobs that are "good enough" rather than the highest possible situation for us. Thus our relationships and jobs mirror back to us our alleged unworthiness.

3. *Inability to Surrender or Trust* based on the premise that the world is "not a safe place." Can we trust that things unfold in divine order? Again, our relationships and jobs may signal that we choose "safe harbors" over the "open seas" of trust and surrender to our own divinity.

According to Braden, these fears show up our personal and work-related relationships and, drawing on the teachings of the Essenes, he cites seven ways in which relationships mirror our fears back to us (see chapter 10).

Why do we go through the human experience? We are God finding out more about Itself. God invests us as Divine Architects, and charges us with going into uncharted areas, writing a life script, playing the leading role, and seeing what happens. We can do this the easy way, coming from love and union with All That Is. Or we can do it the hard way, coming from fear and separation. It's up to us. Therefore, let's rewrite the opening quote for this chapter:

*"What you are is your soul's gift to you.
What you do with yourself is your gift to your soul."*

However, rather than drifting through life, taking whatever comes along, why not use your intent to *determine* what comes along. How do you write the best possible life script? By opening up to love, by listening to your inner voice and by learning from those who share their stories of honor, determination and resilience.

Chapter 3

The Art of Living

"Luck is a matter of preparation meeting opportunity."
— Oprah Winfrey

M OST FOLKS JUST TRY to get through life as best they can but are often like rudderless ships on a stormy sea, pushed hither and thither at the whim of seemingly inexorable forces. Yes, you can be a drifter and let those forces do with you as they will, or you can take control of your life and design a strategy for your life. That brings us to Tony Robbins, America's foremost "success coach." As a speaker, Tony's list of "mosts" is endless: most dynamic, most charismatic, most entertaining, most motivational—you get the picture. I have been fortunate to recently graduate from Tony's "Mastery University," which includes his three courses: Life Mastery, Wealth Mastery and Date with Destiny. A real turning point came in my life when I first met him at his day-long motivational seminar, *Results 2000*.

"Results 2000"

At *Results 2000*, Robbins asked attendees, "What is success? Why do some people's lives seem magical while others' seem like life sentences? Is it the start they get in life?"

In answer to that question, he told the story of the daughter born to a 13-year-old black mother in rural Mississippi. As that little girl grew up, she was molested by four different men and had a stillborn baby at age 13. He asked, "Would you expect a life of hopelessness and drugs when that girl became a young woman?" When the audience nodded, he floored us by revealing that from such an unpromising start in life emerged the star we know as Oprah Winfrey. Clearly, being born into privilege is not a prerequisite for success, so as an example of what Tony Robbins is talking about, let's take a closer look at this remarkable woman.

Born in 1954, her media career began in 1973 when, at age 19, she became the youngest person and first African-American woman to anchor the TV news for a Nashville station. By 1984, she was hosting the *AM Chicago* talk show, which within a year was renamed *The Oprah Winfrey Show* due to her overwhelming popularity. This evolved into today's *Oprah* show, empowering 22 million viewers in 113 countries, topping the talk show ratings for 14 straight years and taking a record 34 Emmy awards.

In 1996, she started *Oprah's Book Club* aimed at revitalizing interest in reading for, as a teenager, the book *I Know Why the Caged Bird Sings* changed her life, taking her from her confused and chaotic childhood to "hope, possibility and victory." She is still amazed that authors can do that with just the written word and holds them in the highest regard. Needless to say, every book featured by her book club is catapulted to the top of the best-seller lists.

The *Oprah Angel Network* funds college scholarships and Habitat for Humanity homes, in addition to awarding $100,000 every Monday to people who have dedicated their lives to helping others. She also has two websites (see Resources) that receive 115 million hits a month and the popular *O, the Oprah Magazine*, fostering personal growth and creative expression for women.

In 1997, *Newsweek* named her "most important person in books and media" and, in 1998, *Time Magazine* listed her as "one of the 100 most influential people in the 20th century."

Following major successes as a critically acclaimed actress and producer, she co-founded Oxygen Media, which has its own women's cable network and *Oprah Online*, a website devoted to exploring how the Web will change women's lives.

As a philanthropist, she pushed for a national database of convicted child abusers and, in 1993, President Clinton signed the so-called "Oprah bill" into law.

Of all her amazing contributions, however, the one I value most is the segment of her shows called "Your Spirit," featuring such topics as the "Phenomenal Women" inspirational stories. In my book, Oprah herself surely tops the list of phenomenal women, and her life-story is probably the most inspirational of all!

Success

Robbins cites: "Success is 20 percent doing the right things and 80 percent being the right things," and this involves:

1. Raising your standards so that you are driven by a hunger for the outcome that consumes you. Self-esteem comes from expecting more from yourself than even you thought possible ... and then delivering.

2. Believing that nothing is impossible. Once you say something cannot be done, you've given up. That attitude didn't get the Apollo 13 astronauts back. In fact, the NASA rescue mission was driven by the maxim: "Failure is not an option." Most of us think that "poor, acceptable and excellent" cover the range of possibilities, but Tony Robbins held out one more option—outstanding, and those winners are rewarded with Olympic gold medals, Nobel prizes and Oscars. Everyone nominated or competing is excellent in their field, but one is chosen as outstanding, i.e., beyond excellent.

3. Being driven by heart and passion, he offered us the quote, "What you fail to give, you lose forever. What you give, you keep forever."

He went on to tell us, "The single greatest force that shapes your entire life is the process by which you interpret the world and create *meaning* for your life. Bill Gates, Mother Teresa, and Nelson Mandela all have or had an extraordinary mindset and a unique way of interpreting the world. They know that to get better answers, you must ask better questions."

Later, Robbins asked, "What do successful people have in common?" They have a plan for making it happen. And it's a big plan, for as Marianne Williamson said (often attributed to Nelson Mandela), "There is no passion to be found in playing small, in settling for a life that is less than what you are capable of living." How many of us, I wonder, are living *as large a life as we can?* Far too few, I suspect.

Once you know *what* to do to create an extraordinary quality of life and have enough *reasons* to compel you to follow through, then *how to do it* is relatively simple, and Robbins gave us a four-step process.

First, *raise your standards* by turning your "shoulds" into "musts." Develop what others may see as unreasonable expectations with extraordinary levels of planning, commitment, persistence, flexibility and action. Go beyond excellence, and become outstanding.

Second, *harness the power of belief*, not wishy-washy hopes but *certainty* about what something means. Identify the beliefs that limit you ("Oh, I could never do that"), and replace them with beliefs that *empower* you to do what you know is right. Remember two things, he admonished. You have the power to *choose* what you're going to believe, and what you consistently say, you will experience. In this context, he downplayed the role of affirmations, instead recommending what he called *incantations*, a different approach to programming the subconscious. This involves summoning up every ounce of emotion you can around the importance of the subject to you, and *then* repeat the words. The intense emotion seems to better carry them through the shields erected by the inner critic, he claimed.

Third, *create a strategy* by writing down the *result* you're committed to achieving, why you must and will make this happen by a certain deadline and at least two *actions* you must take immediately to create initial momentum.

Finally, Robbins advocated *giving back*, focusing on what you can give rather than on what you can get. Live with an attitude of gratitude, for ultimately, no one alive is happy unless they have found a way to contribute beyond themselves. "Life is a gift," he said, "and all of us who have the capacity must remember that we have the responsibility to give something back and make a measurable difference in the world."

At the same event, movie actor Danny Glover asked us, "If a movie isn't a box-office hit, can it still be a successful movie?"

"Yes it can," he answered, "because everyone involved has devoted his or her vision, passion, risk-taking, time and money in it. *That* is success."

I have always thought that success was a slippery subject. We talk of a successful author or artist, which in today's materialistic culture invariably means financially reward. But how many fine movies, books, and works of art have not netted huge financial rewards. Are they still successful? Surely an impassioned creation that changes lives succeeds just as much, if not more, than a piece that entertains millions.

Personally, success is often just grasping whatever opportunities for growth come into our lives. Dr. Nancy Snyderman, a medical correspondent for the ABC News network, said at the event, "The only real failure is not grasping that opportunity. And often, that will take us into uncharted waters, often attracting the criticism of our peers. So do not allow other people's beliefs of how you should lead your life to project onto you and limit you in any way."

Tony Robbins added that often our peer group would resent, even hate, our success for it threatens their comfort zone. And they may try to drag us back down to the group standard that everyone else is comfortable with. If that happens, you can either try to pull them up with you or let them go. Then find a new peer group who accepts your new level as the norm, will expect you to strive for your dream, and support your ever-rising standards. Smart sports coaches, he said, tap into this peer-pressure as a way of getting the absolute best out of their players.

Snyderman also told us, "I was once diagnosed with a rare, incurable disease and was given 24 hours to live. The next day, the problem was re-diagnosed as a parasite from a tick bite, which antibiotics cleared up within hours. Staring death in the face totally changed my life and I now live every moment with gusto and gratitude. But we don't need to go to those extremes. Right now, you can decide to live every day as though it was your last."

That prompted me to wonder what I would do differently if I knew that when I went to sleep tonight, I would not wake up? Would I take my few remaining hours for granted? Would I waste a single moment? Tell any more untruths? Hold back in any way? And how many more "I love you's" would I say?

I later asked Nancy what she thought the greatest human fears were, and she turned the question back on me. I replied, "My greatest fear used to be public rejection, which is why I became a public speaker. This allowed me to face my fear and work through it."

Life Mastery

In September 2000, I attended Tony Robbins' "Life Mastery" event, a nine-day residential "boot camp" with 1,500 other people, all high-achievers. The seminar focused on mastery in three areas: physical, emotional, and relationship. "Emotional mastery is essential to establish a calm, solid foundation for all the other areas of your life," Robbins emphasized, and he gave many techniques for us to achieve a calm inner center. We learned that each day of our lives is a testing ground in which we can become the best we possibly can.

Emotional Mastery

Emotions drive everything in life—violence, peace, love, hate, art, music and creativity—and they all stem from chemicals in our bodies. Emotional mastery calls for us to take charge of our state and rule those chemicals, or they will rule us. Emotional mastery is the ability to invoke any emotional state we wish, instantly, consistently, and in any context.

The trick to emotional mastery is to identify and release any self-defeating patterns that limit us, then find empowering alternatives and finally reinforce the new behavior. For that, Robbins offers us a seven-step process.

First, decide what you really need and identify the pattern that is stopping you from having that need met, such as a belief you're not even worthy of having that need met. Then associate pain with the failure to get a need met, and pleasure with the experience of change. This provides the fuel for change. Use anything as a tool here, such as peer pressure and honest soul-searching. Ask yourself, "What's the downside if I don't make this change now?" and "What are the benefits of making this change now?"

Next, find some way to interrupt this pattern. Say you're trying to stop feeling nervous about speaking before groups. You could imagine your audience sitting there naked. Be as outrageous as needed. At the same time, replace the old pattern with a new one that offers the same or greater pleasure. For example, a smoker trying to quit could pop a mint into his mouth.

You need to reinforce the new pattern until it becomes a habit. For example, if you feel powerless in a particular situation, then "borrow" the feeling from another situation in which you feel powerful. Say you have the boss from hell who routinely cuts you down. Borrow the feeling you have with your mate who makes you feel good and take it to work with you.

Now put yourself in a situation that would have triggered the old pattern to test whether you now default to the new pattern. Then consistently reinforce the new pattern to ensure lasting change.

Finally, give gratitude for the new feeling of enhanced personal power in your life.

Relationship Mastery

Once we had emotional mastery handled, we turned to relationship mastery, and Robbins began with the assertion that, "If you go into a relationship to get something out of it, you're bound to fail, for relationships are as much about *giving* as they are about *getting*. The main challenges are taking your partner for granted, poor communication skills, making your beliefs about how people should act more important than the relationship, and using the relationship solely to get your needs met."

The purpose of relationships, he said, is to expand our awareness of who we are, to practice giving and receiving, and to experience what love is and share with others.

Without these things in our lives, our personal experience is empty, and we are denied powerful tools for growth. "What makes a relationship work," he went on, "is first and foremost the commitment to making it work, through good times and bad. Also, letting go of old hurts, being willing to forgive, and being honest with yourself and your partner are vital aspects of relationship skills."

We learned that having too many rules kills a relationship, so 'don't sweat the small stuff.' Another no-no is to question or even threaten the relationship, which creates uncertainty. Allowing the relationship to become a habit is harmful, as is not making your partner and the relationship the most important things in your life.

Communication Skills

Robbins repeatedly emphasized the importance of effective communication in *any* type of relationship, not just intimate. The main challenge to good communication is that when people treat their beliefs as facts, conflict arises, people react instead of communicate, and emotional upsets occur. Because two people will often have differing beliefs about what's important to them (i.e., different realities), communication is essential to building a bridge between those two realities. If love and respect exist between both of you, communication skills allow you to bridge your differences. It would be a mistake if, every time an upset arises, you questioned the relationship or your partner's intent, for this erodes the bridge, hinders communication, and promotes silent resentment, all of which threaten the relationship. As Benjamin Franklin put it: "The heart of a fool is in his mouth, but the mouth of a wise man is in his heart."

Take the initiative, Robbins suggested, and cross the bridge in order to reconnect at the heart level. The basis of effective communication is to build a *permanent* bridge between your reality and the realities of those you love.

What a different place the world would be if only we could handle our relationships and communication in such a thoughtful way. Well, why not? Then we truly would be Divine Architects.

The Physical Side of Life Mastery

Fundamental to any form of mastery is dealing with our fears, and the event offered us a unique way to face our fears and put them to rest— climbing a 45-foot telephone pole fitted with tiny footholds every few feet, hauling ourselves onto its scant 10-inch diameter and then jumping off into thin air! Success called for emotional control to the max. Before we climbed the perversely named Pamper Pole, we had to define what it was we wanted to let go of; in my case, anger, fear of rejection, and fear of failure. We also had to define a new identity— again, in my case, being a powerful and effective spiritual messenger—and affirm that identity with every step we climbed.

When my turn came, I approached the pole feeling somewhat nervous and had to force myself to breathe deeply. About halfway up, I redoubled my determination to succeed and focused on my commitment and emotional calm. Earlier, I had written my fears on slips of paper, and then, almost at the top, I let the slips flutter off into the wind. Finally, I was there, hands on the flat top of the pole. My teammates 45 feet below were screaming, "Step up! Step up!" and "Look at the ocean." Good advice, for if I'd looked down, it would have been over in a hurry.

Looking out at the ocean gave me time to regain my breath and my muscles time to regroup. With a final push, I managed to get both feet on the top of the pole. Slowly, I stood up, balancing carefully, and was rewarded with the truly breathtaking magnificence of a perfect blue ocean, calm yet infinitely powerful, under a perfect Hawaiian sky. I thought, if I can do this, I'll never fear anything again.

It was then time to leap into my new identity. As I launched myself into space, I declared to the universe, "Today, I am without fear. Today, I am one with God." During the seconds before the tether broke my freefall, the release I felt was indescribable.

Back on the ground, mobbed by my 16 teammates, I felt truly fearless, and saw that fear really is only an illusion that gnaws at who we really are. In my seminars, I joke that to some people, FEAR stands for "False Evidence Appearing Real," while to others it stands for "F**k Everything And Run." Take your choice.

Another important part of the 9-day experience that called for focus and intent was the famous (or infamous) firewalk—40 feet of glowing embers. Before the event, we underwent intense preparation involving several cycles of working ourselves up into determination and, on a signal, immediately switching to calm centeredness. We were instructed to walk briskly and steadily and to visualize cool moss under our feet. Under no circumstances should we run, or we could end up with so-called "coal face," the fate awaiting those who trip, fall into the coals, and eat fire. And above all, we must maintain our "state." After three hours of this exercise, meditation and chanting, we filed out to the huge 16-lane firepit. Compared with the usual 14-foot walks, this one looked as large as a football field.

When my turn came, a staff member gave me the command, "Go!" Standing before the huge expanse of glowing embers, my adrenalin was pumping and my determination peaked. I took a deep breath and stepped out. During the next 15 seconds, I felt like the most powerful person on the planet. And then it was over, and I was again the center of a congratulatory mob scene. As for my feet, apart from a tiny blister from a particularly hot ember, they were just warm!

After the most intense nine days of my life, I looked into the mirror and said, "Step up! Stop your whining!" I had faced every fear I knew I had (and some I didn't know I had). I got on the plane for home totally exhausted but exhilarated. Tony Robbins certainly delivered on his catch phrase: "Life will never be the same again."

He left us with this final thought: "At the end of your life, I don't think you'll remember all the experiences of your life. I think you'll remember certain moments. You can create them or hope they'll show up once in a while. Rarely does the quality of life just happen. It must be created and constructed with conscious thought, caring, and desire. *That's* what makes a great life."

And *that's* what makes us Divine Architects.

Lucid Living

Most of us are familiar with the phenomenon of lucid dreaming in which we are aware within the dream that it is a dream and that we can change any element of the dream we wish. If we apply the same concept to living, with lucid living, we can change any element we wish. Of course, the physical plane is not quite so malleable as our dream plane, so the change may take a little longer to manifest. Creating change in life is a three-step process (we talk more about this in Chapter 10):

1. *Desire*. You must *want* to change.
2. Set your *intent* and impress it on the universe.
3. Give *gratitude* for the change having already occurred.

To change something you don't want into something you do want, you need a plan. You can make plans for the year, the month, the week, and even the day. The reason why Donald Trump succeeds and someone else doesn't is summed up in one word: strategy. Realized architects know the reality they want and how to get it; unrealized architects are creating their reality anyway, but it's an ill-formed, fuzzy reality.

As part of my commitment to lucid living, I joined the Robbins Research Institute's Mastery University, which offers a series of in-depth seminars, all of which have changed my life. I also joined their Coaching Partnership Program where, in frequent one-on-one sessions with a personal coach, you define your goals and review them.

Whether or not you're a Tony Robbins fan doesn't matter. What *does* matter is that somehow you take charge of your life and become your own navigator, helmsman and captain. Then you can chart the course *you* want.

Self-Mastery

Self-mastery—knowing yourself and your motivations—is the foundation for effectiveness. Don't strive to be perfect or beat yourself up if you're not. Success comes from consciously deciding what you *will* do, and then giving it your all, with all the gusto you can summon up. Since you are the Creator exploring itself, you cannot really fail, can you? And as my friend, Robert Gerard says, "Success is a process, not an event."

When I mention the "S-word" (success) in my seminars, a few people challenge me that I'm advocating selling your soul to the devil, and if you define success in the narrow, materialistic way, that may true. But what if your goal is to have healthier relationships, or to become more spiritual?

Now, many spiritual people want to combine spirituality with worldly success, such as having their books or music published. But why do so few actually succeed? Now turn that around and ask, "What's different about those who do succeed?" The motivational coaches will list two things:

1. Those people believe they can, and
2. They make their goal the most important thing in their lives, becoming almost obsessively consumed by it.

There are obvious dangers, however, in becoming so single-faceted that you virtually club everyone over the head with your obsession. There is an easier, gentler way. Nothing happens in your life that does not flow through the beliefs stored in your subconscious mind. You could spend 10 hours a day repeating affirmations into a mirror, such as, "I am wealthy," or "The opposite sex finds me irresistible," and so on. The problem is that a little voice might be saying, "No, you're not," or, "No, they don't." In that case, you're just wasting 10 hours a day. So what is this little voice with the big clout?

As we saw in the previous chapter, before age seven, we uncritically absorb everything we're told and incorporate it in our structure of beliefs in the subconscious mind. But around age seven, our critical faculties come online, and we begin to compare every new piece of information we read or hear with what's already stored in our belief system. This critical "monitor" lives in your conscious mind and colloquially is your "BS detector." Nothing gets by this vigilant sentry, especially affirmations that conflict with the self-image stored in your subconscious. But there is a way around it.

Hypnosis works because in the hypnotic state, the conscious mind (including the sentry), is asleep and implanted suggestions slip by. You can use a therapist or hypnosis tapes, or you can do it yourself. In self-hypnosis, you give yourself induction instructions and suggestions, usually by prerecording them on a tape. There are many ways to self-induce a hypnotic state, so I suggest looking around until you find one that works well for you.

A less well-known way into your belief system is via your handwriting. This is *directly* linked to your subconscious, something analysts have used for decades to analyze your personality. Rather than *passively* reflect your beliefs about you, your handwriting is *interactively linked* with your beliefs. Therefore, whatever you write bypasses your critical mind and reprograms the subconscious. Sometime, try writing your affirmations like an errant schoolchild being told to write one hundred times, "I must not talk in class."

Remember to write in the present tense. "I will get my book published" puts success somewhere in the future. "My book is being published" programs the subconscious to make the necessary connections and stamps your publisher dealings with the aura of success.

Another related trick is to deliberately change your handwriting. If you are a low self-esteem recluse, this reflects in your script. Force yourself to write with bold, flourishing strokes, especially when signing checks. (There's nothing wrong with programming your subconscious for abundance while you're at it.) With daily practice, you will notice your personality opening up within weeks or months.

When is the best time of day to do this? Go for times when you're in an alpha state, just before sleep. Then your subconscious can process the new data while you sleep.

We have spent this chapter looking at how to become the best "you" possible, and I close the chapter with some words to balance out the topic—the Dalai Lama's take on happiness—since, to me, *that* is what it's all about. After all, our very Declaration of Independence says:

"We hold these Truths to be self-evident, that all Men are created equal, that they are endowed by their Creator with certain unalienable Rights, that among these are Life, Liberty, and the Pursuit of Happiness."

His Holiness the Dalai Lama on Happiness

"The purpose of life is to seek and experience happiness; it is our birthright, and all it takes is inner discipline," says His Holiness the Dalai Lama in his book *The Art of Happiness: A Handbook for Living* written with Howard Cutler, MD. These are inspiring words when so many people live in quiet desperation, rising occasionally to mere unhappiness. If what he says is true, and who would argue with the Dalai Lama, how do we achieve that elusive happiness?

First we must realize that happiness comes more from our state of mind than the external events and circumstances that may bring temporary elation or bouts of depression. Look at the lottery winners whose lives fall apart as they adapt to being millionaires. They are still as empty as before, so they soon return to their normal baseline unhappiness.

That baseline is determined by how we perceive our situation and how satisfied we are with that. One technique the Dalai Lama recommends for improving our satisfaction level is *comparison*. For example, compared with the hardships that early settlers in the West endured, most of us have cushy lives. But be careful with whom you compare your life. Unless you're Bill Gates, there'll always be people better off than you.

Another important aspect of increasing the level of happiness in your life is to stay calm, because flying off the handle over every little setback blinds you to your blessings. Accepting that we can't have everything we want in life, it's vital, he says, to appreciate what we *do* have. Witness a homeless person's delight in finding a half-decent pair of shoes in a dumpster, for example.

If true happiness can rest only on a calm, stable mind as he says, how do we achieve that stillness? He recommends visualizing your mind as a calm, deep pool whose bottom you can clearly see. Allow any intruding thoughts to simply dissipate. Hold this state for five minutes, and then let it go.

Another crucial component of happiness is a sense of your own self-worth. It is a source of consolation if you lose everything, as he did when he fled Tibet with the Chinese Army on his heels. If your self-worth is based on *what you have* and not on *who you are*, then a setback appears tragic. True happiness is found in the heart and mind, not the bank account or the prestige of a senior position at work. This also highlights the difference between happiness and pleasure.

Pleasure titillates the senses and is often used as an antidote for unhappiness. It is superficial and transient, and we feel let down when it ceases. True happiness, however, "just keeps on going and going and going."

If you want to avoid unhappiness, the Dalai Lama says, then avoid the mental and emotional states that cause it, such as anger or jealousy, which alienate you from the world around you. And that opens the door to fear, self-doubt and uncertainty. Categorize your thoughts and emotions as either increasing or decreasing your level of happiness. Then declare your intent to focus on only the former and challenge the latter. *And then do it!*

Our brains are infinitely adaptable. If you can learn to type in a few months or shuffle a deck of cards like a blackjack dealer, you can certainly train your mind to look at itself and your emotions.

The disciplined mind, he says, also practices wholesome behaviors, and that changes how we interact with others and the world around us. Unwholesome behaviors are inherently self-destructive, and he recommends avoiding them. Wholesomeness, of course, brings us to the topic of compassion, one of the pinnacles of human virtue. If, as he claims, at its root, human nature is innately kind, gentle and compassionate, then where do aggression, anger and violence come from?

They stem from our intellect, which generates fear and hence conflict. This contradicts traditional Freudian psychology that sees us as a seething mass of ugly, predatory emotions barely contained by a thin veneer of mental restraint. However, psychologists are beginning to find that violence and aggression are *learned* behaviors and not genetic qualities. They are *what we do* and not *who we are*. Deep down, we know that altruistic behavior is important to our survival as a species and as individuals. For millennia, group bonding was the only way we dealt with the natural challenges we constantly faced. Witness today the way a community or country bands together following a disaster.

Spirituality, the Dalai Lama concludes, is not about what you believe or what you do, although these are important. It's about *who you are* deep down. So in a moment of stress, when you're tempted to lash out with a harsh word, you're mindful of the effect it would have on the other person and refrain. After all, it could easily be you on the receiving end next time. Now that's compassion in action. True spirituality has little to do with religion but with the basic human virtues of goodness, kindness and compassion, for those not only increase *your* happiness and health, but that of everyone around you.

As you consciously eliminate doubts and fears from your life, you find that happiness automatically flows in to fill the empty spaces, and an all-pervading peace of mind descends on you. Now you are ready for the next part of being a Divine Architect—waking up again.

Chapter 4

Waking Up

W HEN *HOMO SAPIENS* (literally "man who knows") first became sentient "soul carriers," our species split off from the natural world of "unknowing" primates. Ever since we as soul began incarnating and forgetting our soul nature, we have been trying to remember who we really are and contact those still on the soul plane, our "home base." This was all done according to plans worked out by higher intelligence to explore love and spiritual growth.

Every culture has spawned its own myths about death and the afterlife. The earliest recorded account, *The Egyptian Book of the Dead*, written about 1000 BC, gave detailed instructions for preparing for one's next life. It widely influenced Middle Eastern cultures, including early Christianity but, in the 5th century AD, the emerging Catholic Church rewrote the young New Testament to exclude all references to reincarnation and to portray a much narrower account of the afterlife. While allowing for spontaneous visitations by, say, Mother Mary, the Church prohibited the living from actively contacting the dead.

For many centuries, psychic phenomena flourished underground, while the Church unofficially turned a blind eye. Churches were built on ancient sacred sites, and Holy Days were scheduled to coincide with ancient festivals in attempts to "compete" with and absorb the "Old Ways." But when a 14th century pope declared any exhibition of psychic gifts to be heresy, the stage was set for the bloodbath of the Inquisition. An estimated 9 million people were tortured and killed, often for something as innocent as a precognitive dream or liking cats, as the Church sought to be the *only* spiritual authority in the West.

Painful memories, indeed, for humanity stumbled along in Church-enforced blind ignorance for centuries until one shining light triggered a chain reaction. Emanuel Swedenborg, born in 1688 as the son of a Swedish Lutheran minister, was that light. In 1744, at age 56, this scientist scholar began to have visions that took him to what he called "the other side" and brought back accounts of ongoing growth and activity that conflicted with the Church's "harps and clouds" or hellish images of the afterlife.[1]

Swedenborg's breathtakingly fresh accounts of the other side captured the imagination of millions and eventually resulted in America's Spiritualist Movement and Britain's famous Society for Psychical Research in the late 19th century. The floodgates were open, and millions of psychic mediums "came out of the closet." The countless solid contacts with those who died in the Civil War and WWI changed how we viewed this and the other side. Even left-brained thinkers such as Thomas Edison set out to scientifically prove the reality of the afterlife, and he was working on a communication device when he died in 1931 (see Chapter 11).

Another giant along our hastening path to enlightenment was Edgar Cayce, the so-called "Sleeping Prophet." Born in 1877 in rural Kentucky, he "cured" himself at age 21 of a baffling throat condition by going into trance and giving to a doctor detailed medical procedures to treat his condition. His early readings dealt with medical advice despite having no medical training, but he later branched out into dreams, reincarnation, karma and prophecy. Until his death in 1945, he gave over 14,000 readings on over 10,000 subjects, and more than 300 books have been published either by him or about him. Today, the Association for Research and Enlightenment (ARE), founded in 1931, continues his remarkable legacy (see Resources).

Today, the so-called New Age movement continues to attract adherents and change lives, with an estimated 50 million Americans (about one fifth of the population) now acknowledging that there is

---

[1] As a fitting footnote to Swedenborg's life, he predicted his own death as March 29, 1772. Friends asked him on his deathbed if he stood by his teachings or recanted them. He replied, "As truly as you see me before your eyes, so true is everything I have written; and I could have said more had it been permitted. When you enter eternity, you will see everything, and you and I shall have much to talk about." At 5 P.M. on Sunday, March 29, 1772, he woke up, asked what the time was, sighed and slipped away, leaving the world a very different place for his being here. During his life, he published 18 works, with 25 following posthumously.

more to our lives than our five senses can detect. Books such as those by Dannion Brinkley, Betty Eadie, and James Redfield dominate best-seller lists for weeks, even months. And as I write this, J.K. Rowling's "Harry Potter" books about magic and sorcery have been on *The New York Times* lists for over two years.

Synchronicity

You've been thinking about a friend who you haven't talked to in years, and the phone rings. It's your friend. Coincidence? Of course not. It is synchronicity, a subject I've mentioned before, and now it's time for a deeper look. Why? Because it's often a wake up call that our souls use to get our attention. "Hey, dude, wake up. Something big's going down here."

Swiss psychiatrist, Carl Jung, coined the term to refer to two or more meaningful, related events that have no *apparent* common cause. They just "seem" to happen. I've always referred to synchronicity as "cause-and-effect where we can't see the cause." That's because the cause lies in the soul plane and the effect in the Earth plane. Often the odds against the two effects happening are so outrageous that the event signals that "something weird is going on here" that defies pure chance. And hopefully, an inquiring mind wants to dig deeper to find the architect of the synchronicity. This happened with Tony. The reason he was even in the metaphysical section of a bookstore was to find a book that would explain some odd "coincidences" in his life. Well, he found the book on synchronicity but also walked out carrying *Seth Speaks*.

When synchronicity strikes, it's a sure sign that you're on track and in synch with your life's blueprint, so heads up. In *Conversations with Tom*, Tom Woods discusses this subject at length and points out, "Signs can come in the form of dreams, meditation and intuitive hunches. It can also show itself as the smallest clue that appears repeatedly, such as you glancing at your digital clock whenever it shows 11:11. Synchronicity can fulfill the spirit in many ways. It can teach faith, love, forgiveness and compassion. It can also lead people to their destinies in terms of career, relationships, and life purpose. In addition, it can direct the troubled toward good fortune and blessings.

"For example, two people here had planned before birth to complete a lesson or task together, so their angel guides did everything possible to bring them together. They kept running into each other in remote parts of the globe. After being introduced, each felt a deep, spiritual connection to the other. Hints and clues were sent but neither was 'listening.' Finally, in a last ditch effort to unite them, their guides devised a plan. The woman had a dream in which she was shown a phone number and nothing else. Immediately on waking, she wrote the number down and called out of sheer curiosity. To her utter amazement, she discovered that it was the very same man she had already met on several occasions, and they both agreed that they should become better acquainted. They were married soon after, had five children and completed many life lessons together.

"Again, this assistance is the free-flow of the universe, sent to you by Spirit. I stress the importance of learning to detect this guidance when it is given, and most importantly, to act upon it."

What actually causes synchronicity? The agent who manipulates events in our lives in ways that are far beyond random could be: (1) our higher self, (2) our guides, or (3) another helpful soul. The improbable combination of events is *significant*, often life-changing, to the person involved.

Tony, my co-writer, has two remarkable synchronicity stories. A while ago, the soul of his twin flame told him psychically that it was time for him to meet one of her incarnations to begin a relationship. "I'll try to get her to attend the April meeting (of a spiritual group he attended regularly). I'll make it impossible for you to miss me," she promised.

Nothing remarkable happened at the meeting. "You have no idea what's involved in setting up a complex chain of events so that it looks like coincidence," his twin flame joked. He attended the May meeting and, when a newcomer walked in, the entire room turned gray except for this one young woman who glowed brilliant white. His twin flame was right, and they went on to have an intense relationship in which both of them grew enormously.

Later, after returning from a job as a newspaper editor in Mexico, a series of quirky events resulted in Tony attending a small metaphysical gathering in Denver. There, he got into conversation with three people who told him they were scouring such events looking for a guy called Tony Stubbs who had written a book called *An Ascension Handbook*. Of course, Tony thought they were yanking his chain and played along until he realized that they really didn't know that *he* was the Tony Stubbs they were looking for. At that point, the amazing synchronicity became apparent. It turned out that he had strong pre-life agreements with all three of his newfound friends and entered into a long term relationship with one of them.

The Amazing Story of Gustave and Thayer

One of the best cases of synchronicity I've ever heard of comes from the case files of regression therapist Dr. Bruce Goldberg, documented in *Past Lives, Future Lives: Accounts of Regressions and Progressions through Hypnosis*. Goldberg reports that a client complained of low self-esteem, which a few regular hypnosis sessions didn't really address. In regression, he relived a life as Thayer, an apprentice to Gustave, a fine metal craftsman in 12th century Bavaria (now part of Germany). Apparently, Gustave treated poor Thayer cruelly and took every opportunity to make the boy's life hell on Earth. After several years of this, Thayer fought back one night and, in the scuffle, Gustave lost his temper, grabbed a sharp tool and stabbed Thayer repeatedly in the abdomen, killing him. After the session, with the reason for his low self-esteem now healed, the client was a new man.

Eighteen months later, Brian, an attorney, came to Dr. Goldberg looking for help with his overbearing, arrogant manner. After the preliminary sessions, Goldberg regressed Brian to the lifetime where this pattern of domination was laid down. Guess what? Brian went back to 12th century Bavaria, where he lived as Gustave, a fine metal craftsman, who complained constantly about Thayer, his lazy, good-for-nothing apprentice. Gustave's status as "a mere craftsman" thwarted his social aspirations, so he sought solace by regularly beating young Thayer to within an inch of his life. Goldberg chilled when he heard how, the night Thayer fought back, Gustave lost his temper and stabbed his apprentice repeatedly in the abdomen.

It is inconceivable to me that two souls from the same group could both reincarnate in Baltimore "by chance" with no soul-level intent of meeting. So they either have a future meeting planned, or they missed their cues for a meeting that should already have happened. Or perhaps their souls wanted them to both be treated by Dr. Goldberg. And maybe Dr. Goldberg is also part of the same soul group, and the three souls engineered all this so that Goldberg could write about it in order to convince us, the readers.

In this outstanding example of synchronicity, the spirit realm directed both participants of the Bavarian drama to be born about the same time eight hundred years later, to live in the same city, and consult the same therapist within months of each other. Coincidence? You be the judge.

The point of this story is that before we incarnate, we make a number of agreements with other souls in our soul family to meet up once we are on the planet and it's very important to recognize those agreements when they come to fruition. Through synchronicity and resonance, our souls make the agreement so obvious that it's hard to miss, but you do have to pay attention.

Angels in Spacesuits

For thousands of years, people, prophets and philosophers have witnessed visions that have initiated profound wake-up calls that changed their reality. For the most part, wake-up calls come unexpectedly but, in a few cases, people actively seeking change through prayer or intense desire can invoke a wake-up call, as I did on December 26, 1977.

Having read extensively about UFOs and extraterrestrials, early in the evening, I lit a candle and began with a prayer for divine guidance and protection. With my palms out, I raised my hands to the crystal clear night sky and began breathing and drinking in the energy. I knew that everything is energy, everything is Spirit, and that energy is the matrix by which all thoughts and entities travel, so it made sense to try to merge thought and travel this way. I don't know how I knew to do this; it came from a deep level of knowing. I concentrated on reaching out to those who might hear my sincere request, and then said aloud for emphasis, "If anyone is out there, I'm here and would like to meet you."

I hadn't known what to expect. Maybe a ship would land in the back yard and cosmonauts would step out and say, "Robert, we love you. Do you have any questions?" or an angel in full dress wings would appear.

However, after an hour or so, nothing had happened so I went to bed wondering if anyone had heard me. Discouraged, I grumbled, "No one listens to you when you're twenty-two. It would be a miracle if anyone out there was even listening." Then, I fell into a deep sleep. Little did I know that my call had been heard … and would be answered that very same night.

BOOM! I was awakened by a sound like the shriek of a hurricane's wind. I opened my eyes to see the room filled with iridescent blue flashes bouncing off the walls and ceiling. None of this registered yet on my unsuspecting mind as it was pulled from a deep sleep.

What I saw turned my blood cold. Three huge figures stood at the foot of my bed. Seven to eight feet tall, these "things" wore some kind of silvery suits, the source of the blue flashes. Miniature lightning spiked off them, ranging from a couple of inches into thin air to giant sparks clear across the room that bounced off the walls and furniture. The suits had black visors so I saw no faces. Their gloves were made of the same shiny material. Iridescent waves of blues, greens, and purples washed over the suits and, as each wave passed, the lightning sparks intensified.

Frozen in panic, I tried to shout but there was no air in my lungs. I took a deep breath and, just as I was about to scream, I was pushed flat on the bed and wrapped in a blue cloud that paralyzed every muscle in my body and burned my skin. The more I fought the blue cloud, the more it burned. Suddenly, I noticed that if I didn't struggle, it didn't hurt, so I relaxed.

The blue cloud began to move with me inside it, frozen and helpless. Waves of panic hit me as the blue cloud neared the wall. Just in time, a white tunnel opened up and swallowed the cloud with me in it. With a whooshing sound, I hurtled feet first through the tunnel. Sparkles of iridescent blue, green, indigo, and violet light played around me as I was propelled at breakneck speed to God knows where.

The whooshing stopped, and I was in some kind of room about 30 feet across. The only thing in the room was a huge diamond-shaped object about ten feet high, hovering just above the floor. Diffuse light illuminated the walls, which appeared to be of some blue-gray material.

Somehow I knew that the diamond object was "reading" everything about me—my thoughts, feelings, life experiences. Abruptly, I was back in the tunnel again, hurtling feet first, surrounded by the same light show and whooshing sound. As I continued to struggle mentally and physically, the burning sensation intensified. Suddenly, the sound stopped and I was hovering over my bed, once more encased by the blue cloud. The cloud lowered me to the bed and slowly dissipated, leaving me lying on top of the bed staring at the three figures. But in an instant, they were gone, and the room was deathly quiet. At that point, I passed out.

I came to and crawled across the floor to the bathroom. I looked in the mirror and cried out in horror at what I saw. Someone else was looking out at me. Wild, panic-stricken eyes ringed with dark circles peered out of a deathly white face, topped by hair covered in honey-colored gooey stuff. After a full minute of staring at this apparition in the mirror, my overloaded mind finally realized … it's me!

That experience changed my life and opened me up to a much greater picture in which the question is no longer, "Are ETs real?" They are here whether we like it or not. The real questions involve the implications of their existence, how we can prepare for cosmic citizenship, and what they can teach us.

Extraterrestrial History

History is littered with well-documented accounts of ancient UFO sightings, including Egypt in the reign of Thutmose III (c. 1500 BC), Rome (216 BC, 90 BC and 393 AD), Japan (1180 and 1235), France (1304 and 1461), and England (1322 and 1387) to name but a few.

The most staggering find came in 1938 when archeologists researching a cave system on the Sino-Tibet border found neat rows of graves that contained non-human remains—spindly bodies and very large heads. Carbon-dating would later peg the remains as 12,000 years old.

In the caves, the team also found 717 metallic disks made of a cobalt alloy. Etched on each disk was a fine spiral of unknown characters that, when decoded, told the story of the Dropas, a peaceful race of spacefarers. Apparently, they had crash-landed in the remote mountains, and the impact and fearful local tribesmen had killed some of them.

This remarkable story only surfaced in 1965, following almost 30 years of suppression by Peking and explains the existence of a unique people high in the mountains, still called the Dropas. Experts had long been puzzled by their enigmatic appearance— spindly bodies and very large heads.

During his term as president, Ronald Reagan often remarked that a threat from outer space would unite the peoples of Earth. But are we really facing a "hostile takeover" along the lines of the movies *V* and *Independence Day*? Certainly not, most serious investigators protest. Apart from a few renegade "pirate" groups of ET, they are sophisticated, spiritual, and here to help us advance to the point where we are no longer a threat to each other and the planet.

Who Are Our Off-world Visitors?

In an article on ET theology on his website (see Resources), Dr. Richard Boylan reports the results of 180 interviews with people who have had ET encounters. The consensus among the interviewees is overwhelming and breathtaking.

For example, on the subject of God, ETs see God as a "transcendent matrix of consciousness" that underpins everything and is a manifestation of a supreme being. The ETs, however, do not make a big deal of "worshipping" this matrix but just embrace it as a fact in their science and daily lives.

Despite their vastly superior technology, philosophy and morality, our ET visitors in no way see themselves as superior to us. While they do not have formalized religion *per se*, their highly developed cultures exude compassion for less advanced, albeit sentient, races such as mankind.

ETs also stress our common ancestry and see humans as part of their extended interstellar family. In fact, they frequently mention an organization called "the Federation," of which we are unknowing and non-voting members, an organization in which *all* life is cherished.

Many ET contacts reveal ongoing ET involvement with this planet, including the ancient genetic manipulation of the DNA of a species of primate to create the bodies we walk around in today—bodies sophisticated enough to be "soul carriers," i.e., having chakra and other energy structures that allow us as souls to inhabit them.

ETs unanimously speak of reincarnation as fact and reveal that not all our incarnations are terrestrial. (I myself am aware of Pleiadian and Arcturan lifetimes.) To them, the notion of one lifetime followed by judgment on the part of some deity seems impossibly simplistic. ETs do not label misdeeds moralistically as "sin," but refer to them as "making uninformed choices that bring harm to one another and the planet." They see avatars such as Jesus not as saviors but as teachers of spirituality and moral guidance, here to help us navigate the pitfalls of free will.

Why are they here? As "missionaries," Carl Sagan once claimed in a private remark. Their compassion and caring for a less-advanced species such as us is evident, and, fortunately, they are more enlightened than the Spanish missionaries to South America who gave the Aztecs the choice of converting to Christianity or being burned at the stake.

Given that many species of ET are here, what does their presence mean for us? First, we must expand our worldview from terrestrial to galactic—and quickly—although they will strive to minimize any disruption as we embrace them into our daily lives, for they are limited by a "prime directive" that governs their intervention with less advanced species on a "quarantined learning planet" such as Earth.

So far, contact has been limited to certain individuals and small groups, well out of the public eye. Eventually all peoples of Earth must unite as one planet with one voice. Our political and economic systems must mesh more closely, like the cogs of a well-oiled machine, so that Earth can take its rightful place as a voting member in good standing at the Federation's table.

Just as Martin Luther King had a dream of racial unity, I have a dream of planetary unity in which we transcend petty differences such as race, religion, and color, and see ourselves as just one more species among countless thousands across the galaxy. Only then can we claim our stellar heritage of brotherhood among the stars. And maybe, one day, *we* can serve as missionaries to planets that are stumbling towards toward enlightenment just as we are today.

The second major implication of ET presence is that contact will change our concept of "personhood." ET species seem to be universally telepathic and see consciousness as a collective, a continuum in which it's impossible to have secrets. The inability to hide one's thoughts fosters openness and trust, for what one person knows, all know. Thus we will need to break out of the mentality of rugged individuality that prevails because we think of ourselves as separate. We will also realize that *all* life is aware, albeit with a consciousness perhaps different from our own.

Gone, too, will be the notion that we're born and die once only, having lived a solitary life in between. We will come to see ourselves as a soul that incarnates many times in a variety of roles and bodies, always within a richly textured matrix, where each incarnation is carefully orchestrated to glean wisdom and insight as to the nature of the Supreme Oversoul of which we're an essential part. Because this will include incarnating into different species, the idea of terrestrial versus extraterrestrial will become meaningless. We just happen to be terrestrial for *this* lifetime. In the next, *you* may be the ET!

Many humans will need to adjust to the fact that most of their lifetimes have been ET and that, this time around, they have incarnated on Earth as missionaries dedicated to easing humanity into cosmic awareness, or even as emissaries to liaise between ETs and mankind.

Such major discontinuities in our entrenched belief systems will challenge us to our core. Some hotheads may advocate armed resistance while others will be fearful. Making sure that first contact is a peaceful and joyous affair will fall to people such as *you*. If you've managed to stick with this book so far, you can be sure you have a part in the great cosmic play—and the curtain is about to rise, so take your places!

I for one am excited to be alive during the period when first contact will occur. However, we must approach it with calm, gentle expectation, not fear and hostility for, if the ET agenda were not benign as some fearmongers claim, we would have known about it long ago.

So, when the quarantine around Earth is lifted, let us be ready to reintegrate with our galactic neighbors. What a block party *that* will be!

Wake-up Call #2

Around Christmas 1991, a second wake-up call came in the form of a book on how to change your life. I inhaled every word and that book became my constant companion. I would even rest it on the steering wheel while driving. On January 6, 1992, I didn't even see the car that had stopped at the light in front of me and rear-ended it, wrecking both cars. The irony of the situation was that I was driving to my insurance agent to reinstate my lapsed car insurance. The gods must have had a good laugh at my expense.

Battered and bruised emotionally and physically, no car, feeling like the world's biggest idiot, I was cleaned out financially. Could it get much worse? Could anything else go wrong? Was there any way out?

In an act of final desperation, I began to pray: "Please show me my purpose. Show me my mission. I don't care what it is. I just want to know. I want to be of service. Please show me a direction."

Well, I asked, and the answer came in the form of a psychic at a local metaphysical fair I attended a few days later. "Your guides are telling me something," she began.

"My guides?" I asked, looking round but seeing no one.

"Oh, yes. They're standing right behind you. They say they've been trying to contact you for a long time but you weren't listening."

"So who are these guides?" I asked naively.

"Well," she explained, "we each come into this life with two or three guides who drop hints and ideas into our minds to help us along the path and stay focused on our mission. They nudge us toward people, places, and events that are important to our soul's intended purpose during this incarnation. All we have to do is listen. And right now, they're telling me that it's very simple for you to turn things around. Make up a flyer that says, 'Come hear Robert Perala speak.' Then put this on the bulletin boards of metaphysical bookstores and they'll do the rest to make people come."

Yeah, right, I thought. Like people will really flock to hear a completely unknown speaker. "Is that the best these guides can come up with?" I scoffed.

Over the next few months, I began to have nocturnal visitors—ghostly apparitions who would float around my bedroom, and talk to me about a wide variety of topics such as ascension, the scenario in which the energy making up planet Earth and all her inhabitants is steadily increasing in frequency. Apparently, we are slowly leaving the third dimension, heading ultimately for the fifth. One night, they told me that in the near future, we and the planet would begin to glow as our auras became brighter and brighter. All we have to do is to drop the base emotions like fear, anger, greed, and jealousy from our lives.

Apparently, this is happening according to some vast cosmic time-table and has been planned for eons. Right now, they told me, planet Earth is surrounded by the largest gathering ever of ascended masters, angels, archangels, and ETs from every corner of the galaxy. They are here to observe, help, guide, and generally do whatever they can.

Slowly, I realized that I *did* have a powerful message to share. Maybe people really would come to hear me talk, after all. So I organized my material into a lecture format I called "The Extraterrestrials Are Here." I put together a flyer and sent it to MUFON (Mutual UFO Network), an organization that researches UFO sightings and contacts. After a lengthy phone call with the state director of MUFON, I was invited to speak the very next month at the Divine Science Church in San Jose.

To a full house, I described my abduction experience and conveyed the wisdom of my ghostly guides, and when I concluded over an hour later, the audience of 250 rose to its feet as one body to reward me with a standing ovation. The space brothers had been right 15 years ago. The psychic had been right. The apparitions were right. I had finally found my purpose. I had arrived.

The Visitors

In *The Divine Blueprint*, I recounted how it all began. Briefly, as a young boy, I routinely saw apparitions and was diagnosed as having

Attention Deficit Disorder since that was the medical profession's only answer. Many readers have compared me with the boy played by Haley Joel Osment in the motion picture, *The Sixth Sense*, who uttered the immortal line, "I see dead people. They're everywhere." He's right, of course. The deceased are constantly around us, and the so-called after-life is very much here and now, surrounding us. It is a world full of those we have known and loved, who are now working through many of the choices and decisions they made while in physical bodies. Just because you die doesn't mean you can leave all that behind.

About the age of five, the apparitions started. I'd be lying in bed and would notice groups of men and women in my room talking to each other. I wasn't scared, because their arrival would herald a bath in the warmest, most delicious love I had ever experienced. These visitors were almost solid but occasionally I would see a bright object shining through them. I watched them for hours, eavesdropping on their conversations. I could understand them plainly, but I was never invited to join in. I really enjoyed their visits, more for that feeling of love than anything else.

After about a year of this, I remarked casually about the visitors to my mother, who promptly took me to specialists and counselors who had me stack up little blocks, group things together of the same color, and tell them what I saw in ink blots. After several sessions, they were baffled. I, too, was puzzled because I couldn't figure out what the big deal was. What I didn't know, of course, was that not everyone saw these beings or the colored lights around people's heads. To me, it was just normal.

Next, I was packed off to a hospital where my head was shaved and covered with little wires. I had no idea what an EEG was, but it sounded very important, and everyone was very nice to me so I didn't mind too much. Except that their machine didn't work too well. They found nothing wrong and declared me a normal, healthy ten-year-old.

All this was beginning to affect my school life. With so many distractions in the classroom that the other kids didn't have, I was diagnosed with Attention Deficit Disorder. It was a crock, of course. I had normal attention. I just had a whole lot more to attend to than the other kids, something that parents of children with ADD might check out for themselves.

My teachers were very concerned about what I called "the lights" around people and all those "invisible" people who talked incessantly among themselves without moving their mouths. But even at the age of ten, I knew I was overhearing their thoughts, some of which they were probably implanting in the minds of those they were guiding.

At school, I routinely saw two people standing behind the teacher. They looked just like everyone else except that they were somehow not quite as solid as the teacher. I was often surrounded by my own entourage, who tutored me with a constant stream of thoughts into my mind, often interfering with the thoughts my teacher would rather I had. I wanted to fit in so much that eventually I learned to keep quiet about the crowds of guides filling the classroom.

To get to the bottom of my apparitions, when I was 12, my mother called in a minister with the gift of psychic sight. The Reverend John Henkins began by asking for the protection of the Christ Light and waited to see which being would come in to help us with the session.

"Did Robert have a brother?"

"Yes, but he only lived for three days, and that was several years before Robert was born," my mother replied, puzzled.

"I ask because he's here with us now. And he has been guiding Robert from the other side since he was born," the Reverend explained. "He has something he wants you to know: that Robert has a very special gift and that we should cultivate it. Robert came in with a very specific purpose and he will need that gift as he gets older."

After a pause, the Reverend continued, "I'm seeing Robert, older now, before many people, talking to them. They're listening eagerly to his message. His mission is that of a messenger. It's why he came here—to communicate with people. You do like talking to people, don't you, Robert?" he asked, turning to me. "Later in your life, you will be a messenger with a spiritual message. Your brother is asking me to tell you to study spiritual things so that you will be ready."

My mother listened to Rev. Henkins with rapt attention but didn't express any surprise. Instead, she just nodded in agreement. A psychic was sitting in our living room telling my mother that her 12-year-old son had come to the planet with a mission and was constantly accompanied by non-physical beings here to guide him, and she just nodded. What a mother!

Fortunately, she realized just how real and important all this was and took it very seriously. She never told me that I was just making it all up, the way most mothers would. She took it all in stride and shouldered the responsibility of fostering and developing the gift I'd come in with. But neither did she make the mistake other mothers might have of putting me on a pedestal and treating me like I was somehow "special." I was just her son, with a few quirks.

Following that session, the frequency of the apparitions increased, and my mother and I decided to keep our little secret to ourselves. She read everything she could on the subject and inhaled the works of people such as Edgar Cayce and Shirley MacLaine. One evening, I looked in the mirror and saw behind me a Spanish Conquistador in full 16th century armor. As I turned to confront him, he simply vanished. The apparitions weren't limited to historical characters, though. One time, I saw a neighbor wandering through our house as she astrally projected during sleep.

I would later learn that some of them were ETs who inhabit the astral plane and are here to observe humanity, our behavior and creativity, and our belief systems. They can also inspire our thoughts and nudge open minds with information that will help us take our places as cosmic citizens.

All this activity peaked just as a major paradigm shift hit the West. In the mid-sixties, my heroes, the Beatles discovered Eastern mysticism. Disillusioned by the inability of the Haight-Ashbury drug scene to reveal the meaning of life, they were introduced to Maharishi Mahesh Yogi, who in turn introduced them to Transcendental Meditation. Fascinated, they traveled to Bangor, Wales for TM instruction and their mantras. Sadly, during this time, they received the news that Brain Epstein, their manager, had died at age 32 of an accidental drug overdose and they were intrigued by the irony of Brian dying while they were seeking the meaning of life.

When the press asked how the Maharishi had counseled them, John replied, "He told us not to allow our grief to overwhelm us and to keep our thoughts happy because whatever we think will travel to Brian wherever he is."

A few months later, the Beatles spent a month at the Maharishi's ashram at Rishikesh in India, something they described as a kind of "summer camp with meditation." When they were told that one of them could take a short helicopter ride with Maharishi, John bullied his way on board. Afterwards, when Paul asked John why he'd been so forceful, John replied, "I hoped that if I could be alone with the Maharishi, he would slip me the answer."

With the Beatles returning from India with tales of meditation, mysticism, and mantras, my fascination with the Maharishi deepened.

~ ~ ~

Maharishi Mahesh Yogi

In 1917, a son was born to a middle-class family in India, and was named Mahesh Prasad Varma. Who would have thought that this boy would become one of the shapers of the twentieth century and fundamentally change my life?

For the first forty years of his life, Mahesh studied at the feet of his teacher and, in 1958, assumed a key role in his Spiritual Regeneration Movement, seeking to devise a meditation technique that anyone could master. One day, while meditating on the slow spread of the movement in India, Mahesh received the sudden inspiration to go to the West where people would be more open than his conservative countrymen to trying something new.

A year later, in complete anonymity, he stepped off a plane in San Francisco. The western world would soon hear about the Maharishi Mahesh Yogi. Beginning with small groups in the homes of friends, he taught a technique called Transcendental Meditation (or TM), and everyone who tried it became an instant advocate. TM involves relaxing, quieting the mind, and repeating a mantra mentally in order to center the mind and push out intruding thoughts. Because the mantra has no meaning to the mind, the mind can't fixate on it. Over a few minutes, one reduces the mantra's mental "volume" so that it's almost whispered in the background but is still effective. After about 20 minutes of this, the mind is calm, focused and clear. You come back into waking reality feeling refreshed and raring to go.

Word of TM and the Maharishi spread quickly, and the groups turned into crowds, especially when he relocated to Los Angeles. At his first press conference in April 1959, he revealed his mission to regenerate spirituality worldwide.

The response in Los Angeles to everything about this charismatic Eastern mystic was overwhelming. After a year, he flew to London and gave his first public lecture in December 1959. For the next five years, the TM movement gained momentum. At the same time, another phenomenon was also gaining momentum, and when the two collided, the impact would change the world.

In 1965, while making *Help*, their second movie, the Beatles became involved with Indian music, and George Harrison's fascination with the East burgeoned. His wife, Patti Boyd, attended a 1967 lecture on meditation and was initiated at the Maharishi's London center in fashionable Belgravia. Her enthusiasm for TM rubbed off on "the lads," and they, along with their wives, were also initiated.

In August 1967, John, Paul and George were staying at a London hotel that just "happened" to be the venue for the Maharishi's last public appearance in England. They attended his lecture and, with brilliant foresight, he invited them to his upcoming ten-day retreat in Bangor, Wales, intended for advanced TM practitioners. In return, the Beatles ensured that their arrival was a well-publicized media event that promoted TM. They also arranged for their friends Mick Jagger and Marianne Faithfull to attend.

Involvement with the Beatles turned this obscure Indian into a household name around the world, and he became a sought-after guest on Britain's talk shows. This gave him further opportunities to extol the virtues of TM's ability to counteract life's mounting pressures, and to move practitioners towards inner values rather than materialism.

The tabloid press tried to "dig up the dirt" on the Maharishi and his movement, but failed consistently, leaving older Brits just shaking their heads at this phenomenon sweeping through the younger generation. The Beatles solid endorsement of their spiritual teacher opened the same doors in America, and groups such as The Grateful Dead and Jefferson Airplane quickly embraced TM.

In January 1968, the Maharishi returned to his ashram in Rishikesh with 60 followers, including the Beatles and their wives. Ringo and his wife left after two weeks, but the others thoroughly loved ashram life, coming up with some of their best lyrics in the tranquil environment.

The idyllic transcendental atmosphere of Rishikesh, however, was disrupted when one of John's friends, who was jealous of the Maharishi's influence over John, leveled false accusations of impropriety against the holy man, and poisoned John's mind. With doubt and suspicion in the air, the spell was broken and the Beatles abruptly departed.

Public knowledge of the rift damaged the Maharishi's popularity. As the sixties gave way to the seventies, interest in spiritual matters in general waned, including TM. However, the undeterred Maharishi announced in 1972 his World Plan to have one percent of the planet's population practicing TM, about 40 million people in those days. A few folk were suspicious of the TM movement and the Maharishi's motives, but most welcomed the Age of Enlightenment that the Plan would usher in.

Less in the public eye in the seventies, the Maharishi spent more time with his devotees and in seclusion. Meanwhile, a fundamental Christian backlash was growing against the "satanic" practice of meditation, labeling it as a Hindu religion, which meant, therefore, that it could not be taught in schools. Ironically, but in keeping with the seventies, TM began to be touted less as a spiritual practice and more as a way to hone one's mental powers, thus leading to greater material acquisition.

In 1980, the movement received a shot in the arm when Dr. Deepak Chopra was initiated and had a lengthy personal audience with the Maharishi. Deepak lost no time in publicly endorsing TM and, by the mid-eighties, was a powerful figure in the movement.

Emerging in the early nineties and embracing the TM movement, the Maharishi's brainchild, the Natural Law Party, was launched onto the British political scene. Fueled by support from Dr. Chopra and George Harrison, the party had high hopes for the 1992 General Election but its showing was abysmal, prompting remarks that the Maharishi should never have gotten involved in politics. However, undaunted, he expanded the party to America, saying, "…it's completely within our reach to create a perfect government."

Today, the Maharishi is head of a huge worldwide organization that boasts dozens of universities, hundreds of centers and millions of devotees planetwide. But what will history say of this man? Will he go down as a madman or messiah? To Tony, my co-author, who began practicing TM in the seventies in England, this humble Eastern mystic is certainly a Divine Architect who just saw a whole lot more of the Divine Plan than most of us.

The Maharishi's "ripple effect" certainly washed over me like a tidal wave. The fact that my boyhood idols embraced "things Eastern" was my first wake-up call that drew me ever deeper into mysticism— something for which I will always be grateful.

My impressionable young mind was sparked by two aspects of the Beatles' discovery. First, the fact that the mind transmits its thoughts the way a radio transmitter does intrigued me, which would later prompt my call to the universe for ET contact. Secondly, in retrospect, the summer of 1967 was the birth of the New Age, with the Beatles its midwives. We were catapulted from the postwar era of materialism and white picket fences into a much larger world of mysticism and cosmic consciousness as a completely new paradigm gave us a planetwide wake-up call.

Some wake-up calls go unheeded as John Lennon found out early in 1966, when he lamented to a *London Evening Standard* reporter about the absence of spirituality in the world. His innocent remark, "The Beatles have more influence on young people in Britain than

Jesus does," was received calmly by the Brits, who saw the sad truth in that remark. However, the insecure Christians in the U.S., especially the deep South, erupted at what they thought was a boast and a challenge. In the media feeding frenzy that followed, "Beatles Trash" collections points were quickly established in order to feed the mass burnings of books and albums—Birmingham, Alabama alone had 14 burning centers.

At a press conference on August 15, when the Beatles landed for their 1966 tour, poor John had to apologize for his perfectly innocent and accurate remark. He explained, "I was just stating it as a fact. The Beatles *do* have more influence on British young people than Jesus does. I'm not saying that we're better. But it was taken wrongly."

However, in a chilling TV interview, a Klansman in full regalia said, "The Beatles claim that they're better than Jesus, so the Ku Klux Klan, being a religious order, will be out at the Coliseum and we're going to stop the performance. We're going to put a stop to these blasphemous accusations. We are a terror organization, and there will be a lot of surprises."

The show did go on, but the constant screaming of fans drowned out the performance completely, something that was holding the musicians back in their growth because they couldn't hear their own playing. That, plus the American reaction to John's innocent remark, put an end to Beatles tours. Fortunately, that gave them more time in the recording studio, where they *could* actually hear themselves play, and marked a dramatic increase in the sophistication of their music, culminating in *Sergeant Pepper's Lonely Hearts Club Band*, arguably one of the most complex albums of its time.

George Harrison: In Memoriam

Just as my world stopped when John Lennon died, it stopped again when George Harrison followed him. I called my friend, Louise Harrison, and sister of George to talk about him. She told me that she had a wake-up call when George had given her a copy of *Autobiography of a Yogi* by Paramahansa Yogananda. She was going through a stressful period of her life and the book was so inspiring that she joined the Self-Realization Fellowship, the organization he formed. The Fellowship's teachings greatly helped her deal with the situation.

The Fellowship teaches, among other things, that the divine spark of the Creator is within each of us, just waiting to be found, and that meditation is an excellent tool to find it. Louise told me, "Once you find that spark, you're never alone because you know that the Creator is always with you. There's no need to go anywhere else. Knowing this is a great source of strength in turbulent times. And your thoughts, words and deeds are automatically good and pure because, with the Creator inside you, you can't go behind its back. I will always be grateful to George for giving me the book that put me on the spiritual path."

Much was written and said about George following his death, so let's take a deeper look at this 20th century icon. George was a multi-faceted man. He became involved in politics with the birth of the Natural Law Party in England, which made *consciousness* the basis of government because, as George once said in a *VH-1* interview, "If people were conscious in a spiritual sense, then all underlying societal problems would be cleared up in a few generations."

He went on to talk about the health care field in which great expense goes to fixing people up and most doctors study disease, not health. "We need to teach people to be healthy, so there's less drain on the health care system."

Later in the interview, George revealed what the Natural Law Party stood for: "Everything in the universe works in perfect order. Now if we as individuals and as a society could be conscious at that level, then everything automatically becomes better. This could take generations to happen but look at the increase in understanding from just the sixties. Today we see a much higher level of awareness in just two generations. You have to be optimistic."

Songs such as "Here Comes the Sun" and "My Sweet Lord" certainly captured George's optimism and devotion to a higher power. He was, in fact, the Beatle who drew the group towards Eastern exposure. After the group disbanded in 1970, he maintained strong links with the East and will always be known as "the spiritual Beatle." But because he was also "the quiet Beatle," we must look to others for glimpses of his spirituality.

First, George died as he lived. In fact, his wife later said, " He left this world as he lived in it, conscious of God, fearless of death, and at peace, surrounded by family and friends."

George also lived peacefully despite intense hounding by the media. His friend Jim Keltner said in a *Rolling Stone* interview, "The guy just had a way of handling everything so beautifully. He was deep with his religion, with his spiritual side. He was always talking about how great one of these days it's going to be to get out of these old bodies."

Reincarnation was a major part of George's beliefs. He knew that the soul is on an eternal journey, which includes a series of brief sojourns on Earth, on its way to perfection. In another *Rolling Stone* interview, with Anthony DeCurtis, George said, "The danger is when you become attached too possessively to each other, even to your own body.... The idea is to be unattached to it but still experience it. It's all part of life's experiences. The only God we need is within ourselves."

Finally of course, we must not forget George Harrison the musician for, as one of his friends said of his passing, "The band in Heaven just got a whole lot better."

Shirley MacLaine

We close this section by saluting one of the finest messengers and bringers of the wake-up call to humanity. Her films, TV appearances and stage shows gave her a public platform and spotlight that guaranteed the reception, usually favorable but sometimes controversial, of her spiritual books. She was probably my mother's favorite author and her work was a major topic of conversation in our home while I was growing up.

Shirley landed in show business in an odd way. She had weak ankles as a girl and took up ballet in order to strengthen them. But she found that singing and making people laugh brought her the most joy, which led naturally to musical comedy and a career on Broadway.

Believing that we are primarily spiritual beings, Shirley lives her spirituality. To her, life is a "walking spiritual experience," which she shares in her nine books.

Shirley's newest book, *The Camino*, tells the story of her experiences on the walk of the same name across northern Spain. She tells the story of how, while walking, she became lost and her deceased parents appeared to her and led her to safety. During the 500-mile walk, taking only what she could carry on her back, Shirley got to look at the issue of what we *have* versus what we *need*. In fact, carrying more than only what you absolutely need on the walk can threaten one's survival—a good analogy for life.

Along the way, she saw that Christianity, by denying that the soul exists before birth, locks us into the physical body as our primary identity, needing material possessions to help define who we are. The fear of losing our material wealth stems from our dissociation from our spiritual nature, and that fear limits our soul growth and spirituality.

Shirley defines spirituality as: "the authentic discovery of my capacity to feel the alignment with the Divine." And when this alignment occurs, she says, you learn more about who you are. She saw clearly how religions and science have worked to undermine human emotions, each seeking to muzzle our feelings under its respective dogma, and realized that each of us is morally obliged to seek joy through feeling our own Divinity.

Whether we're talking about the book or the road, *The Camino* is a fascinating interweaving of unexpected events and startling revelations—a well-told tale by one of the founders of the New Age.

Looking back over the last few decades, few have done more to awaken the Western world than Shirley MacLaine. At a time when talk of UFOs, reincarnation and the spirit world in general often brought guffaws of ridicule, this woman had the courage to stand up, look the world in the eye and tell her truth. She paved the way for other messengers, such as myself, to follow in her very large footprints and, without her brave pioneering work, we would be having a much tougher time.

Waking Up Your Sixth Sense

Dozens of new metaphysical books pour out of publishers daily, and movies such as *The Sixth Sense* continue to defy box-office odds. The subject of this movie came up during a recent radio interview, which went like this:

Q. You've often been compared to the young character in the motion picture *The Sixth Sense*. Is this because you see apparitions?

A. No one knows why this phenomenon exists for me. It's something I was born with. It may have had something to do with my mother. As you know, if a child sees something, most parents will say, "It's only your imagination. It's not really there." So the child learns to dismiss this wonderful gift and take on the belief system of the parent. But my mother didn't do this. She had a very open belief system when it came to these kinds of things.

Q. What kind of people do you see?

A. Men, women, sometimes children, even animals and creatures I've never seen in this world. The fourth dimension is full of things you couldn't imagine.

Q. How did your mother react to this?

A. At first, we didn't know what it was. She was fascinated and immediately wanted to pursue it. She was just getting into metaphysics at the time and wanted to know what the phenomenon was so she took me to all kinds of doctors to determine if I was hallucinating or not. After all, direct contact would be an exciting breakthrough for those trying to understand the fine line between the physical world and the esoteric realm.

You must remember that in 1966 metaphysics was strictly taboo. People just didn't talk about this kind of thing for fear of being labeled mentally ill by society's standards at the time. There was nothing on the other side except Jesus or Satan waiting for you! Today that seems just hilarious, doesn't it? The very thought of apparitions still scares some people even today because we don't have any control over it.

Q. Is this why psychologists and psychotherapists consider you to be an anomaly of some sort?

A. Yes, I guess I scare them. Today millions of people are asking deeper questions about our origins and there's more contact with the other side than ever before. This is because, with the deeper questions we're asking and the consciousness raising, greater contact is a natural byproduct of our collective quest. The more questions you ask, the more answers you receive. The more your level of interest in After-Death Communication, the more contact will become a reality for you.

Q. What's life like on the other side?

A. Well, first, being over there doesn't mean they're exempt from what they created here. One of the first things that happens on passing from this world is a panoramic life review where they get to see what they created here that served the world versus serving self, or what they took away from the world or from their self. Now because they're in spirit, they get to experience their life from all sides. So if they harmed someone, they get to be the other person and feel what that person felt. Just knowing that should get a few people to clean their act up down here before it's too late.

People over there understand much more of who they really are on the other side. The self-righteous ones have a hard time. You can imagine the incredible discomfort of discovering that who you thought you were isn't who you really are at all. Say you went to church every Sunday and proudly flashed a hundred dollar bill in the collection plate so that everyone could see you. When you cross over, you expect to be applauded for your righteous ways, and are shocked to find that it counts for nothing because you were seeking approval. But suppose you once gave a starving man a meal and then completely forgot all about it. You're surprised to see that event replayed and held up as a selfless, loving act.

Q. What happens after the review?

A. The choices are wide and varied. You could hang around the Earth plane to influence things with family members and still be part of their life in some way. Or you could resume whatever projects you had going before you incarnated. You can serve in countless ways. Lots of folks help new arrivals to get acclimated, which is really important when we have a major disaster over here and thousands cross over at the same time.

Q. What can the other side teach us here?

A. Three main things. First, just the fact that it exists is enough to dispel the fear of death. Countless people have communicated back that it's not an end but a transition to a far more glorious state of being. Second, their greatest lament during the life review is that they wished they hadn't caused so much harm while here or hadn't wasted so many opportunities to do good. Of course, it's too late then to fix the harm you did, and you'll need to wait until the next lifetime. So the moral of that is to do no harm and take every opportunity you can to spread love and light.

The third thing it tells us is that we're far more than we think we are. We're not these tiny egos in these frail bodies, but vast spiritual beings on field trips to learn more about creation. But more than that, we're sparks of the Creator here to learn more about itself.

Q. Wow. That's a big concept to get the mind around.

A. Isn't it? We are the Creator playing hide-and-seek with itself, and the thrill of finding out more about itself is the whole point of the game. That's why anything anywhere exists, has existed, and will ever exist.

Q. Your contacts seem very dynamic in the sense that they're frequent and very pronounced. Are the veils between the physical world and the other side becoming more transparent?

A. Remarkably so. We're living in a time where there is a merge, as if the astral plane is slowly merging with day-to-day reality. It's very subtle at first and has been unfolding for a number of years now although, in the last couple of years, it's picked up dramatically.

Q. Our world is in so much trouble right now and we're on the brink of destruction. Wouldn't direct contact help us get through this terrible dilemma?

A. My visitors at nighttime have shared with me that there is an overall blueprint for each and every soul entering the physical world here. And, while we have free will to choose personal destruction over ascension, if we were to put the planet at risk of annihilation or jeopardize the balance of the karmic-bound souls already here or due to come here, then there would be very dynamic and direct intervention. This tells us that we must be good stewards of each other, our environment, and the planet, which has just been loaned to us, by the way. It's simply not ours to destroy.

Q. It seems incredible that you converse with people from the other side. How does this exactly happen?

A. In the middle of the night, either voices or activity in the room bring me semi-awake. This pulls me directly into the hypnogogic state. That's the fine line between when you're awaking from sleep, and just when you're falling asleep. With the body's activity out of the way, the subconscious and buddhic mind have a chance to come forth with little interference. This allows my conscious mind to be aware of what the Ajna center, or third eye, is witnessing in the fourth dimension.

This allows me to see what's right beside me on the next level. Scary for some, thrilling for others, I suppose. What I see are men and women in the fourth dimension. Because most of them have been around longer than me, I can benefit from their greater knowledge. This is not always true, but more often than not. Most of them have lived on the Earth at one time or another and they ran out of time because of illness or accident that caused their physical form to stop functioning.

Q. How do your visitors speak with you?

A. In a combination of ways. When you watch a movie, by the end of it, you're able to capture the essence of the entire picture all at once. It works something like that. We humans use words as stepping-stones to get to where we're going with an idea but they somehow bypass this process and give me the entire idea all at once and in a fraction of the time. This can be overwhelming at times as I try to absorb the whole concept while I'm just coming out of sleep. I then write it down as quickly as I can so as to lose as little of the information as possible. I strive to report it as carefully and accurately as I can. I respect the material and the thoughts imparted by those across the veil and, because I honor them, they continue with this unique relationship.

Q. What are some of the more interesting communications they have shared with you?

A. One of the most fascinating informational pieces they have shared with me is the swiftness of the changes in consciousness as we enter into a "new age of enlightenment," or more aptly the time when "humanity wakes up." Those on the other side work tirelessly at readying Earth and its inhabitants to be birthed into the "big picture." This means that Earth is slowly being ushered into more of a multi-dimensional reality.

Q. What does this planet-wide wake-up call mean?

A. We will see changes in our DNA and begin accessing our cellular memory of other lifetimes. And, for those who are in alignment with the Divine Plan, their Ajna Center or third eye will open up. These people will begin to see etherically and have the kinds of experiences we've just been talking about. This is one of the gifts of spirit that the Bible talks about. Other people won't have this gift and won't know what's happening.

Q. Why do you think these contacts are happening more frequently recently?

A. Because the veils separating our world and the next are becoming thinner. This is due to the overall spiritual frequency with which the planet is resonating. We're also at a stage where the spiritual hierarchy that watches over the planet is becoming more evident. Our increasing frequency brings us closer to the frequency of Christ Consciousness and, at some point, those who are open will be permeated by its qualities of love and unity.

Hints of the new world emerging are all around us, such as the crop circle phenomenon. Here, we see etched in wheat and barley fields mathematical equations, astrological designs, ancient hieroglyphics, and even the 23rd letter of the Greek alphabet. Many of these glyphs are giving us new insights into physics, astrophysics and so on. I believe they are placed here to show us that a new culture is emerging. And most importantly, they are intended, over the period of a few generations, to get us used to the idea and comfortable with it.

More Visitors

Recently I had an amazing visit from a group of people who found an opening of some kind of portal in the veil. While many visits happen while in the hypnogogic state, this one was interesting because I stood out side my physical body completely. I saw two males standing in the room who suddenly noticed me. At first they were surprised that I could see them for they immediately asked, "You can see us, can't you?"

I replied, "Yes I can."

They somehow thought this was unique because they understood that most people who still have bodies just don't see them, whether asleep, out of body, or awake. I asked, "How did you get here?"

They looked at each other and said, "We're not sure. We found an opening and suddenly we ended up here. Where are we?"

I said, "You're in Scotts Valley, California."

They were even more curious and asked, "What year is it?"

"It's 2002."

They had the most priceless look on their faces, and then burst out laughing. It was only then that I realized that I must be out of my body. I stepped closer and reached out to touch one of them. I thought, you're real.

"Of course, I'm real," he said. "I'm probably more real than you."

In the back of my mind, I knew this but him saying this made it all seem new again. When I thought the question of where they came from, they said, "We're on a field trip with others and found the opening."

That's when I noticed they were wearing nametags. I couldn't make out their names because I'd never seen their language before. I said, "You speak English but your nametags have characters I've never seen before."

One replied, "When you don't have a body, you use thought, and each person translates that into his or her own language."

Needless to say, I was becoming confused. Just then, several more people were suddenly standing behind me. They were looking around curiously and took great interest in me. They began touching me. Then one stepped forward and said, "You're from the physical world, aren't you?

When I said yes, they looked at the other two and then at me and asked, "Where are we?"

The original two said, "We're in Scotts Valley!"

"Where's that?" the third asked.

The first two said laughingly, "It's in California!"

"California?"

"Yea! And it's the year 2002."

Everybody started laughing, even me. Just then, a few more arrived, looking just as confused as the rest. The room became one big meeting with everybody examining everything. Finally it occurred to me that I might be dead and on the other side, so I asked the original two, "Am I dead?"

"No, yes, no, well yes."

Just then a woman came into view and everyone turned to look at her. She said, "Well, I see you all found your way here."

Amid disgruntled moans, she said, "It's time to go, everybody."

I said, "Wait a minute. I need a few answers. Am I dead?"

She said, "Of course not!"

I asked, "How do you know?"

"That's easy. You don't have all the light around your body. You're much too dense."

Everyone started to laugh! "Well, not dense in that sense," she interjected. "When you're on this side, you are who you truly are. Your colors shine much brighter. If you had been on our side, your light would shine much more brilliant and others would know you just by your light. It's who you really are."

"Then why the nametags?" I asked.

"Well, first they're not nametags. It's the name of the trip we organized. And these two fun guys found an opening that brought them here."

"Where's the opening, and will you all come back?" I asked.

Several started to sit down, as if this might be a long explanation. She said, "Well, first, once in a while, a strong request to connect with this side will make its way to a soul or an area and creates an opportunity between time and space. It's difficult to explain and, while you're in the physical world, your mind wouldn't have room for that. Just consider that your thoughts have a lot more power than you know.

Thoughts travel everywhere and create many conditions in the unseen you wouldn't know about until much later."

She then added, "I'm not surprised that this happened. I can see by who you are that you're a researcher of the fine lines between the worlds. Much of your research is in bridging the worlds. So in a way, you called us here."

Feeling that our time would soon come to a close, I asked, "Are these people from our Earth?"

She answered, "All of them."

One blurted out, "I used to live in New Jersey!"

Everyone laughed. The tour guide added, "Many souls who lived on your side stay here after they've passed for what would be many of your Earth years in order to see things through that they created earlier. They only have a slight influence now and see everything from another perspective. This must have been quite an experience for you."

"Oh yes," I said. I then began to feel quite emotional, as if I were saying goodbye to some new close friends I had just met. How could that be, I wondered.

"Well, everybody, it's time to go," the tour guide said.

I protested, "Wait! I don't even know your names."

She looked at me lovingly. "You'll see us again sometime. It's not our place to interfere."

And with that, they began to fade away as quickly as they came. I felt a rushing motion and was suddenly startled at the change in location. With my eyes open, I was staring at the ceiling of my bedroom, and feeling a warm glow as I lay there. Touching the other side had given me a feeling of being connected and a warmth I will never forget.

For some reason, the veils are thinner in the Scotts Valley area than most other places, which makes it easier for us and those on the other side to travel between the dimensions and through time. Also, many of the locals tell me that apparitions are not uncommon in the area.

Conclusion

This chapter has been about wake-up calls to the fact that amazing times are unfolding—synchronicities, apparitions, ET contacts, crop circles, etc. As a species, we are poised on the verge of the greatest shift in our species' history—an actual dimension shift. However, the planet and humanity will split into two factions during this shift, one moving into the fifth dimension, and the other remaining in the third.

Hallmarks of the fifth dimension are love, creativity, beauty and communion with spirit, whereas the third will rapidly degenerate into chaos, natural disasters, and war as the way of life for all.

What determines who goes to the fifth dimension and who stays in the third? This is not a conscious decision. By the Law of Resonance, your frequency, and especially that of your heart chakra, determines whether or not you go to the fifth dimension. The Law simply will not allow those of impure heart to make the shift. But anyone reading this and similar books who resonate with the material need not fear. Your frequency is already sufficient to carry you to the fifth dimension.

Sources tell us that the split began after the planetary wake-up call of September 11, 2001, which basically made us look within and choose to respond with hate and fear, or love and compassion. Now it is imperative that you do not allow any such subsequent tragedies to put you into fear, but that you use them to reaffirm your choice. Recognize any future tragedies as the final sorting of the wheat from the chaff. For, as a Divine Architect, you have already made your choice. See you there! And save me a seat!

Chapter 5

The Dreaming Room

*"There are more things in Heaven and Earth
than are dreamt of in your philosophy, Horatio."*
—"Hamlet," William Shakespeare

*"The dream you dream alone is only a dream.
The dream we dream together is reality."*
— Yoko Ono

OUR CONSCIOUSNESS FINDS a number of ways of leaving the focal point of our physical bodies, such as Out-of-Body and Near-Death Experiences. However, the first takes training, and the second, a life-threatening situation. So the easiest and safest for my money is a third option—dreaming.

In order to see what dreaming actually is, take a step back. If you tune into a daytime soap opera, you see people like you and I engaged in real-life dramas but, of course, they are "just acting." Behind the scenes, a team of writers decides what will happen to the characters, how they will respond to situations and the other characters, when a new character will join the program, and when an old character will be "written out." To the characters, the writers have almost god-like powers of life and death.

In the dramas we call our daily lives, the writers are our souls, who nightly meet for planning sessions about what will happen next in our lives. For example, you meet someone at a party and feel attracted. Will the two of you start a relationship? If so, how will it turn out? Or if your spouse goes to a party and meets someone, will he or she begin an affair. If so, how will you respond? Will you split up or reconcile?

Tony and I call these meetings "reality factories." That is where committees of involved souls hammer out the realities their incarnations will experience on the Earth plane. In these higher dimensional meetings, entire scenarios are played out, evaluated, and voted on. Our hypothetical encounter at the party is run several times, each one with a different outcome, or with various twists and turns, so that as much "juice" as possible is sucked out of the scenario. In the end, our souls know every possible angle.

Unknown to your waking consciousness (fixated as it is by the intensity of the Earth plane), your superconscious, or higher self, spends much of its time in these planning committees. Your waking consciousness normally goes offline while your body sleeps, but suppose it attended a planning session. What would it make of the experience, especially as, on its return, it must process what it saw and heard through your linear brain? Fantastical images, long deceased relatives, weird events involving people you may or may not know in your life, all jumble together as you lie in bed trying to sort it out. What does it all mean? Why was my dead grandmother riding a unicorn? Who were those people I had that argument with, and what were we arguing about?

Because the dream experience happened in a higher dimension and bypassed the physical brain, the details are not in your short-term memory, so they fade as quickly as the stars at sunrise. While awake, our ego looks out at the world through our belief system which filters out most of what our eyes see, so that we only *notice* what our beliefs tell us can be out there. But our higher consciousness can look at a situation from many different perspectives, unfettered by the blinders of our beliefs. When our ego wakes up clutching a few images that it calls a "dream," no wonder it can't figure any of it out. Since what happens on the inner planes simply cannot correspond to our limited waking reality, we conclude that most dreams are meaningless jumbles of chaotic nonsense.

Dreams seem to break all the rules of our simplistic cause-and-effect reality of daily life, because in the reality factory from which the dream originates, there *are* no rules as we understand the term.

We begin dreaming while we're still in the womb and we continue until our deathbed. Dreaming is as old as mankind itself. To aboriginal cultures, the "dreamtime" *is* reality, while the waking state is just a pale illusion.

The Bible is littered with references to dreams, and the ancients accepted them as just another part of who they were. However, the early church leaders condemned them because they couldn't control the contents of our dreams. But the growth of the Spiritualist Movement in the early 20th century saw revived interest in dreams and after-death contact in dreams (once dismissed as "wishful thinking"). Freud saw dreams as expressions of taboo sexual urges, but Carl Jung legitimized them as a valid means of communication, both within the psyche and with other beings. Let's take a deeper look at this phenomenon we all take for granted.

Sleep is the period when our conscious mind goes quiescent to allow the body systems to regenerate and the being to dream. (I use the word "being" deliberately because, as dog and cat owners know, their pets dream, too.) Freed of the conscious mind's dominion, the subconscious is able to process and connect with the being's soul. Also, the astral/etheric body is free to leave and visit other physical plane locations and dimensions. Now, our minds are cleverly partitioned, each part with its own tasks:

- *Conscious mind*—manages our daily lives.
- *Preconscious mind*—houses knowledge and memories that are accessible with a little effort, such as the layout of your first school or the name of a childhood sweetheart.
- *Subconscious mind*—contains our entire life history, including everything we've repressed because of trauma or would simply prefer to "forget." Access usually requires hypnosis. If you can't remember the color of your first bicycle, you can be sure that memory is here.
- *Collective unconscious*—the hidden repository of ideas, symbols, and archetypes that underpin humanity. First identified by Jung, this level is the source of those rare "grand dreams" that deal with the major issues of the human condition.

We have evolved to the point where our sleep cycle is well organized and predictable (see Figure 5-1):

- Starting in the beta state (14 – 20 cps), we drop through the hypnogogic state (13 cps) as our brain switches from conscious mode to subconscious, and may receive clairaudient and clairsentient input. This is the state when I best see the apparitions that constantly surround us. Initially, we're aware of this but, as the conscious mind begins to shut down, we stop remembering.

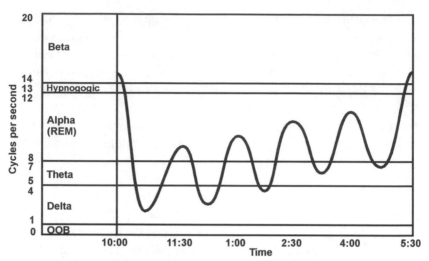

Figure 5-1 Human Sleep Cycle

- We quickly drop through alpha (8 – 13) and theta (5 – 7) into deep delta sleep (1 – 4) where healing and regeneration take place.
- Every 90 minutes, we rise back up to alpha and enter a dreaming phase. Dream duration is between 5 and 45 minutes, and includes rapid eye movement (REM), muscle twitching, variations in blood pressure, heart rate, breathing, and emotional arousal. The physical body can't distinguish dreams from waking reality, and this can be so intense as to actually wake us up.
- Between REM periods, when in delta, we may have psychic visits from Earth plane beings who are astral projecting and beings from the soul plane or higher. We often dismiss these as "just dreams," but they have a different quality. Researchers are not sure whether the dreamer "goes to the other side," the other side comes to us, or we meet in the middle. Those who have had a sleeping contact report that the experience is so much more vivid than dreams that they shouldn't really be called "dreams." Also, they are rarely casual but may convey important information that can be independently verified afterwards.
- At some inner signal, or if woken, the conscious mind comes back online, often catching fragments of the most recent dream activity or psychic visits, which we remember on waking.
- As we pass from alpha to beta, we may once more receive hypnogogic input.

Because the subconscious mind is not normally accessible to the conscious mind, most dream activity goes unremembered. If our soul wants us to be aware of a dream or visit, it arranges for the episode to occur as the conscious mind comes back online at the sleep/wake border.

To the conscious mind, dreams are apparently spontaneous, hazy, meaningless and often chaotic, mental activity below the level of the conscious mind. In fact, they are well-crafted, whole, meaningful, and coherent activities at the level of mind they are created, which stimulate the visual, speech and emotional centers of the brain.

Psychic visits by others include their identity and energy, but your dreams are all your own creation, so they incorporate symbolism that is meaningful to you, although we all share some common, universal symbols by the simple virtue of being human. Ever since Freud began his systematic study of dreams (and messed up a whole generation of psychologists in the process), researchers have worked to help us understand our dream images, and many fine books are available on the subject (see Reading List).

One thing is certain: your dreams provide fascinating insights into the workings of your subconscious mind and are highly worthy of examination, so never dismiss them. The purposes of dreams include:

- Processing the previous day's events for learning or rebalancing.
- Examining previous experience or running various scenarios to help in dealing with present or future challenges.
- Exploring our capabilities and potentials that might be exploited.
- Scenarios woven together by our soul and guides to explore possible options that we may or may not choose to experience on the Earth plane. If you do choose to manifest a scenario in waking life, you may experience *déjà vu* when it actually happens.

Where do dreams occur? In dimensions higher than the frequency of physical plane matter. They are ongoing in those dimensions, although once the conscious mind takes over on waking, awareness of them is eclipsed.

Accepting that the dream state is one where the soul and subconscious are free to explore personal evolution and send signals to our conscious mind, how can you best use this valuable tool? There are three main ways: (1) dream programming, (2) lucid dreaming, and (3) dream interpretation.

Dream Programming

In *dream programming*, just before going to sleep, you can instruct your subconscious mind to:

1. Root out and process any limiting aspects of your self-image or belief system.
2. Bring to your conscious awareness any helpful hints or pointers to promote health of your ego and its ability to cope with daily life.
3. Ask for solutions to a specific problem to be delivered either in the dream or as an intuitive flash the next day.
4. Ask for a physical body condition to be healed during sleep.
5. Ask for a visitation from those on the other side to help with a specific problem. Do this by focusing on the person's energy and then stating the problem as clearly as you can. (This is ideal for inventors whose research has hit a snag, because you can be sure that the problem has already been solved over there.)

In *lucid dreaming*, you know you're dreaming and have full waking consciousness. You can influence the dream, change outcomes and, within limits, reassign meaning to the contents of your subconscious mind. Many excellent books tell you how to master this powerful reality creation technique.

Dream interpretation is such an enormous topic that it usually has its own section in the bookstores. Subconscious-driven dreams reveal our underlying issues, often symbolically. For example, being held back or frustrated can be telling you to set some life goals and develop a strategy for achieving them. Recurring dreams are always a signal that you haven't got the point yet and really need to attend to an issue before it becomes a problem.

Dreams also involve universal symbols, such as the ocean as the subconscious, drowning as fear of being swamped by subconscious drives, your house for your ego personality, being nude in dreams as spiritual emergence or openness, and being chased as part of your needing integration. The list is endless, and many great dream dictionaries are available.

Soul-driven dreams are revelatory or may be giving you a progress report, in which "high" symbols such as rainbows and butterflies are a definite "thumbs up."

Delta state encounters can include healing and meeting your guides and other visits, which we usually don't remember unless we wake up soon after. These delta visitors may give us information or guidance about challenges we face in life. We often then weave this into a dream during the next alpha spike.

Nightmares almost always symbolize a problem that you are not facing and which will not go away until you act on it (with the rare exception of traumatic imagery from a previous lifetime). The more frequent the nightmare, the more urgent the issue is.

After-Death Encounters

We will see how our loved ones who have crossed over want to contact us to let us know that they're okay and to comfort us. We will also see how our grief and beliefs can block that contact. Sleep, however, is the one state where our guard is down and we are open. They can also burst through into waking reality and appear as visions.

A third scenario of opening occurs during serious illness when our mind's control is impaired. This happened to me during a devastating bout of food poisoning on a trip to Egypt. On the Spring Equinox under a full lunar eclipse while staying on the Giza Plateau, I was deathly ill and a door opened up to the other side:

I find myself on the flight home from Cairo to New York, and the captain invites me into the cockpit. He points to the third seat behind the co-pilot and motions me to sit down. This is my first cockpit visit during an actual flight and I'm ecstatic. I look forward and see endless sand dunes, gleaming white in the blazing sun. As I look out the window, I reflect on Egypt, what I've seen, and how glad I am to be going home.

Suddenly the plane shudders once, begins to vibrate, and then shudders again, this time more violently. The nose starts to go down, the angle getting steeper all the time. The pilot and co-pilot exchange clipped phrases and work the controls feverishly as they try to get the plane back under control. The engines are screaming like banshees as the captain tries to pull the nose up. But the desert is coming closer and closer, faster and faster.

I'm going to die. I thought I'd known fear but, in that cockpit, my fear level goes off the scale. White knuckles grip the back of the co-pilot's seat. I'm mesmerized by the fast-approaching ground. My thoughts speed up and I suddenly see very clearly who I am and what my life is about. I'm not ready for this! It's not time! Please let them pull up in time.

The plane is almost vertical now, spiraling down out of control. Just as the plane's nose is about to hit the ground, I instinctively close my eyes and hear my voice saying, "It will be all right. I'll be okay." A calm peace overtakes me, and suddenly there's nothing. Total stillness, followed by a whoosh. I feel as though I'm a million tiny pieces spread across the sky, like vapor, like I'm a part of everything. So this is what death is like, I say to myself.

A voice asks, "Are you all right?"

I think to myself, I know that voice.

Again, I hear, "Where are we?"

I realize that the voice is mine. Somehow I'm hearing myself. I am a point of consciousness trying to find some kind of anchor for itself. When you're part of everything, that's not easy.

I see a mist of sparkling, silvery light that clears to reveal that I'm standing by the edge of a river. The sun is glistening on the water and iridescent sparkles reflect on the surface. I look down to see my reflection and realize I'm alive! Oh, my God, I'm alive. I made it. But how did I get here? There's no wreckage so the plane didn't go down. Somehow they averted the crash and this river is the Nile. No, impossible; there's no plane. So where am I?

I feel fine and begin to walk along the riverbank toward some buildings where I see people going about their business. A man walks toward me wearing a black robe with flecks of gold in it. His shoulder-length brown hair shines in the sunlight. Brown hair and blue eyes. I love that combination! My attraction for this guy grows quickly. Who is he?

The man smiles. "Hello, Robert."

I notice that he's able to speak without moving his lips. How does he do that? And where am I? And who are you?

"Think of me as a guide," he says in response to my unspoken thought.

"Where am I?" I ask.

"You've been brought here."

"Where's 'here'?" I ask again.

"This is where we look at the inequities of the spirit."

The thought goes through my mind that inequity means unfair. This doesn't sound good. "What does that mean?" I ask him.

"This is where those things that have not been realized up to this point in one's life are reviewed. Think of it as a review of what you have already accomplished and where you might go from here."

"Have I died?"

"Yes, in a sense, you have."

Again, I'm fascinated by the fact that he isn't moving his lips. But then the truth of it crashes in on me. I'm dead, Oh, God! Everything I wanted to do and now I can't. How I'll miss my friends back on Earth.

I touch my arms, my face. I still feel like me. Then I think, maybe this being dead thing isn't so bad. It just takes some getting used to.

"What is this place exactly?"

"Many souls are brought here, some when they have died, some when they're living and in transition from the old self to a new self. They come here for review. Some who are here realize that they are here and some don't."

I look around at the people walking by and understand that they, too, are souls. Without being told, I simply seem to understand what this means. I look at one man who walks with his head down and wonder what happened to him. Whoosh—my consciousness runs right into him and merges with his. I feel his entire life, his hopes, his fears, the pain of his childhood abuse, the abyss of his horror at abusing his own children. His sense of desolation about his life is so intense that I scream, "I don't like this!" Instantly my consciousness bounces back at me like a stretched rubber band that's released and almost knocks me down.

"You must be very careful how you use your thoughts here," my guide admonishes gently. "You are much different here. You can feel other people's experiences."

He's right, I realize. You get things on a deeper level here. All that is inside you—the fear, the love, the anxiety, the hatred, the glory, the depression—all those things that you wear in your emotional body, you wear on the outside in this realm, naked to the world. Everybody knows who you are, knows your deepest fears, your highest hopes.

"Thoughts and the words that express them are very real and powerful," my guide continues.

I see a couple arguing and watch in horror as their hurtful words hit their partner's aura like tiny missiles that explode into gray areas. If enough missiles hit, the entire aura turns gray.

I reflect that every thought we have is a tangible thing, sacred and significant. Every thought and word has an impact. We have to be careful how we use our thoughts and what we say.

The guide shows me a tablet with something like hieroglyphics on it. In a way I can't describe, it speaks to me. The tablet is actually talking to me. It is a record of my life. When I look at it, I see silver letters turn to fire. I look into the tablet and see good news. It shows me that, overall, I have lived a good life. I'm not so bad after all. I have lived my life treading gently on the Earth. I have been a generous friend to those in need, a shoulder to cry on when needed, a source of strength to those in doubt. Yes, I can live with myself. That is the biggest question you face in this situation: can you live with who you are?

I also see the inequities, those areas of my life about which I'm not too thrilled. Top of the list is *lust*. I was so lustful that I used to feel guilty about having those thoughts. But I smile because it all looks so different up here. I see clearly that spirit looks at this with great compassion. Everybody has plenty of petty faults and many are far worse than mine. I am relieved.

My next bugaboo is *anger* that is translated as indignant outrage whenever people compromise their integrity or code of ethics. Not too much of a fault, I see.

Resentment is next. My habit of harboring grudges is more of a problem because it locks stale, dead energy in my aura. Yes, that's one I must work on in the next life.

Then my *fears* swim into view: fear of rejection, fear of making mistakes, of not being able to control my emotions. "Trust, Robert. Have faith in your own spirit and in God," my guide telepaths to me.

"Anxiety is a peculiar human condition," my guide tells me in response to the anxiety welling up in me. "It is the background sense of being disconnected from the creator. You yearn so much to feel your intimate union with the Creator and when you don't, you feel forsaken. Trust, Robert. The Creator could *never* forsake its own creation, its own being."

Wave after wave of love hit me, almost knocking me to my knees. "Robert-the-ego feels bad for having these faults," the guide says, "but Robert-the-spirit feels only compassion for you."

He smiles. An overwhelming burst of love hits me and he explodes into a blinding flash of intense white light. At this point, I pass out.

As I come to, one thought consumes me: LIFE IS A GIFT. Life is the most precious thing there is, a magnificent opportunity to come to Earth, to serve humanity and the Creator, to experience unconditional love.

I begin to hear the thoughts of my guide again. "There are many Earths. The one you know is not the only expression of Earth. This is only one aspect of Earth. Many souls go to alternative Earths, where the consciousness and choices are different."

It becomes clear that we reincarnate into situations that help us see what we gave. We are who we are because we are the result of everything we've been. Most souls are actually millions of years old. We reincarnate into what we have created in other lives. I see a Nazi war criminal reincarnate into a life destined to lead to a concentration camp. I see hunters reincarnate as the hunted. All these Earths make up a huge school, designed to let us experience the outcome of our actions. In review sessions like this, you look at the balance sheet: how much have you given and how much have you taken?

As concepts wash over me, I get them in their entirety. It's like after you've watched a movie, you have the whole movie as one huge memory. But I'm getting the encapsulated memory first, without needing to plod through the entire movie.

My guide answers some of my most pressing questions without my even having to ask them. "The ascension isn't going to happen to you. You see, you are going to happen to ascension. It is just a name for something that humanity and the planet are currently doing: raising their frequency to a new expression. As you move up into it, you will realize what I mean. And then it will become a reality. Ascension is not some impersonal product out-there, but a very personal transition in-here," he says, pointing to his heart area. "Yes, there will be planetary upheaval and land mass changes, but humanity will be around for a long while."

I see the big picture in which the ascended planet and humanity take their place within the great galactic community. What joy I feel at seeing this, but I'm saddened at discovering all this too late to relay it to those still alive on Earth.

Just then I notice three odd creatures, like boxes with faces, waving good-bye to me and congratulating me. Suddenly my guide says, "It's time for you to go now."

Whoosh! I'm staring up at the ceiling, hearing my roommate snoring in the next bed. I can't describe how I feel. I'm alive! I'm breathing! I have the gift of life! What a joy to be alive again. Tears of joy stream down my face. It's true, life is a gift, the greatest gift we can know. I have embraced the sacred divinity of life and will live to talk about it. A second chance. A second gift. I had seen the Divine Blueprint had met my own Divine Architect. It was me all along.

Was it a dream or something more? An out-of-body experience, perhaps? Whatever it was, it gave me a new lease on life. When you've had it taken away and then been given it back, you realize how special life is.

That experience was obviously a communication from my higher self and not a precognitive dream that one day will come to pass. What about those dreams that do, in fact, prepare us for some future event?

Precognitive Dreams

Tony, my co-writer, would never have thought of having a dog in his life. Strictly a "cat person," he thought dogs were noisy, smelly, demanding creatures. But that all changed one morning in March 1996 when his mate, Joy, recounted a dream so clear that every detail stayed with her. In the dream, a black Labrador was sitting beside Tony looking adoringly up at him. The whitened muzzle suggested that he was an older dog. When Tony heard this, he said, without thinking, "Yes, that was Shiva," and then wondered where on Earth that remark came from.

At the time, Tony and Joy lived in a fourth-floor apartment in Denver that didn't allow dogs. They could not imagine how that dream could ever come true, so they filed it under "weird but interesting."

In May, Tony was offered a job in Northern California and a start date of October 1 was agreed. About a week before they were due to move, Joy had another doggie dream in which Shiva, much younger this time, was sitting on a shiny floor waiting for them. Joy knelt down and asked Tony, "Do you think this is Shiva?" At that point, the dream ended.

When Joy and Tony arrived in California, they moved on to a horse ranch where three dogs already lived. Three weeks later, they were in PetsMart buying aquarium supplies, and the local pound was offering several dogs for adoption. Right in the middle of the canine chaos, calmly sitting on the shiny floor of the store was a black Labrador exactly as in Joy's second dream. Joy naturally knelt down and asked, "Do you think this is Shiva?" She shivered at the precise reenactment of the prophetic dream she'd had many weeks earlier and over a thousand miles away. Needless to say, they forgot all about the aquarium. They had doggie supplies to buy!

So, what really happened? Shiva, Joy and Tony had made a prelife agreement to be together. Once Shiva had been born in February 1996, his soul began to put events into motion. He appeared to Joy in the first dream as a preliminary announcement to get Tony used to the idea of having a dog. Shiva was then "fostered" to a family who later moved to a "no pets" house and had to send him to the pound. He then instigated the "heads up" second dream and waited for the big day when he would be included in the pound's monthly trip to the pet store.

Right on cue, along came Joy and Tony, who found him and took him home to a beautiful horse ranch. And because he was then about 8 months old, he was fully house-trained, thus avoiding the inevitable "puppy messes" that Tony would not have tolerated. As we are about to see, at the soul level, Shiva had his own agenda, which dovetailed perfectly with the soul agendas of Joy and Tony.

So You Think I'm Just A Dog

Tony and I were curious about how the soul of a dog could intersect with a human soul on the dream plane, so he talked about it with Lauren, a psychic friend. She went into the inner planes to talk with Shiva, and they both got a lot more than they bargained for.

They found that the souls of dogs and cats go through similar pre-life decision-making to the human process we saw in Chapter 1. Shiva explained the routine to Lauren and introduced her to "the Overseer," the master guide who orchestrates the process. In turn, he introduced Lauren to a long line of souls eager to tell their stories. So much information poured from these interviews that Lauren and Tony began a book entitled *The Canine Project*. With their permission, we include portions of the interviews with the Overseer and Shiva. After reading them, you will never look at a canine again and say, "It's just a dog."

We start with the Overseer, but let me warn you, you may shed a tear or two at what you read.

"Being a soul in service, without thought of self, is not an easy road. Not all who choose a life as a dog approach me for advice. Only the ones that choose to leave highly evolved dimensions of living in order to serve a specific need for the people they will adopt. The discrepancy between the two realities is great and often painful beyond imagining. Therefore, it is necessary to seek counsel before making the extreme leap.

"The world of canine service is a large one, filled with souls who wish to help humanity, individually and as a whole. These souls take many forms and suffer many hardships. One of the forms in which a soul can serve is by taking the form of a family pet. Being the family dog is not an easy task. Easier, perhaps, is the role of the family cat. As one of my protégés put it, the cat has the human race conned into believing that it is superior to the human and therefore must be served. The cat smiles internally each time a human rushes to its aid when it emits its tiny, pitiful cry. The dog, on the other hand, is here to serve. It takes what it can get and is grateful to the bone about receiving anything at all. The service a dog performs is, to a great degree, totally dependent upon the whim of its human 'master.'

"Consider, if you have not already, what it might feel like to be left in a house or yard while the family members depart. 'Do I have enough water and food? What if they don't return? What will I do? How will I survive? Will anyone outside this small world of my house and yard know that I exist and come to my rescue?' You are totally at the mercy of the human world.

"I cannot tell you of the tears I have wept at the suffering I have seen. These angels of mercy have given the ultimate to the human race—their unconditional acceptance, love, and devotion. Yet I have seen a beautiful Rottweiller die of heatstroke, chained in a tiny alcove, beaten by the relentless summer sun, left without water. When they found him, his body was covered with sweat. It is not possible for a dog to sweat ... but this one did. He panicked as he died. The moisture in his body was released in a futile attempt to keep him cool until someone noticed that he was dying, which didn't happen. No one noticed.

"I have seen a fabulous soul, an outstanding Collie, die without a whimper as it struggled to breathe in a locked car. I have seen dogs choke to death due to being chained to trees in unsupervised yards. I have seen humans pit one dog against another just for the thrill of watching them die.

"Why would a soul choose to be at the mercy of others to such a degree that, if you are not cared for, you may die a slow and painful death?

"Let me tell you first that these gracious animals have souls and choices. My job as the overseer is to make certain that the souls who are choosing to incarnate in this service are capable of carrying out their missions. They must have the strongest of hearts, the greatest stamina, and utmost devotion to the task. They must learn, if they have not already, that to judge is to forget that unconditional love is all there is. As souls who are in service, they may or may not suffer. If they suffer, they must be able to do so without judging those who cause their suffering. The role is, for the most part, a sacrificial one, in which the soul learns to love without judging the person that it loves. There is no thought put into such things as, 'My human woke up in a nasty mood, and so today I will not love him,' Or, 'My human forgot to put fresh water down for me and so I will hold a grudge and will not lie at his feet this evening.'

"In addition, a soul who takes an incarnation as a dog gives up, for the most part, free will. Can he or she serve without thought of self? Can the daily reality of living every moment at the whim of a human's choices and demands be carried out without resentment? It takes a special temperament to live such a lifetime without resentment or anger. I know of few humans who think along such selfless lines and make such observations, and so this sacrifice is, for the most part, unrecognized. The role of family dog is a major test of a soul. And yet, hundreds of souls make this choice every day. That, I believe, is a testament to the endurance of the soul as it seeks to understand existence."

Sobering words. Here's what Shiva had to say when Lauren asked him about pre-announcing his arrival to Joy in a dream:

"I had been to the Overseer to arrange this journey to Earth and, together, we decided that a lifetime with Tony and Joy would be ideal for all of us. But in order to make that happen, I had to get their attention so that they would be ready for me when I arranged to be picked up by the pound and be in the lobby of the pet store that they frequented. I have been on Earth numerous times. Spirit travel is nothing new to me. I am actually an old soul and, if I may say so, very wise.

"I am in training to be a spirit guide, someone who walks with a soul who is in a physical incarnation. More often than not, spirit guides serve entire lifetimes without any recognition whatsoever. It is not an easy role and I am determined to be the best that I can be when the time comes. This is why I volunteered for my current assignment, in which I have the opportunity to study the human experience from a viewpoint that is totally different than any I might have by actually taking a human body.

"You might wonder why an old soul would choose to be so restricted in its free will choices by becoming a dog. There is much that you learn by being physical but without the daily stresses and obligations of a human incarnation. But sometimes we worry. Like when they leave, we worry about where they went, if they'll come back, and why we couldn't go with them. On a spirit level, we understand these things but, as humans often do, we drop into concerns about the physical and forget the spirit.

"It would take great insight to understand what it takes to give up free will. I'm fairly lucky in that my family supports my range of experience. However, this is not the case with all dogs. The surrender of free will is one of the things that I chose to learn about, and the finest way that I could do that was to take on a dog's reality. But this particular experience with the loss of free will is fairly painless. This is not the case for everyone, I know."

So, the next time you're tempted to aim a kick in the direction of your pet, it's humbling to know that there's a sentient being in there who trusts and loves you unconditionally. Are you ready to honor that trust, for they, too, are Divine Architects?

Before leaving the subject of animals, one of the responsibilities of being a Divine Architect is that of stewardship for the other species on this planet, a responsibility I see being drastically ignored, with the effect that we are short-changing the animal kingdom in a major way.

Can your vision of Heaven on Earth include willful cruelty to thousands of animals daily (dozens have died just while you have been reading this), animals who cannot speak for themselves and must suffer their agony in silence, just so that our toothpaste makes teeth whiter and our army's bullets wreak more carnage on living tissue?

Someone must stand up for the rights of our wise and loving friends. Why not you? After all, you are a Divine Architect ... and so are they.

Chapter 6

You'll See Them Again

"The more I learn of physics,
the more I am drawn to metaphysics."
— Albert Einstein

W E PUT TREMENDOUS ENERGY into defining, shaping
and molding our lives so that we can be happy, find stability, and see ourselves through the wondrous phenomenon
we call the human experience. But we all share one common bond—
the one experience that awaits us all, regardless of race, color, creed,
gender, etc. What is it? *The afterlife!*

Much has been written about the afterlife, but many people don't
realize that it's really an integral part of *this* life. We say goodbye to
our loved ones who have passed over and grieve the fact that we've
"lost" them and that they're no longer a part of our lives. Wrong! My
years of research in this area have led me to one undeniable conclusion: our relationship with them isn't over but has just changed, and
you will see them again.

In our lifetime, we make thousands of major decisions and millions of small ones, and experience an enormous wealth of emotions
and thoughts. Our soul records and stores every minute detail, no matter how seemingly trivial, for that is why we incarnated in the first
place. There are some things that can only be done down here in physi-
cality. However, there comes a time when our physical sojourn is
complete, because we can glean no more experience in a particular life

situation and body so we, the soul, shrug the body off. And we may hang around close to the physical plane, still working and playing with our loved ones. Unfortunately, much to the chagrin of the soul, the numbing grief of those loved ones tends to block its attempts at contact. Fact or fiction? Let's look at what we Americans believe.

In 1991, an ISSP[1] study found that 55 per cent of us believe in some sort of afterlife. In 1994, a Gallop Poll survey discovered that believers in the afterlife had risen to 90 per cent, with 49 per cent saying that they believe that communication is possible with those on the other side. And a NORC[2] poll determined that 40 per cent of us had actually experienced one or more After-Death Communications (ADC).

Reincarnation: Fact or Fiction?

In my talks, people often ask, "Do you really believe in all this reincarnation stuff?" After reading many, many accounts, the answer is obviously a resounding "Yes." However, diehard skeptics will deny irrefutable proof if they don't *want* to believe. For example, probably the most famous account of reincarnation is told in *The Search for Bridey Murphy*, by Morey Bernstein. In Pueblo, Colorado between November 1952 and August 1953, Bernstein, an amateur hypnotherapist, regressed housewife Virginia Tighe to the 19th century life of Bridey Murphy.

Adding to the credibility of the proceedings, Bernstein was initially skeptical about reincarnation but soon had to change his tune. Over six sessions, in a beautiful Irish brogue, Bridey poured out tremendous detail regarding her growing up in Cork, Ireland and her later marriage and move to Belfast. Verifying the many names and places required a trip to the "old country," during which many details, such as the names of stores where Bridey shopped were easy to verify. However, historians disputed many of Bridey's assertions, but more thorough research overturned their every objection and taught the so-called experts much about arcane Irish history. Over the past century, maps, customs, and the language had changed. Even professionals would admit that recall under hypnosis is not one hundred per cent accurate. For example, Marge Rieder (who we met in Chapter 1) tells of one Millboro client who swore that the town had been called Willboro.

---

[1] International Social Survey Program
[2] National Opinion Research Center

When *In Search of Bridey* Murphy was first published in 1956, the debunkers gathered like vultures. A little-known writer for the *American*, an obscure Hearst-owned Chicago magazine, wrote an article dismissing the whole affair as something that Mrs. Tighe made up based on something she had read or heard. Despite a lofty rebuttal of the article in *The Denver Post*, *Life* magazine ran the *American* story as if it were true. Given the prominence of *Life* magazine, sadly the American public now believes that "hoax" is the last word in the Bridey Murphy story.

With all the professional therapists running around hypnotizing people, skeptics ask why it would be left to a Colorado businessman to be the first to document such a case. The obvious answer is that in the fifties, a therapist's training specifically excluded reincarnation, and any professional "going public" with regression was destined for the unemployment lines. As a hobbyist, however, Bernstein had nothing to lose.

For proof of reincarnation that has scholars still shaking their heads in disbelief, we need go no further than Dr. Whitton in *Life Between Life* in which he documents a fascinating case in which his client, Harold, was regressed to the life of Thor, a Viking warrior. Whitton asked Thor to phonetically spell words from his language, who obliged with 22 words. After lengthy research, linguistic scholars identified the words as coming from Old Norse, precursor to modern Icelandic, neither of which Harold was remotely familiar with.

In another session, Harold went back to a life as a scribe in Mesopotamia in 600 AD. When asked to write in his native language, he produced pages of apparently meaningless scribble. However, Library of Congress scholars identified the scribble as the written form of an extinct language that was used in Mesopotamia between 226 and 651 AD, again not something that Harold routinely dabbled with as a hobby.

An episode of the TV show *Unsolved Mysteries* told the story of a woman who went to a hypnotherapist for help in losing weight and came away with a whole new life. In 1979, Sharon Johnson (not her real name) underwent hypnosis with Frank Baranowski. She immediately started coughing and was terrified that "the water was burning." Since childhood, this had also been a recurrent dream that had puzzled Sharon.

As it happened, Baranowski took a group of his clients to Hawaii for a workshop. When the group visited Pearl Harbor and toured the Arizona memorial, Sharon had a panic attack. Over the next few months, she underwent 20 more regression sessions in which an interesting story unfolded in great detail. Sharon's terrifying memories belonged to a John Gillespie, born in 1921, the son of John and grandson of Frank Gillespie. He had grown up on a farm near Omaha, Nebraska before joining the Navy as a crewman aboard the battleship *Nevada*. Like much of the Pacific fleet, the *Nevada* had been a sitting duck when the Japanese attack occurred on December 7, 1941.[3]

Through Sharon, John told of the torpedo explosion, bombs dropping and fires burning out of control, until everything went black. Presumably, John had died at that point. In another session, John listed details such as his Navy pay number and the names of nine shipmates, plus those of the captain and paymaster.

Skeptics might say that Sharon had read voraciously about Pearl Harbor in order to confound the therapist, but she is an ardent pacifist who has never read a book about WWII in her life. And a polygraph test on her and the therapist indicated no sign of duplicity.

Baranowski's research took him to Omaha, where he saw the birth certificates of the three generations of Gillespie men and matched the dates of birth exactly. He also went to Washington and the National Archives, where the crew roster of the *Nevada* showed eight of the nine names Gillespie had listed but, oddly, a ninth was missing, that of an Ensign Tosig who, Gillespie said, had received a serious leg wound. *Unsolved Mysteries* was able to track down Tosig who confirmed that he had been on the *Nevada* and did have a leg amputated. In his case, the Navy's paperwork was incorrect. This is important, because if the therapist and client had used naval records to concoct this story for some reason, they would have made no reference to Ensign Tosig. When a regression yields information that can only later be verified, that to me is certain proof of reincarnation.

So, yes, the jury is back and the verdict is that reincarnation is definitely how it is. Which leads to the obvious question: why don't we know about our other lives? The equally obvious answer is that knowing

---

3   On December 7, 1941, the battleship USS *Nevada* was moored apart from the other battleships, which allowed her to maneuver. The machine gunners opened fire on the torpedo planes approaching her port beam. Two planes were hit, but a torpedo tore a huge hole in the port bow. Her engineers got up steam, and she was able to get underway but, while attempting to leave harbor, she was struck again and was gutted. Sixty men were killed and 109 were wounded.

about the other lives that our soul has lived (and is still living) would ruin the game for us.

All souls have one or more grisly lifetimes and deaths under their belts, and I personally do not want to know all the gory details of every life and death my soul has had. I have enough trouble dealing with one lifetime, let alone several hundred. If I knew of every time one of my incarnational brothers or sisters had stumbled along the path, I'd be a basket case and that would also invalidate the current opportunity my ego personality has to figure things out. No, I enjoy things being fresh and new each time around.

Profile of an ADC

Accepting that our soul lives again and again, each time in a new body, when we leave a body, it's only natural that we'd want to contact those loved ones we've left behind on the physical plane. Given that we no longer have a body, we're limited in the types of after-death communication at our disposal.

In my research, I have profiled the typical ADC. You are awake but alone, possibly feeling sad, lonely or troubled, when you get the distinct impression that a deceased loved one is close to you. You know immediately who it is, even though you're likely to be skeptical. The person contacting you died probably less than five years ago, and more likely less than 12 months ago. The contact experience lasts from 15 seconds to two minutes, and leaves you feeling renewed and supported, as if a newfound strength is with you. If visual, your loved one appears whole, healthy and younger than when he or she died. You will probably keep quiet about the experience because you think others wouldn't understand.

You, the experiencer, are likely to have suffered the loss of a spouse after a lengthy relationship, and statistically are likely to be a woman over 60. Your religious beliefs are irrelevant in governing whether you're contacted. Your family may have a history of ADC down through the generations, so you are less likely to deny the experience.

What Was That Noise?

Researchers Bill and Judy Guggenheim interviewed over 2,000 people who had been contacted by someone who had crossed over, and they documented their findings in *Hello From Heaven*. Unlike professional psychic mediums, experiencers are just ordinary people who may never even have given a moment's thought to the afterlife. That can change very quickly. The Guggenheim's identified the main ways that the spirit world uses to get our attention:

- *Sensing a presence*, a feeling that the person is in the room, often accompanied by a warm, comforting sensation. They may often show up for big occasions, such as weddings and birthday parties, to help assuage grief among bereaved relatives or just to let us know that they're all right.

- *Voices*, either heard through the ears or as thoughts. The message is usually short and sweet, such as, "I love you," or "I'm okay," or they can be extensive reports of life on the other side. In *The Divine Blueprint*, I described how, at the exact moment my mother died, I was driving and heard her say, "Robert, Robert" as clearly as if she was sitting in the back seat. If you stay calm, you can strike up a lively conversation with your visitor since he or she can read your mind and reply telepathically. When Walda Woods (see Chapter 1) was about to give a chest of drawers to a thrift store, she cleared it out, or so she thought. She heard the voice of her husband, who had died a few weeks earlier, say, "Check again." Finding nothing, she told Tom, who repeated, "Check again." A thorough search turned up, taped to the inside top, an envelope containing $1,000. Apparently, Tom had been saving up to surprise her with a cruise vacation.

- *Touch*, ranging from a light tap to a full embrace, usually to reassure or comfort us.

- *Smell*, usually reminiscent of the person, such as perfume or tobacco.

- *Partial appearance*, often a bright ball of light hovering in the room, or the visitor may project his or her face. You don't need to be eyes closed in meditation, either. These are broad daylight, eyes open appearances, albeit it not solid-looking. Whenever I see apparitions, I can usually still discern any bright or shiny objects that are behind them.

- *Full, solid appearance*, which may surprise us because the visitor looks to be in perfect health, and often younger in appearance than at the time of death, with more hair and with any amputated limbs intact. This type of contact, more than any other, convinces even hardened skeptics of the reality of life-after-death. When Walda Woods was looking for her husband's wedding band, he appeared to her and patted his shirt pocket. Sure enough, that's exactly where Walda found the ring, even though the shirt had been through the washer and dryer.

- *Glimpses beyond.* Almost as if you're looking through a window, you see your loved one in *their* actual setting, rather than in your setting. Some people see it as a movie shown on an invisible screen in front of them.
- *Hypnogogic contact.* On falling asleep or just waking, we are open to any form of contact. In *The Divine Blueprint*, I reported how, just as I was waking on the day of my father's funeral, I heard him say to me, "Hi, Rob" so vividly that the shock jolted me fully awake. The assurance that he was still alive and kicking on the other side was a great gift to me on that very sad day.
- *Sleep state contact.* As we saw in Chapter 5, when the conscious mind shuts down and we are free to roam the higher dimensions, our deceased loved ones have the home field advantage and can communicate with great clarity.
- *Phone calls.* Since souls are pure energy, they can manipulate electronic devices quite easily. The experiencers interviewed by the Guggenheims reported that the phone would ring once and they would hear the voice of their loved one on the other end, either clear and crisp or sounding distant, possibly with static. Sometimes, the caller would break into a conversation already in progress.
- *Symbolic signs.* Our loved ones may send us a meaningful sign, such as a butterfly landing on us or a rainbow on the anniversary of someone's passing.
- *Physical signs.* Many times, visiting spirits give us signs, such as turning lights on or off, stopping clocks at a significant time, turning the radio on just when a particular song is playing, or moving things just to let us know they're around. Tom Woods was particularly playful in this way, refusing to leave the TV remote control alone.

As Walda Woods reports in her book, *Conversations with Tom*: "Every light on the third floor was on, too, including a light in my son's room that had never worked, and a light on the underside of my new dresser's mirror that I never knew even existed! Suddenly, the odd waves of emotion shifted to the most incredible feelings of love and peace, further proof that Tom was close by.

"Tom's favorite means of communication, however, was the television. It would turn off and on without anyone being near either it or the remote control. Curiously, it would turn off and on exactly on the hour, according to the cable box digital clock. It would also change channels on its own. I would be watching a favorite program, and suddenly a sporting event (Tom's favorite) would replace it. I swapped cable remotes three times and even bought a brand new TV set, but not only did the occurrences continue, they became even more frequent!"

I heartily recommend *Hello From Heaven* and applaud Bill and Judy Guggenheim for their valuable contribution to our knowledge of the afterlife. The only reason *not* to read their book is if you are so attached to your skepticism that you don't want to risk losing it, because otherwise I assure you that you *will* become a believer. For adamant cynics, the Guggenheims even include a number of contactees' cases in which information was given that only later could be verified.

This is especially true when the ADC occurs before you even know of the person's passing, as when I heard my mother's voice and only got the news later. The Guggenheim's talk extensively about this and give enough examples of solid visual ADCs to convince even the most hardened skeptic. What is compelling about these cases is that the experiencer was not expecting to be contacted. And for the arch-skeptic, *Hello From Heaven* includes a chapter of solid gold evidentiary cases where information was given that only later turned out to be correct, such as the location of documents and valuables that the deceased had hidden for security purposes.

Why do those who have passed over communicate back to us? The main reasons I have found are:

- *To reassure us of their well-being*. When loved ones die, we may be worried about them or wonder what happened to them. Having them visit us can be extremely reassuring. This is particularly important in the case of suicide, where the bereaved may be concerned about their loved one's status in the afterlife.
- *To comfort the grieving*. Although our loved ones may be fine and dandy on the other side, those of us still on this side are left carrying the grief. All too often, our grief causes them great distress. So they appear to us to bring comfort and tell us that we're only separated by a thin veil. When a mother loses a child, for example, the overwhelming grief may be softened when the child's soul tells the mother that everything went according to plan, and it was the soul's time to go.

- *To pass on important information*, such as the location of a missing will or other document, as with Tom Woods telling his wife of the $1,000 in the envelope. This type of contact also reassures us that our loved ones are still looking after our best interests from across the veil. ADCs have known to occur decades after someone's passing. In these cases, we can often see the spiritual growth of our loved one, with anger replaced by compassion and understanding, for example.

- *To give a warning or suggest a course of action*, as when my father warned me about problems with a real estate deal he had begun but not concluded. Another type of warning is to soften the blow of learning from outside sources of the passing of a loved one.

- *To assuage guilt.* Suppose you feel guilty about having put an aged parent in a nursing home. The soul of the parent may return to say that it fully understands the reasons why that had to happen and that there's no reason for you to feel guilty.

- *To apologize for something.* Suppose a parent had a hard time telling you how much he or she loved you, the parent may wish to tell you that you really were loved, even if the personality could not say the actual words. Another reason for an apology is suicide. Not only must the bereaved deal with their grief at their loss but they must also come to terms with the deliberate death. On the other side, the soul who sought relief from earthly problems must deal with the fact that death was not the hoped for solution. But worse, it must accept that the pain it caused was of its own doing, something for which the term "abject apology" does not even come close.

Under the warning category, the Guggenheims report ADCs that allowed many contactees to avoid accidents, crimes, and undiagnosed illness. In one case, when a driver panicked on a railroad crossing, a deceased friend materialized and stomped down so hard on her right foot that she suffered a severe bruise.

Protection also comes in the form of inspiration and counseling in order to prevent a possible suicide in the face of depression or seemingly overwhelming problems. They remind us that suicide is "a permanent solution to a temporary problem," and that no problem is so great that it cannot be overcome.

Crisis visitations warn a loved one of the visitor's recent or imminent death. The tremendous release of psychic energy associated with crossing the veil plus the love that wants to warn are the fuel that can blast through to even the most ardent skeptic. The literature is full of wartime stories of husbands and sons who visit wives and mothers at the exact moment of crossing, often from a distant part of the world. In one case, an airman who crashed appeared to his comrades so clearly that they were mystified when his plane was reported missing.

Since an ADC often happens in a quiet moment, it's rarely shared, and later we may doubt that it actually happened. However, when two or more share the experience, it's less easy to dismiss it as "just my imagination." Of course, those involved should discuss the experience, or everyone may stay silent, afraid of being thought foolish.

When a roomful of people see, smell, or hear the same thing, denial is impossible, although details may differ for each person. However, if others report a contact but you perceive nothing, do not deny their experience. They may just have needed it more than you. Often, family pets will share in an ADC, and their uncensored reaction will leave you in no doubt that something happened.

Knowing of this phenomenon is vital for two reasons. First, an ADC may be unsettling, scary even, and the last thing your loved one wants to do is scare you. Second, if you're not aware that this can happen, you might miss it.

As the terminally ill approach their crossing, consciousness begins the journey hours, even days, in advance. This allows people to see through the veil and begin to greet and converse with those awaiting their arrival. The reaction of loved ones in attendance at a deathbed vigil varies from amusement to horror at the sight of someone they love chattering away to apparently empty space. "Granny's losing it," is a typical comment, but it's vital that this phenomenon is acknowledged so as not to invalidate the experience. Granny probably does not care what her grandkids think, because she knows what she's seeing, and the contact is reassuring. Sometimes, the visitation can be so clear that even others in the room can see the apparition.

Confirmation of visitations comes when those being visited have no way of knowing that the visitor has crossed over. For example, suppose that Granny is close to passing and one of her sons dies. The other relatives may keep the news from her but, when she encounters the son's spirit, the secret's out. Granny knows without anyone on this side telling her. This also happens when a child is close to death and is visited by grandparents who the child never knew in this life.

Our culture does a grave disservice to those about to cross the veil by denying the phenomenon of visits by those who have already crossed. Knowing what we know about the infinite caring and compassion of the other side, it should strike us as ridiculous if we *didn't* have assistance in our crossing. Because our culture's "consensus reality"(or mass belief), is too small to include the interlife (except for narrow religious interpretations), those who have contact with it have nowhere in the scheme of things to put their experiences.

The Bad News Is: My Parents Died; the Good News Is: They're Alive Again

In May 1994, my mother was diagnosed with ovarian cancer, and both my parents were so close to death that I thought they might even die on the same day. That was not to be. On July 28, I had visited my mother in the hospice and was driving home when, from the backseat, she said, "Robert, Robert." I looked round, wondering how on Earth she had gotten in my car, but I saw no one. When I got home, my father called to give me the news. Needless to say, the time of death was the very moment that I'd heard her calling my name.

In the fall of 1994, my father's days were fast coming to a close. The doctor estimated that he might have two or three months left. I decided to spend the short time remaining together in his company, and we discussed everything from the nature of time/space to the mysteries of death.

In his last few days, I approached him with an idea. It was radically different and certainly a departure from anything I'd attempted in previous experiments. "Dad, if as we agree, death really is an illusion and the essence of who you are really does continue, how about trying an experiment? Let's put it to the test. Let's try to continue our relationship, even though you may not be physically present in a body."

The experiment I proposed to my father was based on the premise that, at death, we continue our existence without missing a beat. All we need do is set our intent to continue our relationship and open our belief systems to allow it to happen. We talked more about what that would mean and he agreed to give it a shot. So, together, we set our intent and sealed it with a handshake.

When my sister, Dennie, heard of this, her reaction was, "Robert, you're always experimenting. First, it's extraterrestrials and now it's raising the dead!"

"Dennie," I explained, "many people believe that death is 'the final frontier' that marks the end of existence, that memories are lost, that identity ceases, and that the living cannot communicate with those who are no longer attached to a physical body. But the truth, as I see it, is totally the opposite. Bearing in mind how limited we are stuck in physical bodies, you could say that 'real life' begins only when you *do* die. Forget about life after death. Is there life after *birth*?"

Our experiment began with me facilitating a life review for him, much like we believed he would undergo after leaving his body for the last time. We went over all the major decisions in his life, and he reflected on what they had meant and what the outcome could have been if he had decided differently. For example, what if he had married someone other than my mother? What if he had chosen a life as a politician or military officer? But the most significant outcome from this review were his answers to the question, "If you had your life to live over again, what would you do differently?"

- "My biggest regret was getting sucked into earthly dramas at the expense of my spiritual values, especially my obsession with making money. Money was too important to me. Striving for *quantity* caused me to neglect the *quality* of life. I wish that I'd focused more on who I *really* was and my relationship with the planet and nature. I now see these things as my *real home*. I see now that I was just following the values I had inherited from my parents—that amassing wealth was the number one indicator of a successful life."
- "I wish that I'd read more of the great metaphysical books and attended more lectures and workshops by the great spiritual pioneers."
- "I wish that I'd been able to clear up old grudges when they came up. Listen, son, make sure that you quickly forgive anyone who harms you and that if you harm anyone, you apologize and get their forgiveness."

My father's review left me with three salutary lessons:

- Do not put off your life review until after death—it really is too late then. Try to make it an ongoing process.
- Take every opportunity to immerse yourself in your own spiritual evolution. Read books, attend workshops that interest you, talk to people of like mind, see your relationships as "works-in-progress" and keep enhancing them, for as the old saying goes, "you're a long time dead."

- The most important issue that troubled my father was that of self-love. The first thing you realize on the other side is just who you really are, how awesome a being you really are. If you haven't lived a life full of self-love, you really kick yourself when you realize what an opportunity for joy you missed.

Early in the morning of January 15, 1995, my father knew the end was near, and he was rushed to the emergency room. The prognosis was grim, and he had told me that he did not want life-support to extend his life. So now I had to make the decision that would finally kill him. All my studies into life after death told me that I would be freeing him from that tortured body to enjoy the glories of the higher dimensions. Fine in theory, but now the time had come to put my beliefs on the line. Could I "pull the plug" and end his life?

For two long minutes, I fought with the conflict in me. I grappled with my feelings at losing my father but, in the end, of course, his wishes to be spared a long drawn out death were paramount. Part of me wished that the other members of my family were there to share the burden, but I was on my own.

I took a deep breath and went into Intensive Care. My father was barely visible under the tangle of tubes keeping him alive, the wires monitoring his final battle. "Okay, doctor, I'm ready. Let's do it," I said quickly, "before I change my mind. And I want to be there."

My father was not conscious as I cradled his head in my arms, and the medical staff freed him from his artificial life. I asked that his guides be present to meet him once he left his body. The audible heart monitor was already slow. Soon it began to slow further until it was just a continuous tone. After a two-year struggle with a mysterious disease, he was free.

The sound of the monitor hung in the air, a postscript to my father's last moments. Thankfully, a nurse turned the machine off, and I was alone with my father's body.

I knew that the newly-released consciousness often lingered for a while so, in case he was initially confused, I said, "Dad, look for someone familiar. Is there anyone you know there to meet you?"

I stayed with him for some time until the nurse and doctor finally led me out of the room. As tears streamed down my face, I took one more look at him and said, "Bon voyage. I love you, Dad. We'll be in touch. Remember our agreement." With that, I turned and left.

The memorial service was held at the golf club clubhouse; the 19th hole had always been my father's favorite. As I gave my eulogy, a psychic friend there with me gasped. I continued speaking. Later, she told me that my father had been standing next to his casket, beaming with pride at my words and exuding incredible love in my direction. To her sight, he was just as real and solid as anyone else in the room. Now I know why we say, "Don't speak ill of the dead." Chances are, they're standing right next to you. My father's antics were not over yet.

The minister conducting the service had brought a colleague along who chose to use this occasion to score some religious brownie points. He got up to tell us, "Don was a deeply religious man whose constant words were, "Praise the Lord."

In fact, my father had been a deeply spiritual man, but religious? No. My friend later told me that my father had held his nose and waved his hand as if to say, "You're full of bologna." What she didn't know was that this was a very common gesture my father used at anyone with whom he disagreed. Score one for the after-life!

Remembering our agreement to conduct research, I began to look for signs of communication. It had been a hectic week for me because, even though he had worked hard to straighten out his business affairs, many of them were so convoluted that several tangles had to be unraveled. This left me physically exhausted and mentally depleted on top of the emotional distress of losing a father and a good friend. In retrospect, even if he *had* been trying to contact me during that week, I was probably not in a receptive state.

On the day of the funeral, just as I was on that threshold between sleep and wakefulness, I heard my father say so clearly that I thought he was by my bedside, "Hi, Rob."

Still groggy, I opened my eyes and looked around the room. Then it dawned on me. He had slipped his greeting to me before my overworked mind could get involved in the day's activities. Nice job, I thought. I relaxed and enjoyed the energy of "it's all going to be okay" that he somehow wrapped me in.

With that masterstroke of my father's, seven days of tiredness, grief, worry, and doubt evaporated. Yes, he's still around, I thought. Yes! I bounced out of bed, full of hope, optimism, and joy. I threw on a robe and ran into the kitchen where everyone else was fixing breakfast. "Listen up, everybody. I have an announcement. Dad's alive! He just spoke to me and everything's going to be just fine!"

Twelve blank faces stared at me as though I was a raving madman. They had no idea that I and my parents had a "spooky" side. I could imagine what was going through their minds, "Poor Robert's finally cracked under the pressure. Grief and anxiety over Don's business affairs have pushed him over the edge. We bury the father and commit the son to an institution all on the same day. What a mess."

My sister Dennie said, "Robert, you're tired."

"I'm not tired!" I snapped back. "I'm telling you, Dad's alive."

"Then what in the holy hell is going on here?" she asked.

"What do you mean about everything's going to be fine?" someone else asked timidly, not wanting to provoke the madman too much.

"Well," I said, "it wasn't so much what he said but the knowing that he immersed me in. As though he washed out all my doubts and fears and replaced them with confidence and security. I don't know how he did it, but he just spoke to me. These seven days have been hard, the not knowing. But now I know, it's true. It's really true!"

I stopped there, thinking that my wild babbling might prompt someone to call 911. I decided to bask alone in the warmth of my father's love, to enjoy it without anyone trying to talk me out of it. And enjoy it I did.

After the service, my psychic friend told me that during my eulogy, my parents stood together watching the proceedings and that at one point, my father came over to me and put a captain's hat on me. I guess that meant that I was now the head of the family.

About three months passed before the next contact, despite my daily ritual of reaffirming our contract and restating my intent for our relationship to continue. I woke up knowing that I'd been dreaming about my parents but wasn't able to bring the substance of our meeting to conscious awareness. However, I awoke with the deep feeling of being loved and would go about my day held in that warm glow.

One morning a few weeks later, I awoke with a clear memory. I had met my father and had been aware that, although I was present with him, my physical body was asleep elsewhere. This was my first lucid dream with him, and I remembered every detail. I had hugged him and with tears streaming down my face, said, "I love you, Dad." He'd looked at me with tremendous love in his eyes and I'd felt it wash over me and through me. Without moving his lips, he said something about being emotional. Suddenly, a spinning sensation overtook me, and I was back in my own bed, startled by the sudden change of location.

I then realized what his warning about emotion meant. That my being overly emotional would break our connection to the dream dimension. Breaking the connection is a valuable safety valve when the content of a bad nightmare gets too intense, and you wake up sweating with your heart racing. Any emotional intensity will bring your waking consciousness back into your sleeping body regardless of whether those emotions are enjoyable or terrifying.

I trained myself to avoid excitement during our meetings and would greet him with, "Hi, Dad." Equally calmly, he would reply, "Hello, son." Once I remembered to stay calm, I began to lead two lives: an outer life resolving a very troublesome legal situation I inherited from my father and an inner life with him at night. This led me to refute the deeper reality of death. In fact, I was "dying" myself every night when I met with my father, except it was a "temporary death" because I came back to my physical body afterwards.

At one meeting, I noticed that he was looking younger and slimmer with fewer lines in his face. He was wearing his favorite polo shirt, slacks, and shoes. Telepathically, he asked if I had any questions. "Where are we?" I asked.

"We're right here, son. Because here is the only place we can be."

Of course, I thought. Here *is* the only place you can be. That profound insight had great inner meaning for me, although much of the meaning would unfortunately be lost to my waking consciousness. Don't you hate it when that happens?

"So, how are you, Dad?" I asked.

"Fine, son, just fine." He smiled and began answering my next question about what he did all day even before I'd begun to form it in my own mind.

"I'm going to school right now, playing catch-up on what I missed during my Earth life. And the subject is … me. I'm learning about what I'd hoped to accomplish on Earth versus what I did accomplish. I'm replaying every decision I made to explore what would have happened if I'd decided differently, and which would have been the best decision for everyone involved. I'm re-enacting every experience I ever had to see how it served me, everyone else and even the creator.

"The bottom line is that, apart from the regrets we talked about, I lived a good life, an honorable life. I'm even drawing up some tentative plans for another lifetime and deciding what I would want to learn and accomplish."

My dream-state meetings with my mother revealed that she, too, was conducting her own life review—her life plan, her actual accomplishments, what had and hadn't served her. Her findings were very different, of course, because her personality's attachment to material wealth was different. She seemed to feel more sorrow about unachieved goals, whereas my father could blow that off more easily. I wondered if this was due to our having already conducted a life review while he was still alive. Mother expected more of herself and was harder on herself in her review than my father was.

It occurred to me that after death, it's important not to get too hung up on what had been done or left undone and simply plan to tackle it in another life, which adds a new literal meaning to the saying "life goes on." It's important to accept what is and move on.

The story doesn't end there, however, for I later consulted a psychic medium friend, Marge Cuddeback, and author of *Vanishing Veil*.

Over the years, Marge has conducted hundreds of ADC sessions. In 1970, following the death of her father, Marge began meditating and discovered that as soon as she closed her eyes, she could see into the spirit world. Following her husband's death in 1972, Marge's natural talent really opened up, and she soon began giving sessions for friends and relatives. Slowly, news of her gift spread, and her clientele increased to the point where she "went professional."

In reading her book, I'm repeatedly amazed at how much good psychic mediums do in helping us come to terms with our grief over having lost a loved one. As Marge says, "Know that our loved ones don't really leave us. And, they're always there for our big occasions. They're only a thought away. It's just frustrating for us and them that we can't see them as readily as they can see us … Our loved ones, whether they are deceased family or friends, spirit guides or guardian angels, are always watching out for us. When my father firmly called my name when I fell asleep at the wheel of my car, he saved me from a head-on collision. It obviously wasn't my time to cross over."

Marge continued, "At the time of death, you can either remain close to Earth or move on to the level to which your spirit has grown and is most comfortable. However, most spirits choose to remain on Earth for a short time to help to comfort and heal the loved ones they have left behind."

In one of Marge's cases, the client's birth mother died when she was two, and she was raised by a cruel stepmother. The first soul who showed up for her reading was a woman, and Marge reported, "She's a thin, short lady with long, light brown, straight hair, and large, round, brown eyes. She looks to be around 27 years old. She's sitting in a rocking chair, holding a girl about 2 – 3 years old who has sandy brown hair. The lady is saying, 'I never left you.'"

At this, Marge's client burst into tears and said, "You just described my mother perfectly. She died of cancer when I was two years old. I was really never very happy after that, being brought up by a cold, distant stepmother who I felt never loved me. I always wondered if my Mom was around me as I was growing up."

Not only do mediums like Marge help those on this side, but they're also invaluable to those who have passed over. Imagine the frustration of that mother's soul at leaving her beloved baby daughter behind and not being able to tell her how much she was loved, and then having to watch as the little girl grew up with a cold, harsh stepmother. Imagine the overwhelming joy at having that "one last time" to set the record straight with "I never left you."

In February 2000, I had a reading with Marge with the intention of contacting my father. Apparently, he came into the room with me, and Marge got right into things. "The spirits come in and I describe them. When you say their name, I will see them nod or shake their heads. So, let's see who wants to come in. First is a man, medium height, bald, expressive eyes, medium build."

When I said, "That sounds like my father, Don," he nodded.

"Yes. He's been here all the time. He's standing to your left with his right arm around your shoulder. He's saying that he's very proud of you. Now he's talking about his growth on the other side and how vivid the colors are. He's still learning, and there's so much to do and learn that sometimes he doesn't know where to begin.

"Now he's telling me that you have many guides and angels around you, and that he's asked to become one of your guides. He's around you at least eighty percent of the time anyway. If he doesn't have the answer to one of your questions, he's learning where to go to get it. He says that over there, he can be anywhere he wants just by thinking of a place.

"Now he's saying, 'I'm so glad to be rid of that body. Your mother was there to meet me. When I crossed, she took my hand and jerked it a little to free me from my body.'

"A woman has just come in. She has a petite build and salt-and-pepper hair. She's thanking me for making this communication possible.

She's joking with me that to her, you walk on water, Robert. Not having physical contact is frustrating because she's around you a lot but you're not always aware of her presence. She's learning to project more strongly, though."

"That sure sounds like my mother," I said.

"Uh ho, a huge spirit just came in. It's so bright that the walls have disappeared. She's telling me that you're a highly evolved old soul, that you're accomplishing what you came here to do, and that you're perceptive with people but should trust your intuition more.

"However, she's saying that you soak in other people's negative energy and allow them to drain your energy. You should protect yourself more, she says. Here's what I do. I surround myself with a bubble of white light, and then see a ring of fire around the bubble. Then I say, 'All negativity will burn off before it gets to me.' When you're with negative people, visualize a gold bubble around them and say, 'All negativity will burn off before it leaves them.'

"The spirit's saying that you didn't come to Earth this time for karmic reasons but to help raise the frequency of the planet. She was planning to incarnate with you but chickened out at the last minute. So she guides you now from the other side.

"You have a lot of healing energy around you, and lots of 'wounded birds' gravitate to you, but you've 'been there, done that.' Affirm that you only want people around you who are on your level. No more carrying other people's burdens, because others incarnate with their problems in order to deal with them. No more allowing them to become dependent on you. And in your relationships, strive for the frequency you came here to work with."

I asked, "Is there anything I should be doing to further my mission?"

Marge replied, "Your mother is saying for you to continue with the book and have more trust in your intuition. Listen more to your guides. But apart from that, you're on the right track."

"So, Dad, what actually happened at the moment of your death?" I asked.

"He's saying that the room was filled with lots of relatives, two angels and five guides. Once your mother had helped him out of his body, he went round greeting everyone."

"Was he still in the hospital room, or were they already in a different location?"

"He's saying that they'd already moved to a new location of rolling hills. He and your mother sat under a huge tree and gazed at the colors because they were so vivid."

"Can he tell us about his life review?"

"Yes, he had five guides with him because they knew that he'd be highly critical of himself. They were there to reassure him that he'd done the best he could with his life, which was good because he was almost horrified at some of the things he'd done."

"Will he describe a typical day?"

"Well, first we don't have days, but mainly I go to school, learning as much as I can. I visit you a lot, and think a lot. I'm discovering so much about my own power, so that I get things right when I return."

"What was your soul's purpose for this last lifetime?"

"To give and receive love. Looking back, I'm disappointed in how I did. But I'm receiving a lot of help on this side."

"What message would you like to give to the world?"

"Open up to your spirit. Get out of your ego. Know that your thoughts create your reality. I didn't get that while on Earth."

"When I dream of you, are we really together?"

Marge laughed and said, "I'm seeing the word 'YES!' in forty-foot high letters."

"How can I improve our connection so that I can be more conscious of our communication?"

"Before you go to sleep, simply ask that you remember more. I want to thank you for what you taught me during my lifetime. I really helped."

"John Edward told us not to refer to you as 'dead people.' Would you agree?"

"Of course. I'm talking to you now, and I'm very much alive."

"What happens to those who commit suicide?"

"It sets their growth back for a while because they need to set up another lifetime with the same or similar combination of problems."

"What's the best thing we can do to contact loved ones who have already crossed over?"

"Meditation, automatic writing, asking for and being aware of visitations during sleep."

"When we dream about people who we don't know from this lifetime, are they spirits who we left behind on the soul plane?"

"Sometimes, but others are guides who are giving you information."

"Are any of my guides extraterrestrial?"

"Yes, one of your most prominent guides is Pleiadian. You work with her a lot."

"Is there anything she would like to say?"

"She's here to help you through the transition you're going through at this time, so that you're more aware of the energy shifts as the planet goes into the fifth dimension."

"Dad, did you experience remorse when you crossed?"

"Oh, yes. A great deal. I brought my emotional pain with me to be dealt with over here. I wish I'd dealt with it on the Earth plane, because it's harder now. To make amends now, we have to implant a thought in someone's mind and hope they get it. Trust me, it's easier for you to just pick up the phone."

"What can I do to better execute my mission?"

"Raise your frequency by meditating. Second, ask your guides for their help. Third, trust your intuition more."

"Is there anything we've overlooked for the book?"

At this point, Marge laughed. "For the first time since the session started," she said, "they're being quiet. I'm not getting a thing. Not a thing. I guess that means you're following their guidance pretty well."

What did I learn from this session? First, that it indeed was my parents although I omitted the personal evidential material from this account. Second, when I get an intuitive hit, I should trust it rather than analyze it to death. Third, healing negative emotions and beliefs in the afterlife is largely ineffective because we're doing it from a higher perspective, as when we take a test with the answer sheet in front of us. It is far better to heal those emotions and beliefs when we're still in the "muck and mire" that created them. If you can forgive those who harm you *while you're still here*, you're free and clear. But if you take unresolved anger or hatred with you to the other side, you cannot as easily resolve them and will probably need another lifetime or two to practice forgiveness. As one of my favorite teachers once said, "Turn the other cheek." And lastly, I learned that none of us walk through this world alone for, as the boy said in *The Sixth Sense*, "They're everywhere."

My session with Marge echoed one I had with Melinda Conner three years after my parents died. Clairvoyant and clairaudient like Marge, Melinda sees and hears whoever comes in with the client. In my session, my parents showed up and asked Melinda to sing, "It Only Takes a Moment … to Love." I was shocked for, unknown to Melinda, this was the song I played at my father's funeral. My father also relayed through her that he was with me 80 per cent of the time, the exact same number that came through Marge.

It's Never Too Late

Suppose someone crossed over with whom you had unfinished business. Maybe you argued with the person and didn't get chance to apologize, or maybe you cheated in a business deal and are now consumed with guilt. It's still not too late to right the wrong. Simply focus on the person for a minute or so and know that he or she is with you. Then offer your apology, just as if the person were in the room with you, because he or she is. Be sincere, however, because your heart and mind are open books to those on the other side.

It's important to do this before *you* cross over, otherwise you take the unfinished business with you into your life review—just another piece of unwanted emotional baggage to lug around. Death does not provide the chance to walk away from the harm we have done. In fact, our wrongdoings color our early existence on the other side. Hopefully, knowing and acting on this will allow you to cross over with a clean slate, carrying only the love you generated and the good you did for your fellow men, women, children and animals.

The Bishop and the Ghost

In the ADC classic, *The Other Side*, James Pike tells of how his deceased son contacted him. The story is unremarkable except for two things: it was written in 1968 before ADC was a hot topic, and the author was an Episcopal bishop, an attorney who had worked for US Naval Intelligence in WWII—not a man given to flights of fancy, especially as this story got him thrown out of the Church.

The story starts when Bishop Pike's son, Jim, committed suicide early on the morning of February 4, 1966 in New York. Pike was living in Cambridge, England at the time and began to notice odd things happening. Photographs and books would be rearranged, and the clock would routinely stop at 8:19, the exact time in England when Jim had died in New York.

Pike eventually surmised that Jim was trying to get his attention, so he consulted a psychic medium. To her, Pike was just another client who wanted to contact his dead son, but she proved her worth when, not in her normal voice, she said, "I failed the test. I can't face you. I didn't know what I was doing … too many pills … I'm not in purgatory … nobody blames me here."

Through the medium, Pike began the first of many lengthy conversations with his son, most of which didn't mean a thing to the medium but totally convinced Pike that he really was talking to Jim. Bishop Pike was a high-profile cleric in the Church so, when he went public with his proof of life-after-death, the Church turned around and charged him with heresy of all things.

I include this story because of its unlikely central character. Pike had no leanings towards ADC. In fact, his position in the Church forbade it, which makes the account even more compelling.

One Last Time

Unlike many theatrical mediums, John Edward is a modest, unassuming, guy-next-door and the last person you would expect to talk to dead people for a living. In his book, *One Last Time*, he reveals an early childhood much like mine. Born the son of a cop and a secretary who was a "psychic junkie," he can't remember a time when he didn't hear "the whispers" as he calls them—voices that told him who was on the other end of a ringing telephone or who was at the door. He also saw auras around his schoolteachers.

In reading his book, I was struck by how difficult his job is in that many of those who come to him are dripping with skepticism and demanding evidence. That's why, he explains, much of the material that comes through is mundane, evidentiary stuff in the soul's attempts to melt the skepticism. Of course, with a good medium, that's not hard to do. How many other professionals have to first convince a dubious client that they really can do what they claim? Why, I wonder, do people actually go to mediums in the first place if they don't trust them. Of course, there are charlatans, as in any field, but not this guy. You can hear a pin drop during his public appearances as he reels off the names of those waiting on the other side to get their messages to loved ones in the audience.

John titled his book *One Last Time* after the opportunity ADC gives us to share a precious moment with our lost loved ones, which is particularly important following an unexpected death due to sudden illness, accident or even murder. In these cases, there was possibly no opportunity to say our goodbyes, and we feel "incomplete."

John comments on the *intent* of those on the other side to come through. They are often as headstrong and persistant as they were when on this side, and often wake John up or resort to all manner of other tricks to get his attention.

I recently saw John at a public appearance before a capacity audience of 2,000. He began with a brief introduction in which he described how the auditorium was also filled with those on the other side, eager to get their messages through. "There's two things they all want you to know. First, don't call them 'dead people,' for they're actually far more alive than you. And second, their personalities are pretty much the same on the other side."

John explained that he is given word or parts of a word, symbols, or scenes from a movie as clues. Then he must make an educated guess as to the being's meaning.

After a break, John walked briskly to one side of the auditorium and said, "They're showing me a scene from the movie *Victor/Victoria*. "Is there a Victoria here?"

A rather shaky woman stood up and said in a quiet voice, "I'm Victoria."

"Your husband is telling me that the fact that you weren't there when he died is totally unimportant. He wants to assure you that he's still very much part of your life and has been with you every day since."

Apparently, Victoria had been living under intense guilt because she had not been with her husband when he had died two years earlier. This reassurance lifted the woman's terrible burden of guilt, so that she could get on with her life. Think of the countless millions of relationships that have been severed by death and the bereaved who are plagued by grief and/or guilt.

Writing *One Last Time* was just the beginning of John's good work. He has also made an amazing breakthrough into mainstream television with the *Crossing Over With John Edward* show which is now airing in syndication in both the U.S. and internationally. One after the other, John brings through relatives who have crossed over and have messages for members of the studio audience, and even the production crew. On one memorable occasion, John was pulled to the back of the audience, but no one there seemed to recognize the spirit coming through. It turned out that the recipient was actually someone in the next building!

With an outstanding book and six hours of television weekly, John is bringing ADC into the mainstream and pushing back the curtain of fear that surrounds death. Thank you, John, for your service in healing people.

George Anderson

Let's conclude this psychic "hall of fame" with another great: George Anderson. Born in 1952, he survived a life-threatening childhood illness and woke up with powerful psychic abilities. His devoutly Catholic parents were horrified and shuttled him between Church psychiatrists and mental institutions. Fortunately, he survived the Catholic Church, but being "different" left him with a shyness that today is an engaging humility.

In his first book (many have been written *about* him), *Lessons From The Light*, he thoroughly explores the phenomenon of mediumship and describes a sort of electrical hum that warns him that a message is on the way. He sees his life mission as reassuring the bereaved that their loved ones have not left them but are still watching over them. So rather than angrily shouting "Why?" when someone crosses the veil, he recommends asking, "What growth should I accomplish from the loss of someone so meaningful to me?"

George emphasizes that there *is* a reason for our suffering in grief, but that we probably won't know what it is until we, too, make our own crossing. Nothing happens in the universe by accident, even though the answers aren't immediately apparent. He adds a cautionary note, though, that our loved ones may not give us a sign of their continued existence until we have handled our grief. Otherwise, we might become too dependent on them and "live from sign to sign," something that would hinder our growth.

Our loved ones have only our welfare at heart, and are smart enough to know when an ADC would reopen the wound and pull us back into grief. Once we are finished coping with our grief, then we might begin receiving contacts and signs.

George's contacts have told him that although grief is intended as a growth experience, we will not fully recover until our own passing, and we can be together once more. But for now, he adds, mediums and ADCs are the next best thing.

Anderson's book includes a chapter on violent death, a topic not enjoyed by many mediums. He says that, although it's unlikely that a soul incarnates with a script that includes the express intent to commit murder, a troubled ego can derail a soul's intent, resulting in murder. In these cases, many lives are affected in addition to the murderer and victim, providing great growth opportunities for all involved. Their life scripts must be rewritten with the express consent of all souls involved. Most victims report to George that they've reconciled their violent passing and urge the loved ones left behind to come to the same understanding and forgiveness, while acknowledging that "it's easier said than done."

Anderson describes one session for the parents of Corey, a young man fatally wounded in a shooting incident that really had nothing to do with him. Through George, Corey said that despite his violent passing, he felt no pain since his consciousness had already left his body. He emphasized that he's fine on the other side, and pleaded with his parents not to put their lives on hold following his death. He joked that he was on permanent vacation and does *not* feel cheated by his early passing.

Corey's case involved almost accidental death at the hands of a stranger, but what about cases where the murderer is a family member? George also recounts a session for the mother of Kerry who died under suspicious circumstances just before she was about to leave her husband. Kerry's mother was sure that he'd murdered her daughter and went to George for confirmation.

In the session, Kerry told her mother that she'd put her death behind her but admitted that she had been murdered. She reported that the husband's alibi was phony, that he'd parked round the corner from the house, sneaked back home, and hit her from behind with a blunt instrument. Then he called the police to report that his wife had had an accident. As to motive, Kerry recommended changing attorneys and investigating certain real estate deals and financial transactions.

Soon after the reading, the husband was charged with murder.

Naturally, some of George's most touching stories involve children. One eight-year-old boy who died of leukemia now has dogs, cats, a horse and a bird for pets, attends the equivalent of high school, and is cared for by three generations of grandparents. Two six-year-old friends who died together when they fell through the ice into a pond have a huge, loving support group on the other side, and work together as a team welcoming other children to the afterlife. And when two other children who had already crossed over learned that their parent's dog was approaching the end of its earthly days, they told their parents through Anderson that they already had a home prepared for the family pet. The death of children is particularly heart-rending, but parents can be assured that their beloved sons and daughters are safe and in caring hands, free of pain and limits.

On April 17, 2000 the episode of the TV program *Beyond Chance* told the story of two young girls who were best friends and joined by their love of horses. They were tragically separated when Kristen died in what looked like a freak riding accident. Exactly one year to the day, Emily, the other girl also died from head injuries incurred in a riding accident. The two pairs of grieving parents just thought that this was a bizarre coincidence until they consulted Anderson.

Kristen revealed that she was alive and well on the other side, being cared for by her grandfather. She also said that her death was not the result of the accident but that a brain aneurysm while she was riding had caused her to fall off the horse. She stressed that this was not her parents' fault and implored them not to live in profound grief but to get on with their lives.

In Emily's session, she too begged her parents to remember her with love rather than guilt or grief. She emphasized that she did not suffer in any way, and that she and Kristen were together, sisters in friendship.

The parents were amazed at the wealth of evidential detail through someone who knew nothing about them or their situations, and were warmed by the message of hope that both girls brought. They were also relieved that their daughters' deaths were not meaningless tragedies but carefully planned events.

Conclusion

When we grieve the "loss" of loved ones, we are grieving for them, and for ourselves. My own ADC experiences and those of countless other people indicate that we should not be concerned for the well-being of our loved ones. The old adage, "They're in a better place now" is absolutely true. They are free of any birth abnormality, illness, injury, plain old "wear and tear," or any other limitations.

Those who experience an ADC find it so healing that other people may ask, "Why didn't *I* have one?" The Guggenheims' answer is that you probably did but may have blocked it, possibly by anger, grief, bitterness or guilt. Also, your loved one may know that you're not sufficiently far along in your grief process for contact to be healthy.

It's never too late, though, to pray for contact, whether while awake, asleep or in that open halfway state. Meditation also opens the door wide for contact. If you sense the presence of a loved one, relax, open your mind and wait, but avoid any preconceptions about the form the contact might take. Since most recently departed souls attend their own memorial service, you can practically *expect* an ADC if you're receptive and alert.

After-death communication tells us of the continuity of existence, and being open to them would turn death from a sad end that must be mourned into a glorious new beginning for our loved ones that should be celebrated. ADCs tell us much more than our loved ones are alive and kicking on the other side. They tell us that they are actively concerned for our well-being and watch over us. Because they are new arrivals in the afterlife and have just conducted their life review, what they have to tell us is also significant. Typical of the advice we hear is, "What's important in life is how much you love and help other people. How much you strive to better the lot of your fellow man. So don't wait until your review to say, 'I could have done better.' Vow to begin today, right now."

Realign your life around the values of loving service, integrity, honesty and nurturing others, so that when you face yourself during your life review, you can say, "The world is a better place for my having been in it." You can do it, for you *are* a Divine Architect.

Chapter 7

Meet Your Real Sixth Sense

I F YOU KNEW that you were surrounded by countless unseen people—loved ones, guides, and others—who were watching your every move, what would you do differently? Before you get too worried, please remember that they're here for our benefit, and are completely free of judgment. If you do park in a handicapped parking spot or shoplift that little trinket, you are seen. But it is those who commit serious offenses against their fellow men, the animal kingdom, or the planet herself who might want to think twice.

Our relationship with the dying process is filled with many misconceptions and misunderstandings and, due to our preoccupation with the physical plane, we continue to say things such as, "She's gone," "I lost my husband," or "We buried her last week." Just because we cannot see something doesn't mean that it's not there. It's just a matter of getting used to a new perspective. In your dreams, do you panic because you can't find your physical body?

When, in *Conversations with Tom*, Walda Woods asked Tom where exactly the afterlife is, he replied, "The afterlife dimensions are not 'places' in any earthly sense that you can go to in a car or a boat or even a spaceship, although some of your cults would argue the part about the spaceship. They are non-physical dimensions and exist beyond your five senses. They consist of interwoven levels of energy and consciousness that intermingle with your Earth plane but vibrate at a much higher frequency. The simplest way for me to explain this is to compare these dimensions to radio stations. They each broadcast on a particular frequency, and just because you're listening to one radio station doesn't mean that the other stations aren't broadcasting. You just happen to be tuned into one particular station. You on Earth are tuned into the physical dimension. Because you cannot discern us with your physical senses does *not* mean that we don't exist. We simply occupy another frequency band and are in and around your physical plane."

Accepting that those in the afterlife mingle with those of us on the physical plane, would we not want to bridge the gap? Of course we would. Following the death of my father, this is something I pledged to do. Bridging the two worlds has proved to be an astonishing adventure, one that has made my life immeasurably richer.

As my father lay dying, we made a pact that we would continue our relationship. My end of the bargain involved following three simple spiritual laws that were taught to me in the early nineties by the apparitions that visited me.

The Three Spiritual Laws / Contacting the Other Side

Three laws that govern achieving conscious contact with those who have already passed over:

1. *The Law of Right Relationship*, which tells us to examine our relationship with whomever we're trying to contact. What did this person mean to us while he or she was alive? A loved one who we wish to continue loving, a wise person whose wisdom we still want to enjoy and benefit from, or a troubled relative in whose healing we wish to participate?

2. *The Law of Right Will* calls for you to align yourself with Divine Will, surrender your ego, proceed with all due humility, and allow yourself to be guided by the Light. Central to this law is the question of how much you want to succeed. Is making contact the most important thing in the world to you, or are you just a tire-kicker? Your determination to succeed must be paramount, because success won't come overnight. It will require hard work and diligence on your part, and you may well suffer setbacks along the way. Invoking and surrounding yourself with light is essential, since the astral plane is home to many unsavory spirits that can't or don't want to go on to the higher dimensions.

3. *The Law of Right Intent* asks you to be sure that you are attempting contact for the right reasons. Are you working for the betterment of all concerned, dabbling out of curiosity, or trying to hang

on to a loved one? Is your goal genuine healing, morbid curiosity, or just sensationalism. You are surrounded by countless beings who *will* lend their positive energy to you if your motives are pure.

Right intent sees this phenomenon not as a party trick to amuse your friends but a process that must be treated with respect. Also, what you get out of it will depend on the effort you put in, while recognizing that those on the other side are rooting for you. This involves having:

- A totally open mind, for you are venturing into new realms governed by spiritual laws and etiquette that are new to you and you must know how things work there.
- Humility, reverence, respect.
- Discipline and patience, for you will be using parts of your being that have been shut down for maybe decades and will require time to reactivate. Stick with it, and know that those on the other side *are* hearing you. Hearing them is only a matter of time.
- Selfless love, without a trace of personal gain, greed, revenge, or ego gratification.

Tom Woods says something similar. He gives the three qualities as desire, faith and patience. Under the heading of desire, Tom points out that it's important to *really* want to do this. "Desire," he says, "comes from a place in the heart and brings with it the love needed to cross the bridge to their world. Your intentions are equally as important. If you're looking to spend most of your waking hours connecting with your loved one, the experience will not be productive. You need balance. It's possible to have regular contact with the other side while remaining grounded and centered in your own world. Moderation is the key."

He also stresses the importance of *patience*. "Wanting things to happen right away is a natural human trait because of the physical plane anxiety about never having enough time. Try to let go of the time issue, for it's not important over here. Understand that it may not happen right away."

In preparing for ADC, Tom recommends, "Spend at least a week of regular meditation, using whatever technique works for you. Making contact depends on both of you building your half of the bridge and meeting in the middle. The soul must lower its frequency, and you must raise the frequency of your consciousness, and meditation is the best way to do that."

He gives detailed instructions on how to make contact and concludes with, "Relax and enjoy each other's company. Take this time to share and to love once again ... Know that you now have this new awareness of the spiritual realms and can return at any time ... When you're ready to say goodbye, tell your loved one when you propose to hold your next meeting. Watch as he or she smiles and waves goodbye."

To aid in your ADC process, it's important to watch for appearances, but what if you can't "see" psychically. Can you still make contact? Of course, you can. A professional psychic medium usually has the sight, because he or she must describe the visitor's appearance to the client for identification. But there are other ways to make contact, notably hearing (clairaudience) and knowing (clairsentience). You may actually hear your loved one's voice in your head or even outside in the room, or he or she may drop a thought into your mind in response to a question you ask either out loud or in your mind. They do this a lot anyway, but we just don't notice.

There are many things that anyone serious about ADC can do to increase the chances of opening the door to the other side:

- Become familiar with and use one or more meditation techniques, and learn how to shut off the outside world.
- Clear yourself of judgment and fear, and make sure you see this work as service based on love for humanity, done in a spiritual context.
- Learn as much about spirituality as you can, especially such topics as the energy centers, or chakras, for these are your tools for accessing the higher dimensions.
- Practice techniques such as automatic writing, dream awareness, psychic vision and arranging signals with those on the other side, such as manipulating lights and electronic devices. (This is easy for them since we are all electromagnetic systems on the soul plane.)

The Four Laws

As I see things, we are governed by four laws, which I call the Laws of One, Two, Three and Four, pertaining to our relationships to self, other people, humanity at large, and those in higher dimensions.

The Law of One

The Law of One is about being in right relation with ourselves. To me, this is about honoring the self because, if you don't honor yourself, how can you expect others to do so? We've all seen how people with low self-esteem attract others to them who treat them exactly according to the self-image they project out to the world. The opposite also holds true. If you psychically broadcast to the world the signal that you honor yourself, others will resonate with the message and follow suit.

The Law of Two

Once you've got the Law of One handled, you're ready to explore the Law of Two. Sadly, many people jump into relationships before they've successfully mastered the Law of One, relationships that are consequently doomed to crash on the rocks. How can two people who are not walking their talk hope to come together in a happy, harmonious relationship? It's just not possible for those who don't love the self to participate in loving relationships, for the relationship becomes a dumping ground for their dysfunction, which they look to their partner to fix.

Meeting my twin flame opened up to a whole new level of love, and I was curious about this phenomenon we call love. Through Walda Woods, I asked her deceased husband, Tom, about the love between twin flames.

"Love is the most powerful energy in the universe. It is what our souls are composed of and, in its purest form, it is the *essence* of the Divine Source. It makes up the universe and is in the life source we breathe every day. Only love is real—everything else is just an illusion. If we stripped ourselves of all five senses, love would be the only remaining hint of our existence, the only thing "felt." It is the gift that we come into this lifetime with—and the *only* thing that we can freely take into the next dimension. It has no limits and therefore, being unlimited, is the ultimate energy of creation.

"Love is so intensely powerful that its healing powers have amazed even the most hardened skeptics. Ask the parents of the dangerously ill newborn about how holding, touching, and sending loving energy to the child during its first hours of life cured its disease. When any type of alternative healing is done, it is done through the power of love and it is that intense energy that causes the chemicals in the body to relax and regroup to normal levels.

"When you love someone, it's not *that* person's love you feel; it's the love inside *yourself.* So when you give love, you are actually the receiver. The other person merely serves as a catalyst to set the wheels in motion. When two people fall in love, the act is born out of the pre-life promise they made to one another. The bond is so intense when two people truly fall in love that the umbilical-like cord of energy (similar to the auric material of the spiritual body) that has connected them from birth becomes even more apparent. The heart centers open up to full capacity, and the most intense energy is exchanged.

"This exchange of energy between the heart chakras causes a chemical reaction in the body that brings about an incredible feeling of euphoria. Twin souls particularly recognize instant attraction as if they already know each other! This is the other half of the soul, and the two pieced together make a perfect union. These chemical reactions in the body are natural 'drugs' and the feeling in the body is one of pure joy. These should not be confused with sexual urges. In fact, having these feelings, people often mistake the experience for being in love, and that is quite another situation entirely.

"When true love occurs, it matters not what the person looks like on the outside. The strongest love of all brings with it a spiritual awareness, which can be either conscious or unconscious. This is when each looks deeply into the other's soul and sees the joy and the pain of many shared lifetimes. Remember, it is the desire of the soul to experience love, to *be* love. And aside from the fact that we can give love to and receive love from many different sources during our lifetimes, being *in love* is quite a different experience. Being in love is the ultimate because you share a very intimate part of yourself with another soul. The connection and chemistry is so intense that researchers say that this is why widows and widowers seem to experience the highest likelihood of after-death communication. The bond is so strong, so forceful, that nothing—and I mean nothing—can break it."

The Law of Three

This law governs how we interact with the rest of humanity. As we dip our toes into the water of the new millennium, we are seeing a new paradigm emerge that challenges the old paradigms of organized religion and of science.

Under the new paradigm, reality is malleable. My friend Nancy Stillings taught me a powerful technique to form reality: "Suppose you want a particular outcome to a troublesome situation, with the intent of arriving at the best possible outcome for all involved. Universal Law stipulates that the outcome you seek must serve the highest interests of all participants and be the path with the highest overall quotient of love, otherwise you're just creating karma for yourself.

"Visualize the situation in as much detail as you can: what everyone is wearing, how they look, the actual location where the situation will be resolved, the sounds and smells, the feel of the chair you're sitting in, say. Once you've created the setting in your mind, then play out the situation with what each person says or does, guiding events towards the desired outcome. Try to repeat the exercise every day for the week leading up to the actual event itself."

If one person can do this—and I know it's possible, for I've used this technique to pull off some pretty improbable outcomes—then imagine the power of millions of people focusing their intent on one common goal, such as world peace.

Due to the Law of Resonance, we are constantly exchanging energy with the world around us. It influences us and our moods and thoughts. We influence it with how we feel and what we think about. In 1991, Tony, my co-author, wrote extensively about this phenomenon in *An Ascension Handbook*. It is based on one simple principle—that everything is energy in motion. Like colored dye dropped into clear water, you put your personal stamp on your world, attracting to you whatever you're thinking about *with feeling*.

The problem is that most of us focus on what we don't want and usually fuel that with plenty of fear. Guess what? That's programming reality to deliver *exactly* what you least want to happen. Instead, turn that around and impress reality with what you *do* want—better relationships, an enjoyable job, and abundance. Whatever you want is out there, and *it's already yours*, so it's only a matter of pulling it in with intent and desire. These are paramount!

Another key Nancy revealed to me is that, "Reality scripting works better when the outcome is in the highest and best interest of all concerned." Use caution, because you can use it to plot someone's downfall. However, because most of us are unaware of reality scripting, it can lead to *your* downfall.

I highly recommend that you become aware of this. The next time you take a car or plane trip, simply visualize yourself arriving safely at your destination, and feel the joy this will bring you. Apart from driving with due diligence, do not focus on the possibility of accidents or breakdowns. Your attention is how you signal your choices to the universe. Of course, your soul has its own agenda, too, but your ego has a big say. So why not choose joy? After all, it's free, it's yours, and you can have all you want.

Do these techniques give you an inside edge in the game of life? You bet, but reality scripting and resonance happen all the time, so why not use them consciously rather than living on autopilot? As for misusing it, that's called karma, which could take several future lives to clear. And who wants that?

That's the Law of Three in action. As we will see in Chapter 8 on the Science of Compassion, this is what *real* prayer is about. We are talking here about the emergence of a whole new type of human, the 21st century human, the fully aware Divine Architect. Such a human is free of the limiting superstition of restrictive and suppressive ideologies, and is living in harmony with self, others, and the planet. John Lennon caught a lot of flak for his words, "religion must go," but he was right. Mass religions will inevitably give way to a more personal spiritual path. Which brings us to the wayshowers—the Spiritual Hierarchy, the original architects of the personal growth movement.

The Law of Four

Having mastered the Law of Three and being in right relationship with humanity, the natural progression is to work with those beings who are not incarnate, which includes spirit guides, guardian angels, and the entire spiritual hierarchy. Angels have never incarnated, and work purely with energy, inspiring us and guarding us from the unseen dimensions. We have seen how angels work with energy, but archangels do it on a planetary scale.

My understanding is that Archangel Michael is responsible for the overall energies hitting this planet, and Archangel Gabriel assists any lightworker engaged in helping humanity come back into alignment with the Divine Plan and soul intent. The Divine Plan itself is held by the Elohim Council, who also maintain the energy of certain qualities, such as valor and compassion, making these available on a planetary level for anyone to tap into. Since this is a "free will planet," these cosmic overseers cannot just come in and beam energy into us. We as individuals and as a population must open to it. Therefore, whenever a group of lightworkers get together, I strongly urge that you make your request known and ask for healing at individual and planetary levels.

Ascended masters, on the other hand, have completed a cycle of Earth lives and guide planetary events from the upper reaches of the soul plane and beyond. What we know of the ascended masters comes from them via clairvoyants such as Alice Bailey in the first half of the last century, particularly a Tibetan master named Djwhal Khul. They are in service to the planetary Logos (or soul of this planet), which holds the master plan for Earth and her mobile consciousness—us. These masters work with their mortal initiates on the Earth plane to guide humanity. Initiates may not even know they are serving the plan, for they may receive instruction on their roles while in deep sleep, traveling out-of-body to the soul plane.

According to the plan of the Logos, revealed in esoteric teachings, the human kingdom grew out of the animal kingdom many millions of years ago when proto-humanoids developed sufficiently to become hosts for souls. We as souls had been waiting on the soul plane a long time, working with the genetics of advanced primates to get them ready. That development was pivotal on this planet, for one branch of the animal kingdom began the long transition to becoming spiritual beings, the first step of which was to become "soul carriers." The next step in the plan for our development is to enter the spiritual kingdom and become ascended masters ourselves.

Humanity is poised to make a great leap forward, for we're leaving the Age of Pisces, which emphasized the importance of belief, for the Age of Aquarius, which focuses instead on truth. One aspect of this is that the masters will begin working with us *directly* rather than *indirectly* through religions and mystery schools. So it behooves us to open up to their guidance and consciously begin to accept their direction. How? As always, through meditation, allowing it to bring us:

- *Mental honesty*, in which we discard outworn limiting beliefs and strive for a truth that we allow to guide us.
- *Spiritual directedness*, in which we are guided by our own souls rather than politics, economics, social policies, or other external factors.
- *Detachment* from any specific outcome, so that we can follow the guidance of the masters though our own souls. This allows us to identify with our true Selves rather than who we are in this particular incarnation, the goal being what I call "divine emptiness."

There are certain mortals around the world whose mission is to help raise the consciousness of humanity. Drunvalo Melchizedek, through his workshops, is devoted to awakening us to the mysteries of sacred geometry. I recently attended his workshop where he mentioned the Kogi, a mysterious group living in the Columbian jungle. They are so filled with life force energy that when they look at us, they see us as "dead" in that we run only a tiny fraction of our potential life force. To their psychic sight, there are a few exceptions to this, such as Drunvalo himself. They sent him a message that he would be contacted and invited for a psychic visit to their village in the jungle.

In November 1999, he gave a workshop in Mexico, which was attended by many Colombians. One of them, a woman, spent two hours of telepathic exchange with him in which she revealed the Kogi view of life and reality. She took him psychically to her village to meet them. There, he learned that the woman's body was actually being used by another Kogi woman to make the trip. The second woman's body was in deep sleep in her hut from where she would slip in and out of the first woman's body.

Even more amazing are the Mamas, the Kogi's spiritual leaders, who form a tribe within a tribe and whose communications are almost exclusively images sent across a heart link. They asked Drunvalo to relay a message to lightworkers everywhere who are trying to make a difference on the planet:

"You are changing the world into light. Be not afraid of your innocence and your child nature; it is close to God. Let your imagination soar into a Dream where love surrounds all events, then 'see' it as real. Let the sounds of your heart talk to those who are not alive. You have shown them the way by your example; now 'show' them the way from within. Listen, and your heart will speak. We are with you now. We will help you."

I close this section with some salutary words from my friend Trisha McCannon:

"We, as a people, stand at the brink of a new age, an age that is already bringing sweeping changes. The theme of these changes is Unity, the Age of Aquarius, the consciousness bearer. Thus, we see advances all around us—in holistic medicine, a rebalancing of racial issues, a rehonoring of women as equals, and a slow but sacred movement towards remembering that the Earth herself is a living presence.

"The truth is that we are all connected to the Source by virtue of even being alive. The Source runs through us and through all living things. This Divine Intelligence permeates the Universe. Thus we are all sacred beings—stars, moons, animals, plants and, of course, one another.

"Within us lies the potential of the Universe. Dark and Light, good and evil, involution and evolution. It is our choice, each and every day. Are we takers or givers? Do we run our lives from ego and power or from the higher heart aligned with Divine Will? In this Age before us, we must choose, because the Age itself will not support denser levels of consciousness. Those who do not enter the Domain of the Heart, the Christed Self, will not be able to handle the frequencies of vibration.

"The Divine Blueprint is returning. Our remembrance of ourselves is returning. All time as we know it will change in the next thirty years. The new grids are being activated. Let us stand before the Truth of Love and know its name."

Working With Your Guides

You have a number of sources of information vying for your attention:

1. *Your own higher self, soul, spirit.* You, as pure spirit/soul, decided to incarnate in this time/space in the physical body that you're wearing. You came in with a full agenda of what you wanted to learn and experience, and your soul must manage your ego so that together you accomplish your agenda. You, the soul, might implant thoughts and actually speak audibly, so audibly that your ego cannot possibly shrug it off as imagination.

2. *Spirit guides.* Discernment is especially important here because not all non-physical entities have your highest or best interests at heart. Often they have agendas of their own, so get to know the vibration of your guide if you can.

3. *Guardian angels.* We each have one, two or more guardian angels, which differ from guides in a number of ways. First, they never incarnate so they have no gender. Second, they're less concerned than guides with our life mission. They rarely speak but serve as "morale officers," flooding us with love, hope and inspiration to get us through our "darkest hours." They may often drop a much-needed piece of wisdom into our consciousness. Because they're of a higher frequency than guides, they can move more fluidly through the dimensions.

4. *The inner churning of your mind and emotions.* These thoughts and feelings may be fear-based or lead to separation from others and even cause harm to them if fear-based. These are definitely thoughts and voices *you do not want to listen to.*

~ ~ ~

We come to the Earth plane with a guide to keep us pointed at our life's mission and to nudge us with a thought or intuitive hunch if we deviate too far from the plan. Since communication is a two-way street, you can ask your guide for help with a problem. Make it specific, such as, "Please suggest alternatives in this situation," rather than, "My life's a mess. What should I do?"

Now unless we're really about to diverge from our life plan, our guide won't interfere, so it's up to us to ask for input, and as specifically as possible. For example, don't say, "I need help," but "Guide, I need you to ...," or "I need insight as to this situation and pointers to the next step I must take." Again, guides can't intrude, and you must call them in. Here's how. To work with your guide, calm your mind and withdraw from the noise and confusion of daily life, and then hold the thought of your guide to call him/her in and serve as a bridge between the two of you. Then hold the thought of the situation you want help with. Your guide will pick up on this and may drop ideas, hints, or insights into your mind. Trust these. Stay calm for a while longer in case there's more, and then offer your thanks. Go about your day, being mindful of synchronous events that your guide may have engineered to bring you more information.

Do not feel guilty if you've ignored your guides until now, because they know about the amnesia of the veil. You can begin your relationship anew, right now. Ask for a name and trust the first one you hear or sense, and then begin regular dialogues. My guides were there for me since birth, but I ignored them for 34 years until I was introduced to them in 1992. Since then, we have been in constant contact.

I am unusual in that I see my guides as ethereal or semi-transparent figures. As a child, no one told me that this was abnormal, so I just never stopped seeing them. It wasn't until 1992 that I began a two-way dialog with them. For you to see your guides, either they must lower their frequency or you must stretch your perception, or both. But even if you don't get full figure visuals, they may appear to you as flashes of white or blue energy just to let you know that they're around.

Although guides are usually with us for an entire cycle of lifetimes, we may also have help from deceased loved ones who agree to work with us on specific issues, such as resolving their unfinished business, as happened when my father volunteered for "guide duty."

Tom Woods has this to add about guides: "Spirit guides and angels do not ask that you be perfect. They do ask, however, that you strive for perfection in understanding the principle of love. Your guides are yours and no one else's, and are in perfect balance with your soul's journey. They never scold but are loving and attentive, just as a good parent might be. They guide you gently with soft touches and subtle signs.

"Your guides keep you on the course you chose before birth—the supreme plan, if you will—so do not expect an angel or guide to tell you the future, for they cannot override your free will by interfering with your decisions and choices. However, they will gently nudge you in the right direction, but you must use your "inner ears" to listen to them, to recognize the clues and signs, and to be ever watchful of the synchronicities and miracles that abound in everyday life."

Finally, please remember to thank your guides. They work hard on your behalf and would love to know how much you appreciate their service. And you will feel a whole lot better when you give gratitude.

Protection

We will close this chapter with a note of caution. In no other field of human activity are we more vulnerable to deliberate or unintentional confusion. The main obstacles to clarity are:

1. *Well-meaning but befuddled beings on the other side.* Just because they have crossed over doesn't make them suddenly omniscient. Their lack of understanding of what they are seeing can cause confused reporting.

2. *Different realities.* Suppose three different people living in California were to tell you what they were seeing. The one in Death Valley tells you that California is a hot desert with thousands of miles of barren sand. The person in the high Sierras tells that the state is one of roaring blizzards, with frigid white-out conditions. The one in downtown Los Angeles says that California is a noisy, smelly, crowded place. Who do you believe? Reports from the other side can be even more confusing because it's a reality creation environment, and those there can actually be *creating* the reality that they're reporting on.

3. *Different sense of time.* To those on the other side, things in our future have already happened, and every outcome possible has been explored. If we're told that something turned out a certain way, we can't be sure which outcome is being tracked. Relating to our linear sense of time and not "over-guiding" explains why spirit guides need so much training.

4. *Deceitful beings on the other side.* These can be out to deliberately confuse us or use us. They may give us good information initially to draw us in and win our trust and then switch to self-serving or mischievous disinformation.
5. *Well-meaning but befuddled mediums on this side.* They may have great psychic gifts but insufficient knowledge or discernment to properly interpret what they're seeing and hearing. As these people unknowingly filter everything through their own limited belief systems, they can cause massive confusion on this side.
6. *Deceitful people on this side.* Charlatans are rare but good ones can operate so smoothly that they fool us while emptying our pockets. Recently, a medium, who also ran a business, claimed to be contacting an entity that often dispensed business advice during readings. Coincidently, the "entity" happened to recommend the medium's business. Altruistic or self-serving?

How can we protect ourselves? We have two major tools. The first is *psychic protection.* Surround yourself with white light—the Christ Light—in all psychic work, and ask all those you contact on the other side to affirm that, "I stand in the Christ Light." If they cannot actually say those words, break off contact. By Universal Law, no entity can lie about this, so you know you're safe.

No medium I know would even contemplate holding a session without protection, and it should be as automatic as a welder putting on dark goggles before beginning work.

The second form of protection is good, old-fashioned *discernment* applied to what we're told or what we see. I have an agreement with my guides that if I am to act on their guidance in a life-changing way such as a major decision, I receive two signs through different avenues such as hearing it through a medium *and* an undeniable synchronistic event, such as a friend casually saying the same thing.

Whenever you consult a psychic, ask open-ended rather than leading questions, such as, "What do you see in terms of a new job?" (or real estate or relationships) rather than, "Should I take this job?" (or buy this house, or marry this person). Then ask your guides to confirm or deny the answer through another medium or some other event in your life. Of course always do what feels "right" in your heart. You'll know what this feels like after a little practice.

Conclusion

If an ADC happens to you, try not to be afraid. Instead, learn how to begin a dialog with whoever is contacting you. Learn also the subtle signs that those on the other side use to get your attention. If nothing seems to be happening, use the techniques in this chapter to at least open the door to ADC. But the most important thing of all is to learn to trust and to not walk in fear, for you are a Divine Architect.

Chapter 8

The Science of Compassion

Science: *The observation, identification, description and explanation of natural phenomena.*

Compassion: *the deep feeling for another, prompting the inclination to offer loving aid.*

> *"Miracles are natural. Something is wrong*
> *when they don't happen."*
>   *— A Course in Miracles*

OR THOUSANDS OF YEARS, the ancients have pointed to this moment in time as the bridge between the worlds of duality and unity, and they left us detailed instructions on how to cross the bridge. All ancient calendars point to this decade (2000 – 2010) as *the* time to wake up. A few people, such as those we've talked about in this book (and its readers, of course) are a few years ahead of the majority, but by 2012, *no one* will be able to hit the snooze button.

As that majority realizes that some really big changes are happening, they will have only a few years to adjust, whereas those in tune with the changes will have had one or two decades. What we did gently with fun, grace and ease, those currently asleep will have to accomplish in a crash course that could be painful. The implication for those who know what's happening is that those who don't know will need our *utmost compassion*. They will be struggling to make sense of the kind of material in this book, operating procedures we already take for granted. Hence this chapter on compassion.

Like charity, compassion begins at home, so we'll begin with input from Gregg Braden on self-compassion, move on to reality creation skills, and then look at compassion in action, courtesy of material provided by the Twilight Brigade, an organization started by Dannion Brinkley for hospice volunteers. To me, this is of vital concern, because death is probably still the area of greatest ignorance and misunderstanding, and compassion is essential for all those involved in the process.

Between the Worlds

I have always maintained that every life experience we undergo is an opportunity to practice unconditional love. In Gregg Braden's book, *Walking Between the Worlds*, he states that the purpose of life is to practice compassion, which he defines as the convergence of two technologies: one "out there" and the other "in here." Mankind is out of balance, he says, because of too much focus on the "out there" world. For example, when flu season comes around, we rely on shots and other medicines rather than on boosting our immune system—"out there" stuff rather than "in here" measures.

Another point he makes is that we live during times of the greatest rate of change ever. To the extent that we embrace the lessons that change teaches us, we develop compassion and will be able to handle change effortlessly and gracefully. He says, "If you allow life to show you yourself in new ways, so that you may know yourself in those ways, and you reconcile within yourself that which life has shown you, then you become compassion."

At the heart of compassion is experiencing duality without judgment. Experiences are not good or bad, he says. They are just experiences. Even those we would prefer not to have teach us a great deal about ourselves, and that's what it's all about. Our greatest mirror is our relationships and, drawing on ancient Essene wisdom, Gregg identifies seven mirrors, or ways our relationships reflect back something about ourselves and our mix of the three Universal Fears (see Chapter 2):

  1. *Reflection of who you are in the moment.* In this mirror, other people or situations reflect back to us whatever we're radiating out to the world via our thoughts, emotions, and actions.

2. *Reflection of judgment.* Look at the people in your life and the buttons in you that they push. Then ask, "Are they reflecting something about which I hold judgment?"

3. *Your missing complement.* When you meet someone and "click" with him or her in a magnetic attraction, it could be that this person has a trait or quality you seek for yourself, so you find the person attractive. But rather than fall in love with the person, Gregg recommends that you allow the other person to awaken that same trait in you.

4. *Reflection of addiction.* Our addictions and compulsions to substances or behavior patterns (such as control) take from us, little by little, the one thing we hold most dear in life. For example, those addicted to conflict hold harmony most dear.

5. *Our parents as mirrors of our relationship with the Creator.* How you *perceive* that your parents regard you is how you perceive that your Creator regards you. Our earthly parents are then surrogates for the Creator. As a child, were you constantly judged, criticized or berated? Or were you praised, encouraged and rewarded? How you remember your parents treating you as a child actually mirrors your expectations of your relationship with the Creator.

6. *Mirror of Duality.* We will all undergo an experience that confronts us with our greatest fear—the so-called "dark night of the soul"—and when we do, we must remember that it is the ultimate opportunity to know ourselves, reclaim our power and heal the part of us that we least want to acknowledge. In being plunged into pain and eventually coming back to a new balance, we have thoroughly explored ourselves and come out with a larger identity. Once you embrace the dark, it becomes your ally, and it is impossible to feel fear or experience illness. Compassion is only possible once we're able to reconcile light and dark within us and see that they both have the same source. If we see them as separate and in opposition, we live in duality and not unity.

7. *Mirror of the Perfection of Life.* If you judge any aspect of yourself or your life as less than successful or perfect, you are judging yourself according to some external yardstick or standard. Self-acceptance is what Gregg calls "our highest act of compassion," because we are far more critical of ourselves than of others. Life is the opportunity for experiences that bring insight. We succeed simply by learning more about ourselves. Do you love enough to see the perfection in life's imperfections, he asks.

Compassion is a state of no attachment to outcome, no judgment, and no emotional charge on anything. As we go through whatever life brings us, if we can acknowledge that *everything* comes from a single source, Gregg offers a technique he terms "blessing." When we can bless every experience, no matter how painful, we give thanks for its teaching, for its divine and sacred nature. It doesn't mean that we agree with it or condone it. It simply allows us to move on with our lives.

Can you look at the most painful event in your life, see it as sacred and divine, and bless it? Doing this releases the charge on the event, moves us out of victimhood, and allows us to go forward.

Gregg concludes *Walking Between the Worlds* by bringing all this "inner technology" together in a way that is stunning and breathtaking in its simplicity and clarity, so I won't spoil the surprise. For those who are ready to change their life paradigm, this is a "must read." But as he warns, once you read the book, you can't "unread" it. You *will* be changed and that carries a responsibility.

The Nature of Death

Nowhere is the science of compassion more important than in dealing with the subject of death, both for those about to take the final journey and their loved ones who will be left behind. Let us take a look at the nature of the beast.

Two things have happened over the last hundred years that have clouded our understanding of death. First, we are more materialistic and less spiritual. "More materialistic" means that we identify more strongly with what we *have* than with who we *are*, and we fear no longer having a body with which to enjoy our possessions. "Less spiritual" means that we've "neglected our studies" of our spiritual nature and of the other side, resulting in an unwarranted fear of the unknown.

In the United States, an estimated 20 million people belonged to the Spiritualist Movement in its heyday between the Civil War and World War I. Now that's a lot of folks attending ADC meetings and actively contacting the other side. In just a couple of generations, the pressures of two world wars and working two jobs to make ends meet have relegated such activities to "woo-woo land."

In the last half of the 20th century, death became institutionalized. Most of us will not die at home, surrounded by friends and relatives in a familiar setting. Some, like my father, will be in a sterile hospital, surrounded by tubes and wires. And rather than "lying in state" in the front parlor for a day, the body will be whisked from bed to morgue as the doctors chalk up another "defeat." Pledged to save life, every failure is a personal affront to the doctors involved. Driven by a refusal to accept death as a natural part of our lifecycle, or afraid of the wrongful death suits of greedy relatives unless they eek every last painful breath out of us, doctors hold their patients "hostage" against the Reaper way beyond our rightful time to go. Fear of death is a dreadful weight we bear. Expensive, too. Eighty per cent of all healthcare dollars spent on you during your life go towards prolonging that life by just a few days—and often not very pleasant days at that—all to defy the specter of death for a few hours.

I have no problem with medical practitioners as people and have found them to be, on the whole, caring and compassionate. However, the legal and administrative belief systems within which they must work often force them to misinterpret the word "harm" under their Hippocratic Oath, "Do no harm." Forcing dynamic, vibrant people to exist like vegetables on life support is more harmful than letting them go when it's their time to go. Changing the mass belief that death is the ultimate "bug-a-boo" must come from outside their profession, from the society it serves.

Ironically, it is Western medicine's ability to "bring people back" that has brought us the most compelling evidence for the afterlife—the Near-Death Experience—thanks to brave pioneers such as Dr. Raymond Moody who took the phenomenon seriously back when no one else did, and opened the floodgates to NDE investigation.

Queen Victoria mourned the loss of Prince Albert for the rest of her life and, in her day, mourning a loved one for a year was the norm. This has evolved today into a "week's personal time off" from your job and "grieve on your own time." Why? Because as a culture, we are afraid to stare death in the face and acknowledge it as inevitable. Helpless, we hide from it and turn away from those in grief, lest we be somehow contaminated. When it's our turn to grieve, no wonder we're often alone.

Back when the West was "being won," women often died in childbirth, and children often died of illnesses that are curable today. Death was all around us, and the bereaved were supported by society. Today, however, our fear of the Great Beyond has us ostracizing the bereaved.

Nowadays, though, there is a glimmer of hope as new "after-death" books are published to augment the hundreds already available, many of them riding high on the bestseller lists for weeks. Many are written by those in medicine, such as Drs. Melvin Morse, Raymond Moody and Elizabeth Kübler-Ross. Today, we are seeing moves towards greater social awareness in which the terminally ill are less likely to be "warehoused" until they die, the bereaved will not be so quickly told to "get on with life," and ADC contactees will less likely be shunned or dismiss the contact as "just my imagination."

Central to this increasing social awareness are the hospice movement and their support organizations.

Compassion in Action; The Twilight Brigade

The Divine Blueprint told the story of Dannion Brinkley and his NDE as documented in his book *Saved By The Light*. Dan and I have been friends for a long while and I've heard him speak on many occasions. I am always impressed by his sincerity and passion for helping those in their twilight years. He has this to say about death:

"What I learned from the process of dying helps me to bring comfort to others. The fact that I'm not afraid of death helps dispel their fear, which changes the quality of their final days. If we can deal with our own mortality and that of our loved ones, then we change the way the world sees itself. My experience over the last twenty years has given me a strong spiritual base, and I'm able to pass that on and tell people that death is a safe and comfortable journey. This takes away the fear with which they view death."

In order to provide a framework in which like-minded volunteers can help those about to make their crossing and support the loved ones they'll leave behind, Dannion created a nonprofit organization that musters volunteers called the Twilight Brigade, and works closely with hospices and the Veterans Administration.

Twilight Brigade hospice volunteers undergo intensive training that, as a volunteer myself, I've been through several times. Training covers the full spectrum of what volunteers need to know: listening skills, medical concerns, the nature of grief, and the spiritual aspects of dying. The training emphasizes that our purpose is not help the dying person (the client) and the grieving loved ones to solve the ultimate mystery but may involve just being a shoulder to cry on. Running errands, non-judgmental listening, and maintaining positive attitude and a pleasant disposition are often all the family members need. Volunteers are precluded from initiating discussion about spiritual matters so as not to offend the clients' religious beliefs but, if clients ask for our opinion, we are free to give it in a gentle and non-invasive way.

Volunteers are trained to respond to the needs of the dying and other family members. For example, the dying need to talk about their fears of abandonment and concern for the surviving family members. The client is told that dying is natural and that it's okay to go. Family members are encouraged to treat the client as a whole person, emotionally, physically, culturally, spiritually and financially, and to include them in conversation rather than talk *about* them.

Family members are encouraged to understand, accept and honor the client's mood swings. They are also warned that anger and depression are natural responses to the client's imminent loss of everything that is important to them. It's important to know that his or her life had meaning and that even death will contain growth.

Clients also need to be at home or at least in an environment that is as home-like as possible, surrounded by some familiar things rather than being in a faceless hospital room. They also need reassurance that surviving family members will be okay without them and that they are not leaving any unfinished business behind.

Surviving loved ones also need someone with whom they can talk and have their feelings accepted without judgment or anger. They need to be reassured that it's okay to mourn and withdraw from the world for periods, to be warned that grief is personal and will manifest in unpredictable ways, and that this is okay. It's helpful to have someone with whom they can work through the barriers to expressing grief, such as guilt, having to remain in control or protect children from death, financial worries or anger at being left to cope alone.

When a person first hears that death is the most likely outcome of an illness, initial shock sets in, and possibly denial, followed by a sense of helplessness that may prompt the person to try to control circumstances and other people. Anger is also common and can be directed at anyone or everyone, accompanied by such questions as, "Why me? Why did this have to happen to me?"

Anger is usually followed by sadness and depression over the impending loss of relationships and maybe guilt for any unmended fences. As clients come to terms with the fact that life will go on without them, they may withdraw emotionally and physically from surroundings. However, with the right counseling, they can move into the Growth phase, as they begin to look forward to what is to come.

I have found my work with the dying to be invaluable to me, in terms of giving me a personal sense that I am making a difference. It is rewarding in ways that are impossible to describe, and I urge everyone to at least consider becoming a hospice volunteer.

The Stages of Dying

Dr. Elisabeth Kübler-Ross in *On Death and Dying* identifies the five stages of dying and gives us an outstanding model of the process a client goes through:

1. *Initial Shock and Denial*, in which clients grasp for straws that death is not inevitable.
2. *Anger* about why the client is "chosen" for death while other people are not. Clients may be angry at God, family and the medical profession about losing everything they have worked for and cherished relationships. They may go through anxiety for loved ones and puzzle over why he or she has to go, including possible bargaining, in which clients promise God they will behave well in exchange for a time extension, "Let me live through this and I'll be a better person."
3. *Depression*, in which clients mourn their approaching passing and wonder why they should even bother with anything at all. This may be accompanied by bouts of loneliness, panic and guilt.
4. *Detachment, resignation and apathy*. This is the stage of "surrender to the inevitable."
5. *Growth phase*. Hopefully, the client makes it through to acceptance, optimism and quiet expectation: "Okay, I'm ready. What happens next?"

Clients need to be allowed to work through these stages in their own order and at their own pace, with open honest communication, free of "heavy" scenes with family members.

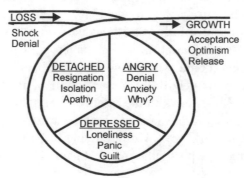

Dealing With Grief

One of the best ways to deal with grief in the future is to know what to expect before it hits us. It's important to remember that grief is a *normal* human response to *any* loss or emotional injury. For healing to begin, grief must be expressed and shared. Grieving is a personal journey of moving from *survival* to *healing* to *growth*.

When an elderly parent succumbs to a slow disease or a child loses a battle with leukemia, say, those left behind have time to adjust to their loved one's crossing. But when a loved one dies suddenly in a tragic accident or from a swift illness, our first reactions are usually shock, numbness, disbelief and perhaps denial. One moment, our loved one is a vibrant, active part of our life and the next moment is gone. Coming to terms with this puts tremendous strain on our psyche.

The loss of a loved one is a very real emotional wound, as real as any other, and it must first be acknowledged and then treated. Funeral and memorial services allow the bereaved to acknowledge their loss so they can begin their healing process, with the goal of coming out the other side able to remember the deceased fondly without emotional pain.

When someone who is part of your life (and hence part of you) is suddenly gone, you may feel angry and lonely, for energy has literally been ripped from your aura. Eventually, you will accept that this is a permanent change, that your life is forever different and that you must move on. But in the meantime, you must strive to find meaning in what may seem a meaningless tragedy. That is why a healthy, not morbid, approach to death is important.

Adjusting to *any* life change takes time and is stressful. It's vital, therefore, to remember that this is normal and not fight it, to recognize that a painful loss has occurred, and to know that you have the inner strength to bear the pain.

Know also that you are not the raw emotional wound you're suffering and that there will come a time when it no longer hurts, however difficult that may be to believe at the time. Your healing will be a process, with a beginning, a middle, and an end. You are now at the beginning. One day, it will be over. This positions you to begin grieving.

Remember also that you're not alone as you enter your grief process. You're not the first to grieve, nor will you be the last. Find a friendly shoulder to cry on and a kind ear who will let you express your grief fully. And if you have a friend who is grieving, why not be that shoulder and ear?

~ ~ ~

In his book, *Lessons from the Light,* George Anderson says that grief can hit us hard, and we may not fully heal until we, too, make our crossing and understand why we pulled in that particular growth experience. Apart from major adjustments that the loss of, say, a spouse causes, being deprived of his or her company is painful. He sees the dichotomy of, on the one hand, the departed living whole and healthy on the other side, and on the other hand, those left behind having to deal with their loss.

There's no fixed pattern. We must be prepared for grief to come in waves. Just when we think we're on the mend, another wave knocks us down again. We must get back on our feet and try to look the world in the eye again because, if we don't, he warns, self-pity and bitterness will consume us. George recommends expressing grief rather than bottling it up. Crying is an excellent relief valve—for men, too. Men who try to "tough it out" open themselves up to problems such as workaholism and alcoholism.

Talk about the good times you shared, for the deceased love to hear themselves discussed, especially in a kindly way. Pulling together and sharing your grief rather than crawling away to grieve in isolation is particularly important for parents who lose a child, for one half of these marriages end in divorce within two years.

If the deceased is a child with surviving siblings, pay particular attention to them, because they may resent the deceased being in the spotlight. This is not a time for parents to retreat into their grief and ignore the other children. It's important to discuss matters openly with the surviving siblings.

Anderson cites the example of Connie, whose daughter Michele was killed as a passenger in a car wreck. Connie was plunged into profound, inescapable grief, coupled with intense anger at the careless driver who killed her daughter, to the point where she was non-functioning.

Michele came through Anderson to tell her mother that she had to get a handle on her grief and that the time would come when she would know why Michele left early and why she (Connie) was having such a hard time. She added, "Good has already come out of this. You've lost all fear, for what's the worst that could happen now?"

Added to Connie's grief was guilt over not being able to protect her daughter and self-punishment as she relived the accident a dozen times a day, thus ensuring a constantly fresh, raw wound. Of course, Michele assured her mother that it had all been planned that way, and nothing she could have done would have prevented the inevitable.

Anderson added that Michele had left because she had completed all the tasks that required a physical body, so she no longer needed it. It's not the body of the deceased we love but the personality and soul, and they are still alive and kicking.

So, should you find a psychic medium and have a session with a loved one? As Tom Woods pointed out in Chapter 6, we must be in the "right space" for that to benefit us. If we're not far enough along in our healing, contact could trigger a whole new cycle of grief. Contact is not a cure for grief, and we still need to work through the pain of loss so that we come out of our journey through darkness stronger and more committed to life. What contact *does* do, however, is remove one piece of the puzzle that is the Great Mystery—the issue of what happened to our loved ones. Knowing that they are living in blissful joy on the soul plane may hopefully allow us to pick up our lives and march forward, knowing that we will see them again.

Ongoing suffering is not the memorial our loved ones want from us. The best memorial we can erect to them is to continue living, cherishing our finest memories of them, showing compassion for those around us and truly appreciating the opportunity that the Earth plane offers.

Organized Religion as Support

Traditionally, the bereaved have turned to the Church for support in dealing with their grief. However, not everyone finds the comfort, solace and explanations they seek for, as Tom Woods says, "The Church is not equipped to deal with grief and bereavement. At one time, the gifts of prophecy and wisdom of discerning spirits were an everyday part of religion, but this came to an abrupt halt when the major religions decided that, by allowing their followers to look outside the standard texts for their answers to life and death, they were giving away too much power and, of course, revenue, both of which the Church needed to survive.

"Religion *should* teach that people are responsible for their thoughts, words and actions—this is what will determine how and where they will live when they enter the next world. Instead, the clergy preaches fire and brimstone, hell and fury, judgment and punishment from an angry God as a means of control. My all-time favorite is that if you are not a member of a particular church, the gates of Heaven will be closed to you! Now, I ask you, does that make sense? By equating death with torment and eternal damnation, no wonder most people are afraid of dying. This deeply saddens us.

"Major western religions do not, as a rule, have any satisfying answers for the grieving. Tissue thin quotes such as, 'It was God's will' leave those who are saddened with more questions. This forces them to see the Divine Source as an angry, judgmental being that randomly chooses who lives and who dies. Not being rooted in love, this creates more fear.

"While organized religion is a source of comfort and faith for many, there will come a time when mankind will turn away from the rigid teachings and move toward the Inner Light that shines within all of us. The Source is pure love, and anything expressed otherwise is not of the Light."

Woods also has unique insights regarding the death of young children and the grief of parents:

"When someone prays to a higher power for a miracle, something will result from the request, but it may take an unexpected form. The outcome will reflect what is perfect for the soul, and that may differ greatly from what's requested. For example, a mother may be distraught over her young daughter being close to death following an accident. So, in the hospital chapel, she prays to God to please let her daughter live. This would be her miracle. The child dies soon after, and the mother is angry with God for not saving her daughter's life. In her grief, she does not realize that the miracle was actually allowing this child to die, because the little girl would have had severe brain damage and maybe other health problems, and the resulting suffering, anxiety and pain for her and her family were not part of her soul's plan.

"So where is the miracle when a child *does* survive an accident but must live with various handicaps? The miracle is the love and devotion of family and friends, the specialness of this child who teaches everyone around her to live life to the fullest, taking nothing for granted. Her great sacrifice and strength will teach many valuable lessons. Do not focus on the tragedy, but on how you react to and confront it. It is in this experience that you will see the miracle."

Walda Woods also asked her husband what impact people's grief has on the one making the transition and whether he had any advice to those suffering from excessive grief.

Tom replied, "As we begin to make the transition, we find ourselves frustrated with your grief. We want to reassure you that we're okay and have just 'gone into the next room.' If you're worried about our pain immediately before death, you should know that most of the time, we never feel a thing. In the case of terminal illness, during the last stages of life, the spirit goes in and out of the body, and during the 'out' periods, we feel no physical pain. In the case of accident, know that the spirit usually exits the body moments before any body trauma ever occurs.

"Getting back to the subject of grief, most of us still have earthly emotions during this first stage and, although they're not as intense as when we were in our bodies, we still resonate with your grief. However, our guides are with us, gently helping us through it and encouraging us to the next step. For you see, our journey onward to new heights of awareness is a vital part of our growth here on this side. Prolonged sadness and 'unhealthy' grief on your part may prevent us from going on.

"Grief is necessary for those left behind, and we are coached on the stages of grief you must go through in order to heal. As you discovered, Walda, your spiritual foundation allowed you to process your grief, otherwise the wound would never have closed. We worry about you when your grief becomes unhealthy and threatens to hold you from your purpose and us from ours.

"Instead of protracted grieving, we need your love and faith to carry us to a higher level. Detachment does not mean forgetting us, for we know that love is eternal and our connection can never be severed. But there is a difference between holding on and hanging on. Remember, we know that accepting that your loved one is no longer physically with you does not mean that you've forgotten about them.

"For those who suffer from excessive grief, we suggest you start your healing by committing yourself to a whole new awareness. Open yourself to spirituality through prayer and meditation to open your heart, which will bring you to accept who you are in terms of what's happened. This new spirituality will help to dispel your suffering and loneliness. And because prayer and meditation are rooted in the heart, they will help to maintain the realization and love of the Source."

While it's vital then that we work through our grief process, we must remember the effect it has on those who cross over. Our grief "anchors" their energy, holding them back from fully completing their transition. Instead of hanging on to our loved ones with our sadness, Tom asks that we send them on their way with loving memories of the good times we had with them.

Working through our grief process quickly is not "selling their memory short" but seeing death as a temporary interruption in a relationship that will all too soon be resumed when we make our crossing.

On his TV show, John Edward frequently says of those who have crossed over, "Know that they're all right." So, by all means grieve your loss, but do not worry about your loved ones, for they are in a "far, far better place."

Last Words on Compassion by His Holiness the Dalai Lama

We conclude this chapter by looking at the issue of compassion through the eyes of His Holiness the Dalai Lama as put forth in his book *The Art of Happiness: A Handbook for Living* written with Howard Cutler, MD.

According to the Dalai Lama, compassion is based on understanding that we as a species are all deeply connected. In today's complex world, you depend on others to refine the gasoline you put in your car, to stock the supermarket shelves, drive your bus, pilot your plane … the list is endless. It is only because of this continuum of cooperation that we survive at all. We depend on other people, so no matter how independent you'd like to be, there's no way. Every aspect of your life depends on the kindness and caring of others.

According to the Dalai Lama, the foundation for compassion is empathy—the ability to relate to another's suffering. One technique for boosting this is to visualize a loved one or beloved pet in pain, and imagine being in his or her position.

He defines compassion as a sense of commitment, responsibility and respect for others, leading to a non-violent, non-harming wish for others to be free of their suffering. Begin by wishing that for yourself and then extend it out to others. But be careful there's no attachment involved, for that will lead to control, which flies in the face of respect. Genuine compassion is not concerned with outcomes except the right of others to be free of pain.

He adds that if your compassion leads you to organized volunteer work such as in a hospice, you will probably experience, as do most other volunteers, a kind of "high," an energized glow, a feeling of euphoria. This reduces your own stress level and enhances your sense of self-worth, all of which increases the level of happiness in your life.

Spirituality, the Dalai Lama concludes, is not about what you believe or what you do, although these are important. It's about *who you are* deep down. So in a moment of stress, when you're tempted to lash out with a harsh word, you're mindful of the effect it would have on the other person and refrain. After all, it could easily be you on the receiving end next time. Now that's compassion in action. True spirituality has little to do with religion, but with the basic human virtues of goodness, kindness and compassion, for those not only increase your happiness and health, but also that of everyone around you.

My experiences as a hospice volunteer personally underscore the Dalai Lama's words. The feeling that I get in this work is indescribable and leads me to ask just who is giving here, because I always receive far more than I give.

Chapter 9

New Science/Ancient Wisdom

B RACE YOURSELF! The contents of this chapter may surprise you, shock you even for, if true, this material may contradict the very foundation of your belief system. Personally, I have great honor and respect for traditional sources of knowledge and wisdom such as the Bible, but the information in this chapter just cannot be ignored. Therefore, I simply present the material and leave the rest up to you.

The Ancient Architects

Let's begin by looking at where humanity came from in the first place. In *The Ancient Secret of the Flower of Life*, Drunvalo Melchizedek, the prominent sacred geometry expert, weaves together what his sources told him in 1985 with Zecharia Sitchin's translation of the ancient Sumerian account of our origins. Sitchin's work was published many years later in *The 12th Planet*. The accounts mesh very well, although other researchers are quick to dismiss the whole thing as science fiction. I leave you to be the judge. I remain open to it all.

Drunvalo recounts that Sitchin decoded the cuneiform writings on ancient Sumerian stone tablets that are 5,800 years old. The history they depict goes back millions of years and place the emergence of *Homo sapiens* at 200,000 years ago. They present a puzzle in that the tablets describe details of our solar system that have only been "rediscovered" in the last few decades. So how did these so-called primitive people know these facts?

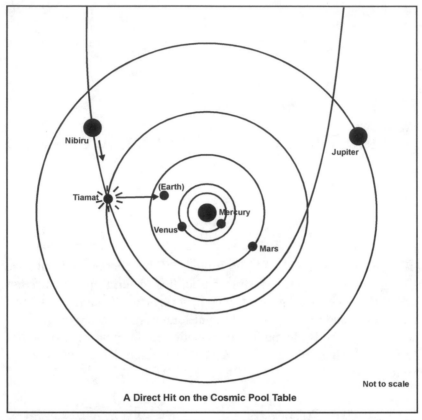

Not to scale

A Direct Hit on the Cosmic Pool Table

They tell of the planet Nibiru which has a wildly eccentric orbit around the sun that brings it close in every 3,600 years, before it swings way out again into space. They also tell of a large planet named Tiamat orbiting the sun between Mars and Jupiter. On one of its passes, billions of years ago, Nibiru collided with Tiamat and about half of the latter fragmented to become the asteroid belt just beyond Mars. The other half was knocked inside the orbit of Mars to form Earth. (See the diagram above for an idea of what this cosmic pool game must have looked like.) The mystery of how the Sumerians even knew about the asteroid belt, when it cannot be seen by the naked eye, is further verification of their written accounts.

Much later, about 450,000 years ago, Nibiru was home to a people that the Sumerians called the Nefilim, a tall race with a lifespan of about 360,000 years. They needed vast amounts of gold to correct a problem with their planet's atmospheric shield. On one of their passes, they left a team on Earth to mine gold from the rich deposits of the

Zambezi Basin in South Africa. The team consisted of 600 miners on the surface and 300 on their orbiting mothership, and was headed by 12 overseers led by a Nefilim named Enlil. Every time Nibiru came in close, the gold was shuttled to their planet. This apparently went on for 100,000 to 150,000 years (accounts differ), or 27 to 40 passes, until about 200,000 years ago, when the miners were getting fed up with the hard work and threatened to strike. To resolve the problem, the overseers came up with a brilliant idea.

Life had been seeded on this planet millions of years earlier (some say by those who carved the Sphinx out of solid rock as their "calling card") and by now evolution had, with a little help from extraterrestrials, produced advanced primates and primitive proto-humans such as the Neanderthal. Using one of these species and their own DNA, Enki, the Nefilim medical expert, engineered a species new to this planet to serve as worker drones. They were temporarily housed on the now-sunken island of Gondwanaland, off the coast of Africa in the southern Atlantic. The female component of the DNA came from the Nefilim, and they called upon another ET species from the Sirius system to provide the male component. Nefilim females volunteered to act as surrogate mothers, because the first female worker drones were sterile.

Eventually, this new species was ready to be put to work and was transported to the mines. This would explain, according to Drunvalo, why the bones of *Homo sapiens* have been found in deep mines that date back 100,000 years and how primitive man could have pulled off the advanced engineering involved in deep mining. Simple. They didn't.

It would also explain another mystery. The worker drones were around our height today, dwarfed by the Nefilim's 12 – 16 feet, which explains the Old Testament references to "giants called Nephilim" and "the sons of gods" (plural in the older versions) who "found the daughters of man fair" who in turn bore children to them. But how was that sterility problem solved?

Apparently, some of the drones were transferred from the mines to served in the Nefilim cities in what is now Iraq. Enki found a way to make the females fertile, thus starting a whole new subspecies. His first success was with a couple of drones named, would you believe it, Adam and Eve. (Remember that the Sumerian scribes literally carved this into clay 2,000 years before Moses is alleged to have written the Book of Genesis.)

This account resolves another major puzzle—why our evolutionary timeline contains a major discontinuity. Primates evolved slowly on this planet over millions of years but, almost overnight, *Homo sapiens* appeared, with a brain capacity, adaptability, skills and language that should also have taken millions of years if left alone. We are still left with the question of at what point did we become "soul carriers," i.e. when did our physical bodies develop chakras and other etheric structures that were complex enough to allow us as souls to attach?

When the landmass known as Lemuria rose above the waves, some of the fertile humans were taken there. According to ancient sources, Lemuria consisted of thousands of islands, and our ancestors flourished there. They had strong psychic abilities and knew that one day their land would disappear beneath the waves, so many of them dispersed to high ground such as Lake Titicaca and Mt. Shasta, taking their culture with them. As the Lemurian islands began to sink (it took a long time), the large landmass of Atlantis arose in the Atlantic Ocean.

Countless millennia later, Drunvalo goes on, when Atlantis sank, the disaster was accompanied by a pole shift that erased human memory and caused the level of our consciousness to plummet. Humanity had to start over, without a clue about what they were doing. Worse, the entire planet and population were moving into a part of a vast 26,000-year cycle of consciousness (the precession of the equinoxes) that pushed psychic awareness to new lows.

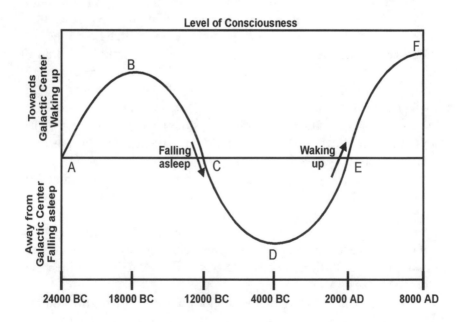

Our level of conscious awareness is subject to 26,000-year long cycles. Because the Earth wobbles in its orbit around the sun, for 13,000 years, it moves towards the center of the galaxy, and we are in a "wake-up" phase, rising up through the dimensions. Then for 13,000 years, it moves away, and we drop down the dimensions, akin to falling asleep.

In the diagram, points A and E are the wake-up calls when we begin an inbound movement. These are times of great change as consciousness begins to flourish. We are currently at point E, just emerging from several millennia of darkness.

At point C, we fell asleep around 10500 BC, coincident with a pole shift and the collapse of the unity grid, and hit rock bottom at point D around 4000 BC. Point B marks the apex of ancient consciousness on this planet as prehistoric cultures flourished, a level we will achieve and exceed in our future. (Note: point F is higher than B because, each time around, we go higher.)

If this brief account of our planetary history is true, what does it mean to us as Divine Architects? First, it means that humanity is not alone in the universe, and that Earth has been visited for perhaps millions of years by races who are further along than we are. Second, it means that we are here on purpose—our souls' purpose—and are being guided by higher-dimensional beings, such as Drunvalo's sources, towards an exciting future for our species.

What you have read here barely scratches the surface, and I strongly recommend Drunvalo's *The Ancient Secret of the Flower of Life* and Sitchin's *The 12th Planet* but not at bedtime if you plan on getting any sleep.

We live in a reality of cycles within cycles, the two most obvious being the annual cycle of the four seasons and the human cycle also with four seasons: birth, life, death, and the interlife.

Due to the precession of the equinoxes, we are also subject to a much vaster cycle. As the Earth rotates round the sun, its north-south axis wobbles slightly and, each year, it points to a different area of space. For 2,150 years, it points to each sign of the zodiac so, every two millennia, the planet comes under a different influence. Currently, we are in transit from Pisces to Aquarius. With 12 signs, the entire cycle takes about 26,000 years to complete, or a Cosmic Year.

As the following diagram shows, the Cosmic Year also has seasons, and we are just now in the Cosmic Spring as the Light of Aquarius

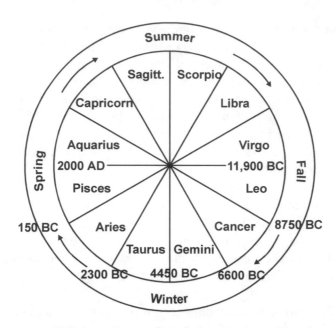

pushes back the darkness of the past 13,000 years to allow a new level of consciousness to spring forth.

Ancient wisdom points to cataclysmic turbulence around 12,000 BC as Atlantis finally went down and the Ice Age ended, causing massive flooding. The Earth probably underwent a magnetic pole shift that erased much of the wisdom of humanity, and we were plunged into 13,000 years of darkness and ignorance. As the millennia rolled by, we sank further from the glorious memories of our divinity, so that around the time of Christ, much of humanity was reduced to animal-level subsistence or slavery to giant war machines such as the Roman Empire. Our divinity was firmly established as "out there," imbued in mythological concepts we called gods. We had shrunk back as far from our own "god-ness" as was possible.

Then, like a supertanker trying to change course, something amazing began to happen towards the end of the Age of Pisces. We began to free ourselves from the stranglehold of our mythological gods-out-there. Teachers such as Swedenborg and Blavatsky, prophets such as Cayce, and higher-dimensional beings such as Seth began to remind us that our primary identity is our eternal soul, not our flesh-and-bone Earth suits.

Today, teachers such as Drunvalo and Gregg Braden are rephrasing ancient wisdom in contemporary terms, reminding us of truths that humanity took for granted until the last Cosmic Fall just 13,000 years ago. Those of us who incarnated to participate in this current Cosmic Spring are alive for the most spectacular event imaginable, for the spring is not just a replay of the previous one 26,000 years ago. The Cosmic Year diagram is not just a wheel but also a spiral, and each cycle takes us higher. This will be the best Spring ever in the history of this planet. And you chose to be here for it!

Research has shown that between 1850 and 1950, the Earth's magnetic poles meandered around at about two miles a year. In just the last 50 years, they have moved about 200 miles, causing chaos for human and marine animal navigation. What can this mean?

Over Earth's history, the North and South magnetic poles have reversed over 170 times, the last one being about 10,500 BC, triggering the latest Cosmic Winter. What geophysicists don't know for sure is what causes pole reversal. Theories include massive solar flare activity and asteroid strikes causing major wobbles in the Earth's rotation, even to the extreme of planetary "rollover."

The fact that rollover has happened many times in Earth's history explains the mystery of woolly mammoths being found flash-frozen where they stood and with undigested tropical flowers in their stomachs. One minute they're grazing in a tropical meadow and the next they're at the new North Pole. Brrrr.

Now, whether this will happen within our lifetime is unknown, but every ancient tradition points to dramatic events afoot between today and 2012.

Astrology and the Divine Architect

My friend and intuitive astrologer Serena Wright is one of those modern astrologers who practice their craft as a science. This is what she has to say about its relevance to our lives today:

"At the present time in our evolution on this planet, many people no longer consider astrology to be 'fortune telling' but a path by which we may actually become the architect of our own destiny. Our astrological chart is a blueprint of our consciousness up to the completion of our last life, as well as a manifestation of the choices we made in spirit for the next steps on our journey.

"The path of our spiritual progress is joyful and exciting when we can see the complete picture. Focusing on only the part of our life that may not be going very well, and pushing and fighting against it, can be frustrating. This is the time when we go to an astrologer or psychic and ask, 'Why is this happening?' or, 'When will it be over?'

"A wise astrologer or intuitive counselor will alert us to which areas of our life need healing. This may not be what we want to hear at the time but it is usually the quickest way to get the result we want!

"These days, we are expanding our awareness about the world in general and asking the same questions about why things are happening and when they will be over. It is good that we're now validating our link with the rest of the world and thinking about healing problems on a larger scale. However, I suggest that we still look within ourselves to see what needs healing in order to actually summon the power for positive change in the larger world.

"According to Vedic or sidereal astrology, Jupiter is exalted in the sign of Cancer from July 2002 until August 2003, which creates an influx of compassionate healing energy to support our activities. An inauspicious eclipse in June 2002 brings in its wake the obvious need for major change from deep within our hearts. The old ways will no longer work but, as with any process of healing, things may well get worse before they get better. This is a time to ask ourselves questions such as:

- In past lives, could I have been one of those people on the 'wrong side' who caused harm to other people?
- Could I have lived during some of the great civilizations on this planet and can I bring some of that wisdom to my present life?
- Where and from which body of knowledge do I find my greatest inspiration?
- Can I accept that other people may get their inspiration elsewhere?
- Are there hidden truths that are about to be revealed that would change the world, and will I recognize them as true?

"The year 2002 also sees Uranus strongly in Aquarius. Everything is ready for positive change and enlightenment. It is certainly possible to be an architect of our own destiny. If we do not take positive action, we will only be pushed back and forth by our own karma and may fall into activities that create even more karma.

"I suggest living in balance by dividing your life into thirds: one third work, one third service and spiritual activities, and one third recreation and relaxation. This helps us to think about why we are here and to be a good example to others.

"On a personal level, I am happy to have the opportunity to help others get in balance with these times and help them recognize and remove blocks that have caused painful patterns in the past. We always have the choice to be a victim or climb up to the next step.

"Through Vedic astrology, inner guidance and years of spiritual practice, I have found that I can usually get a clear picture of a person's life choices and help them feel better about their situation. We magnetize people and situations into our lives that match our state of being. Once we have healed and recovered from past traumatic events, bad choices and negative beliefs, we are free to move forward with clear and positive perceptions. This brings the most wonderful results, which previously we may have thought too good to be true for ourselves and the world.

The Hopi

Living on the 3,000-foot Black Mesa in northern Arizona, the Hopi have practiced harmony with Nature since before recorded history. The word "hopi" means peaceful, kind, and truthful. They believe that we are currently living in what they call the "Fourth World."

The First World was created in perfect balance, but the people misused their spiritual powers and fell out of balance with nature. So major earthquakes destroyed the world, and the land sank under the oceans. The survivors started the Second World, but they made the same mistakes and suffered a great Ice Age, which only a few people survived to start the Third World.

The Third World lasted a long time, and the great nations became technologically advanced, while the people used their powers only for good. However, over lengthy eons, they became enamored of their technology and turned their backs on nature, eventually scoffing at the very spiritual principles that had helped them advance. So the world was destroyed in the Great Flood of ancient legends. Again, a few survived to begin the Fourth World and today we are repeating history. We poison the land and oceans, worship our machines, thoughtlessly consume natural resources and wipe out species that we don't even know about, and let millions of children needlessly die of hunger.

The Hopi see two roads leading from this time. The path of technology is a jagged road leading to chaos, ruin, and destruction. The other path is that of harmony with nature. At this moment in time, a third line joins both paths. For the next few years, it's possible for us to leave the jagged path and cut across to the path of harmony, but once we move past that crossover point, there will be no turning back. Our home, the Earth, will be irreparably damaged and unable to sustain life, human or otherwise.

The Mayan Calendar

The Maya, once occupying what today are southern Mexico, Belize and Guatemala, are shrouded in mystery. Archeologists believe that they crossed the dry Bering land bridge, whereas others (including Edgar Cayce) claim they were emigrants from Atlantis. The great Mayan civilization emerged around 2000 BC, peaked around 850 AD and slowly disintegrated until its demise around 1400 AD. Oddly, many great cities were abandoned, some just left half-built for the jungle to reclaim. Why this happened will never be known because Spanish missionaries destroyed all but a handful of the Mayan books.

Mayan accomplishments were legion. They used complex hieroglyphic writing, were master stonemasons and brilliant mathematicians who used a sophisticated numbering system with which they calculated the distance to the sun to three decimals, and predicted eclipses. Their greatest achievement was the famous Mayan calendar based on their precise observation of the heavens and sensitivity to off-world influences.

The calendar is actually two in one. The mundane calendar, the *Haab*, governed daily life, especially crop-planting and was more accurate than our Gregorian calendar. Their year had 18 months of 20 days plus five "unlucky" days at the end to make up the 365 days. The *Tzolkin*, or sacred calendar, used two cycles. Twenty named days repeated 13 times gave each day a special meaning, making for a 260-day sacred year that governed rituals and ceremonies. Thus every day had two meanings—its *Haab* meaning and its *Tzolkin* meaning—and any particular day took 52 years to come round again.

Central to the calendar is a cycle of 22 of these 52-year Rounds—13 "Heaven Rounds" (676 years) followed by 9 "Hell Rounds" (468 years). The arrival of the Spanish Conquistadors on April 21, 1519 just happened to "coincide" exactly with the first day of the first of a Hell Round series. Also, by coincidence, the last day of the 468 years of those 9 Hell Rounds fell on August 16, 1987. That put the first day of the next series of 13 Heaven Rounds on the exact day of the Harmonic Convergence!

The Harmonic Convergence was an unprecedented phenomenon. Unheralded by the media and unexploited by merchandisers, it crept up on an unsuspecting world as a spontaneous coming together of spiritual seekers—the coming out party for the New Age movement, if you will. It was only later that people turned to the Mayan calendar for an explanation of what had just happened, and found that humanity had just been placed on a 20-year collision course with its own destiny.

The calendar also features a Great Cycle of 5,125 years, five of which incidentally yield 25,627 years, which is *their* calculation for the Precession of the Equinoxes. Since the Mayan calendar began with the start of the current Great Cycle in 3113 BC, the 5,125-year period gives us the year 2012 as its close—December 21, to be precise.

What's significant about the close of a Great Cycle? It points to a tremendous shift in human consciousness that will synchronize us with much larger cosmic patterns—esoteric researchers have always known that the Mayan calendar was aligned with something far larger than just our tiny planet, but whether this signals full-blown ascension into the fifth dimension remains to be seen. For now, in the last *tun*, or 20-year cycle of the calendar (1992 – 2012), we are seeing unparalleled frequency shifts as more Light pours onto the planet. Those who choose to jump aboard will enjoy great transformation amidst the chaotic collapse of old, outworn systems. Those who rigidly hang on to those old systems will perish along with them.

What else can we expect? The falling away of duality, increasingly direct experience of who we are as spirit, the speeding up of time, synchronicity and paranormal experiences becoming commonplace and a grand sense of completion. We can also expect to see the UFO cover-up collapse as more countries join France, Belgium and Brazil in full disclosure to their citizens. The Internet will continue to grow as people find access to information increasingly empowering, and education reforms as the school system is confronted by Indigo Children who demand more control of their lives.

And beyond 2012? What can we expect as we enter a new 26,000-year cycle? The Mayan calendar is silent on this but, because the current cycle is all about preparation for synchronizing with a *much* larger cosmic game plan, we can expect full, open contact with our extraterrestrial neighbors, already gathered around the planet for the celebration. This will lead to free energy, radical improvements in health care, help with pollution clean up, and a new brotherhood that will change our lives completely.

Yes, the last few years of a Great Cycle of this fascinating blueprint should prove very interesting. Bring it on!

The Ultimate Mystery

To me, no mention of Ancient Wisdom is complete without discussing the enigma sitting out in the Giza Plateau, just outside Cairo. We all know the traditional story of them being built as burial chambers for Pharaohs Khufu, Khafre, and Menkhare between 2700 and 2500 B.C. The story also goes that the Great Pyramid alone took 100,000 laborers about 20 years to build, using an estimated 2.3 million limestone blocks that they dragged or pushed up mud-slicked ramps.

The blocks vary in weight from 2 tons to 100 tons, yet fit together with only a 0.02 inch gap, meaning that you cannot slip even this page between them. The whole thing weighs an estimated 6 million tons yet has sunk only 1 inch in 12,000 years. It's aligned to the North Pole to within 0.5 degrees, and that discrepancy is because the pole has moved over time and not a builder's error.

Conservative scholars think the pyramid was an important religious shape for the Egyptians, with the shafts symbolizing the slanting rays of the sun and the sloping sides assisting the soul of the king to join the gods.

Is the traditional account of the age of the pyramids just deliberate disinformation on the part of the Egyptian tourist industry to claim the monuments as "property of Egypt" rather than part of our planetary heritage, and something left behind by off-worlders? For example, the traditional account conflicts with just about every other ancient record that date the pyramids as many millennia before Khufu found them.

Further, according to Joseph Jochmanns, the Egyptian claim is based on inscriptions allegedly found in the King's Chamber by a 19th century explorer named Col. Howard-Vyse. Apparently, in 1837, he needed to curry favor with the Egyptian authorities so he clumsily forged Khufu's signature, or cartouche, in the chamber. However, he made two glaring errors. First, he spelled the name Raufu, not Khufu, and second, he used terminology that would not evolve until 2,000 years later. Even genuine stela from Khufu himself admit that he only *discovered* the pyramids and the Sphinx, repaired some damage, and then dedicated the pyramid to Isis, not himself. So the only actual claim Egypt has to having built them goes out the window.

How old are they? At least 12,000 years, for around 10,000 BC when the last Icc Age ended, the Nile flooded to a height of several hundred feet, leaving behind three compelling pieces of evidence:

1. Ancient records tell of a prominent watermark *halfway* up the Great Pyramid, or about 250 feet up but, of course, this vanished when the original white casing was removed.
2. When the pyramids were first unsealed, researchers found sea salt encrusting the inner passages to about halfway up.
3. The pyramids are surrounded by a thick layer of marine silt that has been carbon-dated to between 9,600 and 10,200 BC.

So it's obvious that the pyramids were already fixtures in 10,000 BC when the Ice Age ended, and the Fourth Dynasty simply adopted them 8,000 years later. Later rulers tried to copy the building techniques, but not one of the 23 attempts even approaches the sophistication of the originals.

Beyond the puerile burial chamber notion, let's look at some other reasons why they might have been built. A more plausible reason is that they were used for mystery school initiations. Having laid in a sarcophagus myself, I can envision that 72 hours alone in one would leave you enlightened or crazy, or both. But the initiation theory doesn't explain why the builders hauled millions of tons of limestone and granite for long distances.

In his book, *The Giza Power Plant,* Chris Dunn presents a fascinating theory—that the Great Pyramid was a huge energy generator. Citing facts such as the Great Pyramid's base being 365.24 cubits (the exact number of days in a year) and that the ratio of height to base perimeter being *exactly* that of a circle's radius to its circumference, Dunn believes that it was built to *resonate* with the planet.

We know that the Earth is constantly active and has its own resonant "hum." According to Dunn, the ancient custodians of this planet knew that and built this enormous energy collecting device and amplifier to capture the Earth's energy and convert into usable form such as microwave energy.

The two main interior chambers are connected by so-called "airshafts" to the outside world. A long inclined gallery approaches the upper chamber. The entry shaft also leads below ground to a subterranean chamber from which a passage dead-ends.

The structure poses more questions than it answers. Why, for example, are the two main chambers topped by huge granite blocks?

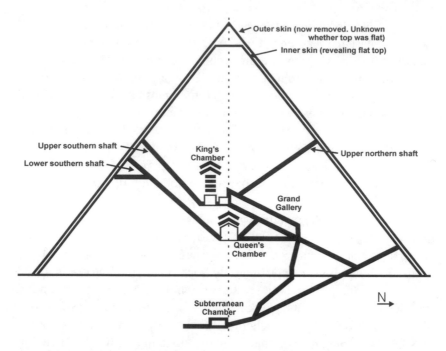

Why does the sloping Grand Gallery have slots in its floor that hold more granite slabs, and what are the latter doing there anyway?

The shafts are also puzzling, for they take unnecessarily circuitous routes through the structure *if* they are just airshafts. Odd settling of the blocks in the lower southern shaft suggests the existence of another chamber. This shaft is closed by a highly polished block that appears taller than the shaft, as though the block could be raised or lowered to open and close the shaft. But where are the controls, and why go to the enormous effort and complexity of building diagonal shafts through the horizontal layers of stone only to close them off?

The shafts do not seem to have an astrological purpose (e.g., allow starlight or sunlight in) because bends prevent line-of-sight. And why risk allowing access to the elements (rain, sand, etc.) and animals (snakes, rats, etc.)? Finally, why does only the Great Pyramid have shafts? What is so different about this one?

Dunn theorizes that the Great Pyramid was a huge machine and that chemicals were pumped into the Queen's chamber and reacted to produce hydrogen that filled the sealed structure. Pulses of energy at Earth's resonant frequency were applied until the whole structure vibrated in harmony with the planet. This resonant coupling allowed Earth's energy to flow out, like water escaping through a break in a levee. The energy was focused in the King's Chamber, where the crystalline content of the granite converted it to electrical energy via the piezo-electric effect, whereby pressure applied to a crystal causes it to generate an electrical spark.

The King's Chamber was designed so that its resonant frequency was also that of the hydrogen atom, which was thus broken down in a controlled fission reaction (much like today's hydrogen bomb) and released a huge amount of energy. With further amplification and conversion to electromagnetic energy in the Grand Gallery, enormous power would be released through the shafts to the outside world, available to be picked up by anyone with a receiver tuned to the correct frequency. (Wireless distribution of energy was also a passion of Nikola Tesla, discussed in *The Divine Blueprint*.)

Dunn is a machinist and maintains that his profession allowed him to see the pyramids as machines, and all he had to do was figure out what they did and how they worked. That they were giant quartz resonators, he claims, also neatly explains why, when most of the pyramid is limestone, certain key areas are of black granite (of the quartz family) slabs polished to 0.0001 inches and with *perfectly* square corners.

So what went wrong? Dunn theorizes that scorch marks on the roof of the gallery point to a huge explosion that ignited the hydrogen and destroyed everything except the outer shell of the power plant. If the plant came online around 10,500 BC and the Egyptians began recorded history around 3750 BC, the Giza pyramids could have operated for many millennia before the explosion. Is it also possible that the explosion was the reason for the builders' departure, I wonder? One thing is obvious, however; this planet was once occupied by a group of beings of unknown identity whose understanding of the laws of nature far, far exceeds our own today and, for some reason—planned or catastrophic—they either left Earth or "went to sleep," forgetting the secrets of their own technology.

Schools of Divine Architecture / The Mystery Schools

Traditionally, a mystery school is an environment in which a master teaches a student the ancient mystical secrets concerning life, death, immortality, and healing that are withheld from the general public. These teachings are passed down through the ages and shared only with those "who have ears that are ready to hear."

Over many decades, those initiated into a mystery school worked to shed the personal side of their being in order to become impersonal, to cast aside the limited in order to expand and allow the God within to manifest itself. How this was done depended on the culture and era, and the history of humanity is replete with various mystery school traditions. Behind its secular government, every civilization has had these clandestine organizations, although many doubled as secret societies that had agendas other than the enlightenment of their members. However, deep down, there is really only one mystery.

Atlantean Mystery School

Believed destroyed in 9600 BC, Atlantis was home to probably the earliest mystery school, run under the aegis of the god Poseidon. For countless millennia, the school was custodian of human knowledge in astronomy, mathematics, and science that far exceeded ours today. In the beginning, its religion followed the Law of One in which all is united and forms the Source of All That Is. Symbolic of the Source was the sun, which played a central role in their religion, although it *per se* was not worshipped.

It is believed that over several millennia, dissention crept in and rival factions began vying for secular power and control, which led to a wedge being driven between man and his intimate relationship with the spirit realms. This eventually opened the door to black magic and misuse of technology that led to the destruction and sinking of the series of islands that made up Atlantis.

Long before that, large numbers of Atlanteans had seen what was coming and emigrated, taking their culture and beliefs with them, most notably to Egypt and the Yucatan, where they continued their practice of building huge pyramids for arcane purposes.

The Mystery School of Serapis

Some sources believe that the Atlanteans who went to Egypt demonstrated their skill and technology by building the pyramids at Giza about 12,000 years ago, but then they merged in with the locals and "went to sleep" spiritually for almost 10,000 years. However, the mystery schools kept the old knowledge alive during that time, and it began to reemerge during the centuries before the birth of Christ.

One of the most closely guarded schools was based on the teachings of the Atlantean deity, Osiris, also known as Apis, later combined to form Serapis. The philosophy was divided into the freely taught Lesser Mysteries, honoring Isis, and the Greater Mysteries, sacred to Osiris and revealed only to the high priests. Tragically, the details of the mysteries were lost when certain factions burned the Serapeum Library at Alexander in 385 AD in order to eliminate all opposing thought.

Hermetic School

Based on the teachings of Hermes Trismegistus (thrice majestic), arguably one of the "fathers" of human civilization. Known to the Egyptians as Thoth and Tehuti, to the Jews as Enoch, and to Rome as Mercury, the Greek Hermes was nicknamed "Messenger of the Gods." He wrote over 40 books that were also tragically lost in the sacking of the Library at Alexander. Today, only fragments remain.

After a lifetime of wandering meditation, Hermes was finally rewarded when he tapped into Universal Mind, and all the mysteries of life were revealed to him. He was shown the process of Creation, told the reason for it, and given great scientific, philosophical and mystical truths. His teachings influenced countless civilizations for millennia and still live on in the symbolism of Freemasonry and Tarot cards, and as an active body of philosophy.

The Egyptian Mystery Schools

In ancient Egypt, initiates went through three schools: the Right Eye of Horus, dealing with male principles, the Left Eye of Horus dealing with the feminine realm of emotions and feelings, and the Third Eye of Horus, which is life itself and considered the most important of all.

The Egyptians built a series of initiatory temples along the Nile, each working with a different chakra of the initiates who underwent various ordeals to put them into a state of fear, on the basis that we become stronger by facing and overcoming our fears.

The primary mentors of the Left Eye mystery school are the legendary Hathors, beings of the purest, loving Christ Consciousness energy. Apparently, they incarnated on Earth many thousands of years ago to help guide humanity and specialized in healing with sound tones. The bodily form they took was about nine feet tall, about the same size as the Nefilim, as depicted in the few remaining statues in the Egyptian temples.

Eleusian Mysteries

The best known mystery school of all was the Greek school dedicated to Eleusis in honor of Demeter and her daughter, Persephone. The school taught that the higher world is the true home of soul, and likened the human condition to a quagmire of misery. It saw birth as death in a larger sense and death as a rebirth either into perpetual misery or joy, depending on whether one made an effort to improve oneself during life.

The outer interpretation for the masses treated the mysteries as explanations for natural events and a moral code, while the esoteric side conferred initiates with spiritual power and wisdom based on great and eternal truths. In testament to the excellence of its philosophy, the Eleusian Mysteries underpinned many civilizations, including the mighty Roman Empire.

Pythagorean School

This Greek mystery school was based on the wisdom of Pythagoras who studied under Hermes Trismegistus and, as every schoolchild knows, founded the discipline of geometry. He taught that command of geometry, astronomy and music was essential to understanding the nature of God and Creation.

Born around 600 BC, the father of modern mathematics and sacred geometry was unceremoniously killed at age 100 by a disgruntled student whom Pythagoras deemed unfit for initiation to the inner mysteries.

Qabbalistic Mystery School

Hidden within Hebrew theology, this school teaches the most esoteric of the three branches of that theology. (The other two are (1) the law, taught to everyone, and (2) the soul of the law, revealed to Rabbis.) Some believe that the mysteries were initially given to Adam by the angel Raziel, and that a succession of angels have privately coached subsequent patriarchs such as Isaac, Moses and King David.

The Qabbala is probably best known for the Tree of Sephiroth, the network of ten circles representing qualities or states of being, and the 22 lines representing paths for achieving wisdom, the whole making up the AIN SOPH, or *unconditional* state of all things. Its influences are found in Rosicrucian and Masonic esoterica.

Druidic Order

Based on a deep understanding of Nature and her laws, Druidism leads to skills such as using herbs in healing. The sun was a key feature of their beliefs due to its importance in an agrarian culture, and Druids were accomplished astronomers, as witnessed by Stonehenge, the great clock that ticks off the days of the Earth's annual rotation.* They believed in reincarnation and that, on death, the soul goes either straight to a realm of perpetual happiness or first stops off in purgatory for purification.

Like all mystery schools, Druidism consisted of an outer moral code taught to all and an inner esoteric doctrine taught only to initiates who had proved themselves worthy by undergoing a series of grueling tests of character.

Druidism's deities were Hu and Ceridwen, based on Isis and Osiris, the influence possibly coming from frequent contact with Mediterranean miners visiting Cornwall's tin mines.

Native American School

The first residents of this continent did not really have mystery schools *per* se because how they lived their daily lives was testament to their beliefs, including such phenomena as reincarnation and guardian spirits. The more esoteric mysteries were documented in the *Popol Vuh*, written in Nahuatl, the language of Quetzalcoatl, also known in Peru as Amaru, or the Plumed Serpent. (Incidentally, Amaruca, which means Land of the Plumed Serpent, is the origin of the word "America," although other sources maintain that the word comes from the name of explorer Amerigo Vespucci.) The ancient book is mainly allegorical accounts of Creation.

The *Popul Vuh* underpins aboriginal philosophy in the Americas but, south of the border, the black arts dominated the mystery schools, probably a perversion of the Atlantean sun mysteries.

---

* Other researchers disagree, claiming that Stonehenge was already ancient when the Druids came along. The mystery still stands, however, as to how, during 2700 – 2000 BC, a small army quarried the extremely hard Blue Stone in Wales and dragged 100-ton megaliths about 250 miles to Salisbury Plain. And why? Stonehenge stands at the confluence of England's ley line network, so was it built as an energy amplifer that allowed its builders to control the country through its ley lines? Or was it just an astronomical counter?

Conclusion

From the Great Pyramid of ancient times right up to today's crop circles, we gaze in wonder and awe at these mysteries. We can only ask, in utter humility, "Who, how and why?" These great enigmas of our planet tantalize and tease us with much larger truths about the universe we live in. I close this chapter by paraphrasing a remark made by the Q entity to the crew of the starship Enterprise as they began their epic voyage: "There are wonders out there the likes of which you can't even begin to imagine."

Chapter 10

Reality Architecture

Architecture: The art, science, style and method of design;
an orderly arrangement.
Reality: The totality of all things that exist ...
as you perceive them.

D O THINGS JUST HAPPEN in the world, or is the reality we share subject to some enormous cosmic plan? And if so, who's the planner? Some entity out there who drops the occasional "act of God" on us or is the source a lot closer to home?

For most of the last 2,000 years, religions have nudged us towards their God as the Divine Architect, but something happened recently that throws all that up in the air and points to *you and me* as the real Divine Architects—the shocking revelation that in 325 AD, the early Church rewrote the rules and stole our cosmic legacy from us. In the greatest conspiracy ever perpetrated, we were stripped of our divinity, and most of our power was stolen.

In earlier chapters and in *The Divine Blueprint*, we saw how a group of men in the Middle East did something that still dramatically affects our lives today. They assembled a number of documents into what would become the Bible and then edited those documents so that all the power in creation passed from humanity to a God that was in turn based on much earlier God myths.

Probably the greatest power theft involved a particular technology that we used to take for granted back then—the ability to control our environment. This violation left us weakened and vulnerable to the very external forces we used to manipulate. So those of the day had no choice but to go along with the only power they saw—the God concept. What was this technology, why did the religions do what they did, and how do we know all this?

The technology hinged on our mind's ability to impress itself on reality and change the outcome of an event, an effect that escalates exponentially as more minds join in union with a common goal. This technology had been known and used throughout time, as our ancestors used it to manipulate the weather, earth changes, and other natural events. This science is what prayer is *really* about rather than pitiful pleas to some mythological deity to "please fix things."

The reason this group covered up this technology was that they were birthing a new religion and needed to give to their deity the power to control human destiny. They reasoned that, if humanity knew of its own inherent awesome power, the people would not need religions or their deities. By transferring our reality creation technology to the deities, they plunged humanity into a dark dependence that still continues to this day.

Out of these conspiracies grew the most powerful organizations this planet has seen, for they stand between us and our innate divinity.

The religions unleashed unparalleled attacks on every source of knowledge other than their own. They began centuries-long orgies of destruction, burning every library and book they could find, thus wiping out the sum total of all the knowledge available at the time and setting humanity's progress back almost two thousand years. Religions cruelly targeted pagans, and centuries of Inquisition and witch-burnings wreaked untold pain and misery on mankind, all in the name of God.

We know of this because a few ancient texts survived, those of the Essenes, a mystical religious sect of men and women who lived beside the Dead Sea in Biblical times. They buried their sacred texts in caves at a place called Q'umran. Known as the Dead Sea Scrolls, these texts have not been subject to the same rewriting and editing that has obscured the truth. Written in the original Aramaic, they are being freshly translated by scholars with no agenda other than the truth, and they reveal a very different picture of life a few thousand years ago.

Discovered by Bedouinis in 1947 in a network of caves at Q'umran in what is now Jordan, these thousand or so documents and fragments created major waves in theological circles.

They included six new books attributed to Moses and even the direct words of Archangel Michael. In addition to earlier versions of the "biblical" books taken into the Old Testament are countless fascinating glimpses of life 2,000 – 3,000 years ago. They also tell of contemporary astrology, prophetic visions, messiahs and antichrists, and even buried treasure.

Organized religion denies us knowledge of our inherent power, ascribes this power to a mythical external being and then "sells" access to this power back to us. Suppose, through your property, runs a river so powerful that you can generate your own electricity from it. Then your neighbor diverts the river, generates electricity from it, and tells you that you must now buy water and electricity from him.

That is exactly what happened long ago, only the power was our ability to manipulate reality. This is what religions have kept secret for almost two millennia—that *you* are the Divine Architect of your reality but don't even know it.

Religions, however, are very important in that they provide an "in door" to spirituality. This is a beginning until we open up to a deeper cosmic consciousness and the universal principles that surround us all. Religions have been at their best when disseminating values, morals, and such fundamental qualities as compassion, service, selflessness, and purity. So let it not go unsaid that organized religion has an important place. It's just that, sometimes, man gets in the way.

The Science of Prayer

At one time, science was based on determinism, or the fact that the future is predetermined by past events and is immutable. Today, however, in stark contrast, some theoretical physicists are speculating about an intelligent field that contains all possible outcomes to any given situation. But what determines which outcome is selected for our third-dimensional reality? That's where the science of prayer comes in, a technology we use to *impress* our desire on to reality.

In *The Isaiah Effect*, Gregg Braden describes how, in a Tibetan monastery, a holy man told him that feeling wasn't just a part of prayer; it *was* the prayer. The implications of this are staggering. In order to explore them, we must clarify the differences between thought, emotion and feeling, Gregg says. *Emotion* is the source of power that impels us towards our goals and is closely allied with desire, the force that drives our imagination to achieve our goals. Without *thought*, however, our emotions may be scattered. Thought is the guidance system that directs emotion. *Feeling* is the union of the desire of emotion and the imagination of thought. To have a feeling, we must have an underlying thought and an emotion, i.e., destination and fuel.

Braden points out that in order to bring something into our lives (such as peace or abundance), we must identify with it and become it, living as though it had already happened, and feeling every nuance of it. (This is exactly the technique my friend Nancy taught me and what Tony Robbins means by "incantations" in Chapter 3.)

A thought without the fuel of emotion is simply a wish, Braden claims. To be empowered, we must give it energy; emotion energizes the wish. But when most people pray for abundance, the underlying emotion is usually fear rather than love, for they are really focusing on the fear of lack rather than the joy of abundance.

Do not focus on what you *don't* have but on something you don't have *yet* but is already yours in the simultaneity of time. Since you already have it in the future, you express gratitude in the present. The miracle has already happened, so give thanks.

Braden observes that since all possible outcomes exist in any situation—good or bad health, abundance or poverty, war or peace, love or hate—it's our job to let the universe know which we choose. The absolute worst thing we can do is focus on what we *don't* want. Because we don't realize our power of reality creation, we do that all the time.

So how do we input our choice into the great computer we call reality? Real prayer, Braden says, involves four steps:
1. Honoring all outcomes.
2. Gratitude for the opportunity and ability to choose.
3. Your chosen outcome, in full and absolute detail.
4. Gratitude for the blessings and joy that the outcome will bring.

Prayer, then, is a forgotten language that our forebears used for countless generations to mold and shape their reality. Rather than stand helplessly by as life just "happened" to them, they were proactive in unifying thought, emotion and feeling, and blending mind, body and heart to impress outcomes on their lives. Because they were keenly aware of their power, they did not misuse it by inadvertently creating unpleasant realities. For example, a Native American shaman is never caught in a sudden storm. In the first place, he would not unknowingly conjure one up by his confused emotions the way we do, and, secondly, if a storm did brew up for some reason, he would steer it and harness the energy of his natural "ally."

Ancient prayer technology, which Braden has termed "The Isaiah Effect," was based on four tenets, which he identifies as:

1. You are already healed. In any given situation, many possible outcomes already exist. Prayer is just a matter of choosing one of them by what you focus on.

2. There is only one of us. In the collective web that binds all humanity, there is no such thing as "acting alone." Every thought and deed ripples out and affects the web. When we care for a fellow human being or tend a sick animal, we raise the planetary "love quotient" a notch, and that love is available to everyone. When we execute a criminal, a piece of each of us dies. It is via this unity web that the Isaiah Effect works.

3. We resonate with our world. Through the web, we attract to us people, events and circumstances that mirror our inner state. Have you noticed that neurotic people usually have neurotic pets and crazy relationships? And that calm people have just the opposite? Magnified, whole communities determine their crime rates and even their weather. But rather than complain that these things "just happen," it behooves us to ask, "What are they mirroring?" and "How can we rework reality?"

4. Prayer allows direct access to our creativity. Just because the early religions robbed us of the *knowledge* of how prayer works, they couldn't take away the *effect*, so it still works constantly but unknown to us. The tragedy is that for almost 2,000 years, our fears and hatred have been fueling some pretty horrible realities— wars, plagues, and so-called "natural" disasters, to name a few.

If you doubt the power of scientific prayer, read up on the many experiments conducted by researchers into the power of active meditation in reducing a community's crime rate. Suppose a desperate armed man robs a convenience store and points his gun at the clerk. Will he pull the trigger or not? What determines the outcome? Two overlays influence his actions: a love overlay and a fear overlay. Experiments have convinced even the most skeptical police chief that a group of people in meditation who are blanketing a city in a love field can dramatically reduce crime. For example, it may well influence the robber to just grab the money and run rather than adding murder to his rap sheet.

Many of the books that were candidates for canonization into the Bible were dropped because they were "too mystical" or "too empowering" for the masses. So despite Jesus' words that, "the Kingdom of Heaven is within," the Kingdom was removed from our hearts and projected "out there" somewhere, along with our reality creation powers. For example, the original Aramaic instructions for prayer read:

> *"Ask without hidden motive and be surrounded by your answer. Be enveloped by your desire, that your gladness be full."*

This emphasizes purity of intention, intense visualization of the desired outcome, and gratitude. By comparison, the abominable translation is useless gibberish:

> *"Ask and you shall receive."*

Two final components to the reality creation recipe are *detachment* and *faith*. Having impressed your choice for a particular outcome, *leave it alone*. Do not worry it, for your energy may interfere with the unfoldment. When a Zen master shoots an arrow at a target, he turns and walks away for his work is done. He doesn't bother the arrow on its path.

You may ask, "What if the chosen outcome doesn't happen?" Well, its manifestation may be a matter of time, or it may not be in the highest and best interest of all involved. If you pray for the ideal mate to come into your life but, after a month, you're still alone, maybe you have unresolved issues around relationships. If so, you might pray for the blocks to be revealed so that you can work through them, and *then* be ready.

Is there any scientific basis for all this? Plenty, claims Gregg Braden. The 4th century clerics may have driven a mental wedge between us and outer reality, but that did nothing in real terms. Scientists know that our moods and emotional states greatly influence our body chemistry, and the Seth entity frequently said that, on a mass level, our moods determine the weather. Of course, the Native American shaman has *always* known that.

According to the old saying, "A loving relationship isn't about *finding* the right person; it's about *being* the right person." So is it enough just to know how to use prayer technology? In order to impress our desired outcome onto reality, we must be able to form that outcome clearly in our minds and transfer that to our hearts and senses. Just as my friend Nancy taught me, we need to be able to see, touch, taste, hear, and smell the outcome. But more than this, we must *become* what we desire. An angry person cannot pray for peace and hope to succeed.

To bring about peace, you must be peace. To bring about abundance, you must feel abundance in every cell.

This impressing effect, which Braden dubs "The Isaiah Effect," goes on all the time, and as the media ply us with fearful images of war-ravaged countries and disaster-stricken regions of the world, death, doom and disaster become our *expectation*. We begin to carry these negative outcomes in our prayer fields and are therefore unknowingly programming reality to deliver such self-fulfilling prophecies. Thus the cycle continues.

Most people see prayer as passive and not the same as "actually doing something." But this reclaimed technology paints prayer as active. So joining a worldwide prayer vigil for peace is every bit as active as marching in the street to protest war.

"Can it be that simple?" people ask me at my lectures.

"Yes, it can," I reply, for think how wars begin. A dispute over a border or a natural resource such as water or oil festers for years, decades even. The hearts of thousands, if not millions, of people, harden against the neighboring country, and public opinion eventually gives the country's leadership a mandate to declare war. Thousands of soldiers choose to follow orders, and the bombs and bullets start to fly. But if all those hearts and minds had not hardened, the conflict might have been resolved diplomatically.

Big problems need big solutions. Regional wars begin with relatively small groups of angry people—a few thousand, a million maybe. In promoting Transcendental Meditation, the Maharishi Yogi claimed that if only a tenth of that number, even a hundredth, unified in a mass prayer field, the outcome could be changed from war to peace.

Closer to home, if you're not enjoying an optimum level of prosperity in your life, if you accept that you caused it, you can not only stop programming for poverty but also start programming for abundance. After all, you *are* a Divine Architect, so what *can't* you do?

Prayer and Reality Creation

Traditionally, praying to a deity is a petition to something outside yourself for intervention in your affairs regarding something you either don't think you deserve or are afraid you cannot have. Therefore, it is usually self-defeating.

A prayer is actually a thoughtform, every bit as real as the nose on your face but just not as visible. It is a thought backed by desire and

Prayer

fueled by emotion, and is the tool of choice of reality creators. Your intent, based on your desire for an outcome and faith in your capacity to have that outcome, is the most powerful tool that exists.

You create your reality from your thoughts, backed by desire, but sometimes you may be surprised at the results. If you set your intent on exploring unconditional love, for example, you may find yourself experiencing intense jealousy as your partner takes a lover. The universe, in the form of your partner and this third party, has rearranged itself to provide you with an opportunity to *really* explore unconditional love. Not exactly what you had in mind, is it?

This possible outcome may plunge you into despair (on top of jealousy), because you think you've failed. In fact, you've succeeded brilliantly and taken a major step towards manifesting unconditional love—finding out where your love is conditional. So your perceived failure at one level is really a success on another.

Reality creation is based on two things:
1. Intent, which is a blend of vision and desire, and
2. Faith, or the inner knowing that it's possible but with no anxiety as to the outcome.

It is imperative that you involve your soul or spirit in setting your intent. In light meditation, ask your soul for its vision, requesting the highest outcome with the most love. Allow this to come in its own way—maybe an immediate thought, or a conversation with a friend a few days later. Whatever your part is in the vision, accept it joyously. It may involve activity or sitting at home holding a thought in your mind. Whatever it is, embrace it with gusto.

Faith differs from belief in that faith is *knowing*, and belief is *hoping*. With belief, your ego is fabricating a part of your reality in the hope (or fear) that it's true. Faith is a deep inner knowing that comes from your spirit. There is no doubt, no question. It just is. Faith goes beyond self-confidence because it's larger than the self. It is a knowing of your "rightness" in the universal scheme of things, so be grateful for having a part in the divine plan.

Blocks to Reality Creation

Before embarking on reworking reality, it's important to assess, accept and embrace your current reality. Is there anything in it that's stopping you from fully expressing your soul in your life, such as fears or attachments? We all have a few simply by virtue of our egos not being fully in sync with our souls. As a condition of incarnating, we had to accept the illusion of separation, which leaves us vulnerable to feelings of inadequacy, because we can't do everything our soul can. We may even feel a sense of shame at having been "kicked out of heaven" for some imagined transgression.

However the sense of separation manifests, it's ours and we must embrace it, come to terms with it, and then reclaim our divinity. How? By stating that you *are* divine, and then standing back as your subpersonalities start listing all the ways you're not. Let them have their say and thank them for having held you back all these years. Then tell them that it's time to rework their identity and job description, for you are a Divine Architect, here to co-create your vision of Heaven on Earth.

You have just started on a painful journey of identifying all the ways in which you feel separate from your soul. Try not to deny the pain, for how can you then heal it? Accept it fully and know that it just comes with being human. But you do have to take responsibility for it because, until you own it, you can't heal it. You volunteered to come down here to explore the *perception* of separation and the fears that separation brings up. Didn't it all look so easy from the soul plane?

Fear is only possible when ego feels separated from soul. Ego then tries to project the fear onto others or deny it. Here are some of the ways our egos manipulate themselves and others. If you catch yourself doing any of these, love yourself a little more, for you're operating from fear:

- Agreeing with someone in order to win approval. Trying to impress, acting "properly," withholding your truth or how you're really feeling in order to be accepted.
- Identifying with a group simply to share their glory or to establish a sense of belonging.
- Comparing yourself with others.
- Looking for outside authorities to tell you what's true and give you their approval.
- Feeling obligated to complete a commitment even though your heart isn't in it.
- Lacking in trust in yourself or others. Withholding intimacy because of fear of opening up.
- Blaming others, especially if they are weaker than you or less able to defend themselves.
- Feeling that you can't trust others so you must do it all yourself; that accepting help obligates you to return the favor.

Belief Rework

We have already seen how difficult it is to change a deeply held belief, which you have tended and nurtured over the years and have much invested in. And how, because your belief allows you to see only evidence that confirms it, your experiences seem to prove it correct.

Because we are a self-aware species, the human mind *can* examine its own beliefs, like a flashlight turned inwards. The mind is a hostage to its beliefs only as long as it *thinks* it is. For example, baby elephants need be tethered by only a thin rope, but when the elephant is a 5-ton adult, the thin rope still works because the elephant is tethered by its own childhood memory.

How does the self-examination process work? Here are three preliminary warm up steps:

1. Distinguish between you and your beliefs: "I am *not* my beliefs. I just inherited them."
2. My beliefs are just my *opinions* about reality and are not facts: "What I believe is not necessarily the way things are."
3. Because they are *my* opinions, I can change them without the world ending: "It is safe to change what I believe."

Do you have trouble with any of the above? If you believe that your beliefs are synonymous with the laws of nature, you would have thrown this book out of the nearest window by now, so I'm going to assume that you're open to changing them. Having given ourselves permission to change, how do we proceed, bearing in mind that beliefs can be slippery little weasels that wiggle around together? For example, people trying to lose weight may thwart themselves by believing that thin people are not taken seriously *and* are more prone to illness. Both beliefs must be turned around before even the first pound comes off.

Step 1: Inner Conversations

Make a list of your beliefs regarding such topics as gender, aging, religion, sex, work, friendship, your body, self-worth, etc. Over the next few days or weeks, hold inner conversations such as, "What I believe about _____ [topic] is _____."

Write down your answers and accumulate them in a notebook. If you find a conflict, then rejoice for that is payoff.

Another common trap is that material wealth is not spiritual (yes, people still believe this), but spiritual people still need a roof over their head and food on the table.

Step 2: Change the Habit

Beliefs are simply mental habits, things that were drummed into you as a child, which you could not and did not question. If you were told repeatedly, "You're worthless," you now have a mantra on an endless tape in your head that says, "I am unworthy."

For every belief in your notebook, look for even the tiniest hint of fear, lack, limitation, judgment or condition. If you find anything, you know that the belief is coming from your ego and not your soul. So, think of the exact opposite, conjuring up as much emotion and intensity as possible. Then, *just for today*, live as though that opposite is true. It will feel strange, but tell yourself that it's only for *today*. See how you feel at the end of the day.

Step 3: Get a Soul Perspective

For a real fun experience, learn to meditate and ask your soul for its insights on the topics: "Higher Self, show me your truth regarding _____ [topic] so that I can manifest you more in my life."

Beyond Separation: The Divine Architect!

You cannot create reality if you feel separate from it. It behooves us to foster as intimate a union as possible with it. To help you gauge how "in the flow" you feel, this section examines what it actually feels like to be a self-realized Divine Architect. But don't despair if you don't measure up in every one—most of us are still recovering from separation.

The following statements present a glorious picture of what being a Divine Architect feels like. Use them as signposts to point the way from where you may be today and where you might want to be tomorrow. And love yourself for being courageous enough to make the trip. Say the following out loud and see how true they feel in your heart:

- I follow my soul's urgings and visions without hesitation. I do not edit my actions or words in order to be accepted by others.
- I am a master of my reality and relate to others as masters of their reality. I honor that we have different pictures of reality and do not feel compelled to force a consensus.

- I know my mission and honor the missions of others without judgment.
- I joyously accept the perfection of my life. Whatever happens to me is a gift from my soul, and I accept it gladly. I delight in not knowing what's going to happen next, and trust that whatever does happen is in my highest and best interest, otherwise it wouldn't have happened.
- I am a powerful being, a creative force in the universe, and I use my power in the service of the Source.
- I participate willingly in reality, not because it serves me personally but because it serves the Source's evolution, of which I am part.

If you resonated with any of the above, then you are on the way to realizing your identity as a Divine Architect. Even though you may not yet see the "big picture" of your soul, you have sufficient faith in your soul that you live an anxiety-free life. You joyously accept life as it happens and, as a master, take full responsibility for it. If the above didn't yet feel true to you, rejoice for the next step of your evolution has just been revealed.

Conclusion

This has been a difficult chapter because it discusses the separation we feel from our soul and the gap between the Divine Architect we aspire to be and where we are now. As always, have compassion for yourself, because you deliberately incarnated here to explore separation, duality and fear with the intent of transcending them and knowing unity and love.

You knew that coming to such a dense planet would be challenging, yet you did it anyway. It's not easy to find love and unity on a planet that magnifies differences, but that doesn't stop a Divine Architect from trying. So face your fears and thank them for helping you play hide-and-seek with your soul. For you are a Divine Architect.

Chapter 11

Journey to the Other Side

DURING OUR LIFETIME, our ego inhabits a physical body with five senses. Our soul also inhabits a body (the etheric double) and its senses and personality are our consciousness. Our waking consciousness is only a tiny fraction of the whole, for we also have the subconscious and the superconscious.

When we're awake, our waking consciousness is anchored in our brain and is busy dealing with our daily lives, while the rest of our consciousness roams free and is aware of what's happening in other dimensions. In the case of psychic mediums, that non-waking part can "talk" to the waking part, which is why mediums can also be aware of the non-physical world. (That's what happens when I see the apparitions floating around my house.)

Technically, we "die" every night when we sleep, in that our consciousness is no longer tied to our body and kept busy with the physical world. As we saw in Chapter 5, it is free to "tag along" to the other dimensions but cannot always figure out what's going on. This freedom is exactly what death is, except that it's a one-way ticket. Whether our transition is fast, as in an accident, or slow, as in a coma, our soul and its consciousness cease to have a physical focus, so it and its etheric body slip out of the physical body one last time.

All regression therapists' clients report consistent elements in the death experience. Once the consciousness (soul-personality) and the etheric body slip out of the physical body, many experienced souls just seem to know to go to the tunnel and let themselves be pulled into it. Other souls may suffer disorientation, not realizing that they have just died or feel reluctant to leave Earth plane attachments. In these cases, a guide is always on hand and possibly one or more relatives whom the soul recognizes.

The person is then led to the tunnel and the group is drawn into it. The tunnel doesn't actually go to a different *place* but to a different *frequency*, much like an ascending elevator. (By way of analogy, to a two-dimensional being, you and the elevator would simply "disappear," leaving just an empty elevator shaft.) So the higher dimensions are "right here" within and around us, and just operating at different frequencies.

At the other end of the tunnel, souls often encounter an intense white light that seems to emanate from everywhere. Many subjects report feeling healed by the light. Oddly, they can look back through the tunnel and still see the Earth plane clearly.

What happens next seems to depend on what the person *believes* happens at death. A devoutly religious person may encounter a religious icon such as Jesus or angels. This is a temporary welcome, however, to minimize disorientation, and guides quickly explain that the believed-in heaven and angels are not how things really are on the soul plane. After getting oriented, all souls find themselves on the same soul plane, regardless of what they believed while alive.

Addicts and souls who arrive badly traumatized following, say, murder or a fatal accident may need to go straight to a healing level, and could be there for days, weeks, or months in Earth time. On the other hand, an experienced soul may be fully aware of what happened and is eager to move on. It may skip the whole welcome thing and hurry to its destination in the soul plane.

The soul often wants to visit the Earth plane, maybe to reassure those left behind. Until it learns a few tricks, such as telepathy and frequency adjustment, this proves difficult as we'll see with Stephen's case below. It took him about four Earth months before he was able to contact his mother clearly to begin dictating their book. However, souls may be able to leave a "calling card" to announce their presence, as Tom Woods did.

The arriving soul discovers that it has complete freedom regarding the appearance and age of its etheric body and is delighted to find hair loss, any amputated limbs and health fully restored.

All arrivals go through some form of life review in which they watch a "movie" of their life, with the often painful added extra of getting to feel the emotions of those they harmed. Souls who went through some form of deathbed redemption are disappointed to find that it did no good. They must still sit through the entire show.

These, then, are the basic elements: the tunnel, light at the end, maybe celestial music, meeting a guide and a welcome committee of friends and relatives, and a life review, although the sequence may vary, and an interval may occur between them.

Levels within Levels

According to Tom Woods, the soul plane actually has seven major levels. He reports that the *first* or *lowest level* is occupied by murderers, rapists and other heinous figures, whose energy takes them there through resonance. They will stay there, he says, until they realize their oneness with the Source, learn their lessons and choose to move on. Guides and angels are on call in this cold and gloomy place, but a soul may stay there for thousands of years in Earth time before it's ready to leave.

Tom says that the *second level* offers the special healing that suicides, traumatic and sudden deaths may need and is staffed by healing specialists. After its stay, the soul is ready to move to the next level and the life review. Following his sudden death, Tom himself spent some time on the healing level.

Level four seems to be the main interlife "living quarters," he reports, complete with schools, libraries and museums. Here, souls also meet with their guides and other members of their soul group to continue learning. Tom notes that the opportunities for R&R are endless, such as riding dolphins, mountaineering, and even golf!

Most souls reporting from level four are aware of even higher levels, and may visit them briefly while meditating or for a special initiation but have no direct experience of them. They seem to be accessible only to souls who have completed their entire cycle of lives and have no further need of incarnating.

What Dying Is Like

In *Stephen Lives*, Anne Puryear tells of how, with no apparent warning, her son Stephen, at the age of 15, took his own life . On March 18, 1974, after climbing a neighborhood tree, writing a series of short notes in a notebook and putting a noose around his neck, he jumped to his death. The discovery of his body the next day plunged his mother into a grief that only a bereaved mother can know.

Stephen describes his last few seconds to his mother. He felt a moment of pain, and then he floated gently up and looked down at his body still hanging from the tree branch. In a moment's confusion, he wondered whose body it was and, when he realized that it was his body, panic set in as he thought of all the trouble he was in. He had hoped to dodge all his problems, but that was not to be. At this point, he realized what he had done and burst into tears. Then he noticed a large group of people around him, relatives he recognized from family photo albums, many of them long since dead. Each one in the group greeted him and "a sweet lady dressed in white" took his hand. As he and the group started to float upwards, he fell asleep.

Stephen woke up in a strange room, sure that he had had an odd dream about someone hanging in a tree. He fell back into a fitful sleep, aware that other people were in the room with him, talking to him, but was unable to make out what they were saying. Then the woman in white woke him and told him that the police were at his house to inform his mother of his death. He jumped up and asked her to take him there, which she did in an instant.

At the house, Stephen shouted and screamed that he was there, but the woman gently told him, "They can't see you. They can't hear you."

At this point, the truth that he was dead hit Stephen hard. Even worse, he got to feel the enormity of his mother's pain, "her heart crying inside his," and ironically wished that he could die to make that pain go away. He pleaded with the woman to turn the clock back, but she told him that what had been done couldn't be undone.

Back at the house, he begged and pleaded for them to see him, and when he realized it was hopeless, he broke down in tears. Then everything went blank.

Walda Woods asked Tom, her deceased husband, what it was like to die. At a Labor Day barbecue in 1996, he suffered a major heart attack and was rushed to the hospital. Tom reports that when he first left his body, he was confused as to what had happened. As he watched the other people at the party render first aid, part of him was shocked that this could have happened to him at such a young age and without warning. As the paramedics worked to bring him back, he drifted in and out of his body. Then he was pulled into a tunnel with walls that sparkled. As he floated along, a figure appeared that introduced itself as his guide.

Tom begged to be able to go back to be with his wife, but the guide told him that he had ignored the signs that would have warned him to say his goodbyes. Not having been able to say goodbye pained Tom so much that he implored the guide for that final chance. He came out of his coma for a few short hours, long enough to look in Walda's eyes one last time. Then Tom's body began shutting down.

Fortunately, Walda was informed enough about spiritual matters to have the presence of mind to telepath to Tom to go into the light. So, when Tom saw a pinpoint of light in the distance, he moved towards it, and his fear and confusion disappeared. As he got closer, he saw some glowing beings who said, "Hello, welcome home!"

In my father's case, my mother, who had died shortly before, came to meet him on his deathbed, and took his hand to pull him fully out of his body. In many cases where the soul slips out of the body following an illness or accident, it hovers around trying to comfort those now grieving. If you are ever a deathbed attendee, please remember that the departing spirit will stay in the room with you until prompted to leave by a guide or welcoming committee. As we saw with young Stephen, the soul may be confused at not being seen or heard by the grieving family members and may need your guidance. Keep calm and, as I did with my father, offer advice such as, "I know you can see and hear us, but we can't see or hear you. You may not realize this, but you have just died. There will be plenty time for you to come back and visit with us but, right now, can you see anyone waiting to meet you? If anyone is there, go with them for now, and you can come back to see us later."

An elderly patient slipping away in a hospice or hospital bed is one thing but, when a young child dies, the outpouring of grief can make the soul's departure hard indeed. Of course, the child may be a wise old soul who knows exactly what's happening, but the consciousness (or soul-personality) may not have that lofty perspective and will require much coaxing by its guides to leave its beloved grieving parents. Again, a few well-chosen words to the soul would really help.

Some souls report staying close to the Earth plane for a few days, until their funeral or memorial service, whereas some leave immediately, often depending on soul age or awareness. Young souls, to whom the experience of dying is still new, may want to hang around to see who attends the service or what people say in their eulogy. Older souls who have "been there, done that" many times before may want none of that humbug, and just return to the soul plane to start taking care of business.

What Next?

George Anderson's contacts tell him that what happens next varies widely according to our vibration. There are no "higher" or "lower" levels *per se*, as many other mediums would have us believe. It's more a matter of existing closer to or further from the light, depending on the spiritual growth one has attained. However, all souls are equal in position in the love and compassion they receive from the Infinite Light.

Those who caused unresolved hatred or anger, and have knowingly veered from their spiritual path, see the damage they have caused others and voluntarily pull themselves away from the Light until, through their own good works and spiritual growth—such as working on forgiveness and understanding—they feel they have earned the Light.

"Souls who have placed themselves farther from the light because they feel they have not yet earned it," Anderson says, "always have the opportunity to move towards the Light when they feel they are ready."

It seems that forgiveness and understanding are the hallmarks of the hereafter and that souls do not necessarily need to return to the Earth plane to make up for lessons unlearned on Earth. So the opportunity to grow spiritually will always be available to souls even if the process is longer because of the lack of struggle involved.

Other souls add that one may need further healing, as in the case of alcohol or drug addicts, or to remove the effects of traumatic death. This may take weeks or months in Earth time but will feel like a short nap. Many need emotional healing of some sort, especially if they died in traumatic circumstances.

The Life Review

We have all got to go through it, and how much it hurts depends on various factors. Those reporting back all emphasize one thing. It is not our "judgment day" but our personal, private "Well, how did I do?"

In marking our report cards, we are often our own worse critics. Recall how when my father had his review, his guides were there specifically to make sure that he didn't "beat himself up."

In *Stephen Lives*, Stephen relays details of his review to his mother. He reports that the review may be conducted in stages, possibly beginning with the larger events. At first, the soul might be hard on itself but soon loosens up as it switches from blame, shame and guilt to what has been learned from those situations in which it caused pain to others. Those in for the biggest shock are self-righteous hypocrites who expect to be greeted by God Himself and congratulated on a life well lived. Instead, they get to watch all the pain that their deeds caused, even the times when they could have acted to help another but didn't. So what we *don't* do to help others is just as important as what we actually do.

During the review, a soul's guide is on hand, gently prodding with, "Well, what did you learn?" The overarching question of the review seems to be, "What did *you* do to help your fellow man and humanity in general?" Stephen admits that seeing one's life with 20/20 hindsight, the pain caused, and the golden opportunities to help others not seized can be extremely distressing.

Stephen, being a suicide himself, got to see how, when he chose that lifetime, there was more than a 50/50 chance that that's how it would end yet, at the soul level, he had been eager to give it a shot and beat the odds. That was not to be. Stephen emphasizes that suicides are not singled out for punishment or retribution in any way; just knowing that he could have better dealt with the problem situation is punishment enough.

The Transition

In her book, *On Life After Death*, Dr. Elisabeth Kübler-Ross gives us the benefit of decades of working with the sick and dying. After countless near-death experiencers have confided in her, she has broken down the transition process into three distinct stages:

1. The etheric body and soul consciousness are released from their earthly cocoon like an emerging butterfly.
2. The soul consciousness realizes that it is whole again and is aware. She cites the countless documented cases where a returning NDEr who died on the operating table can describe the surgical procedures undergone. The soul can also visit any location on Earth simply by thinking of it. The second stage usually ends with entry into the tunnel but could also be, say, the crossing of a bridge.
3. The soul encounters a bright, white light that fills it with indescribable love. At this point, NDErs are met by a being who may lead them through a "mini-review" and then tells them that they

must go back since they still have earthly work to do. However, if the silver cord has been severed, the soul is fully embraced by the light and moves on.

Dr. Kübler-Ross emphasizes that it's never too late to prepare for the review while we are still here on Earth. Life's adversities are simply opportunities to grow in unconditional love. If we allow them to make us bitter and resentful, we have wasted a magnificent opportunity, a waste that we get to mull over for a long, long time. So, look on adversity as a wonderful gift, she advises, "for it will give you the strength and teach you things you would never have otherwise learned."

According to some of George Anderson's contacts, the process of dying can be so simple that it may take a while for someone to realize what has happened. Some people may get the tunnel and waiting relatives but for some reason, occasionally we may be left to figure it out for ourselves.

It's important that we know what to expect, or we may find ourselves wandering around in a daze, unsure of what to do. It's vital that you know to go through the tunnel, because the bright light at the other end washes away the low frequency Earth plane vibrations. Then, you can return without risk of attachment to people or places. After all, you do not want to become a "ghost."

Marge Cuddeback has helped countless earthbound spirits to get to their intended destination after they had somehow become confused and lost. The implications of this are:

1. Many mediums report that their contacts have told them that the immediate post-crossing environment largely depends on your belief system, so we should know what to expect when we cross so as to avoid getting lost.

2. Because our consciousness doesn't miss a beat, that should change our behavior while we are here. For example, murder and suicide do not change a thing but only cause problems later.

3. If we are with someone who is making the crossing, we can advise him or her to go to the light, or to look for the tunnel or someone to meet him or her. Also, we should pray for their speedy passage or for them to be met by a relative or guide.

Reporting Back

When we cross over, our desire to reassure those we have left behind that we are alive, whole and healthy (coupled with our thoughts of them as targets) gives our intent fuel and destination. Emotional intensity and shared love are the fuel that creates the energetic bridge across which consciousness on the Earth and soul planes can contact each other. Initially, we may need some help from a guide but, if we meditated while on this side or could astrally project, we will feel right at home with the technique.

These "reassurance visits" can be so tangible to us that they feel as warm and solid as when they were on the Earth plane. In a 1982 interview published in *People* magazine, the widow of Anwar Sadat reported that her deceased husband returned, and she held his hand as if he were alive. She thought it was a dream but, when she opened her eyes, he was still holding her hand.

Another common reason to build a bridge from the other side is to reassure those who are about to make their own transition. While the terminally ill are drifting in and out of lucidity because their consciousness is not strongly anchored to their body, it is easy for them to "slip across the border" for a sneak preview of their new home and a brief reunion with old friends.

Unfortunately, those reporting such visits are usually ridiculed or pitied, but the lack of payoff for inventing such accounts adds weight to their truthfulness.

Let us look more deeply at the phenomenon of spirit communication. For two people on the Earth plane, successful conversation requires certain agreements:

1. To use the same mode, such as verbal, written, Morse code, or sign language.
2. To speak the same language, such as English rather than French.
3. To have a similar vocabulary set, such as everyday terms rather than scientific.
4. That one will speak while the other listens, and then switch.

If these things are agreed, two people can talk to each other. But suppose they are on different sides of the veil. The one on this side also must quiet down his conscious mind so that he can receive the other's thoughts.

Communication in the interlife is much easier. You just think of someone, and that person "hears" his or her frequency and follows it back to its source. Once telepathic contact is made, one or both of you can teleport anywhere for a person-to-person meeting.

What's Next?

At some point following the life review, the portion of the soul energy that incarnated may meld back with the soul energy that stayed behind, augmenting its "database" with everything that was learned in its most recent lifetime. However, your soul fragment still has the etheric double, and you may continue to use that when interacting with other souls who knew you in that lifetime. In *Conversations with Tom*, Tom tells his wife, Walda, that he looks exactly as he did in Earth life.

The relationship between the total soul entity and the incarnational selves is hard for our limited brains to grasp. By some miracle of organization, each of those selves still exists yet is intrinsically part of the whole. Like blobs of mercury separating out from the whole, soul-selves can split off for whatever reason and then merge back with the oversoul.

In a touching moment, Walda confesses her concern to Tom that he might reincarnate before she gets to the afterlife, and she would miss him. Tom explains gently that "it doesn't work like that" and that the "Tom-self" will not reincarnate "as is" even though his soul still intends to put down more incarnations which may or may not contain a piece of the Tom-self. This explains why long-dead relatives can be waiting to greet us, long after we would have expected them to have merged with their main soul entity. They may well have merged, but they still exist as a separate identity. Do not worry. Those you have loved will be waiting for you.

We have seen how the returning soul fragment wears its etheric body but, in the realms where everything is created by thought, you can manipulate that body however you wish. In *Stephen Lives*, Stephen recounts how his etheric body is trim and lean, with no trace of the weight condition that was one of the reasons he committed suicide. You can also choose to appear at your favorite age and to look in tip-top condition, as did my father.

Most of George Anderson's contacts are involved in some form of "community service" at one point in the interlife, such as welcoming new arrivals or working to ease suffering on the Earth plane. Life is busy over there, although not one single contact had even the slightest complaint about the interlife. Their spirituality involves just a profound personal peace and joy based on deep faith in Creation.

Martin Heald and Destiny

Our final glimpse into the interlife comes from Martin Heald, as told in his book, *Destiny*. Born in 1962, the son of working class parents in Manchester, England, his life was anything but normal. He has an NDE when very young and a being of light introduces himself as David, and tells Martin that his near drowning was unplanned and that he must go back and finish his life. Resuscitation attempts pull little Martin's consciousness back to his body, but his relieved parents will hear none of his wild ride into the light and meeting David. This is to become the story of his life, during which he has odd flashbacks of being in an aircraft that explodes, after which everything goes black.

After a failed marriage, many mundane jobs by day and psychic adventures by night, Martin meets Jennifer, who accepts his psychic gifts and encourages him to develop them. Once they emigrate to Holland, his gifts really open up.

Wanting to solve the exploding aircraft mystery, Martin finds a regression therapist, and they are taken immediately to the life of a Richard Seymour. Martin is taken through Richard's life, his joining the Royal Air Force in WWII as a wireless operator and his death when his bomber explodes in midair. He knows that that lifetime had been about sacrifice and that he had returned as Martin to continue Richard's work.

After many inquiries to WWII experts, Martin receives details of the incident. Richard Seymour had been born in England in 1921. He had joined the RAF, trained as a wireless operator, and died on July 20, 1942 when his Halifax bomber was attacked by German fighters. The plane exploded in mid-air and crashed just off the coast of Holland, with the loss of all crew members.

So far, Martin's story is just another verified reincarnation account, but now it gets interesting. Martin learns self-regression to be able to follow the story after Richard's death. As Richard, he wakes up feeling refreshed and is greeted by Juliette who shows him around his new soul plane home. He attends classes on reality creation, point-to-point travel using his thoughts and special psychic skills he will need in his next incarnation. For what seems like several Earth years, he works alone and with others in the interlife to perfect his thought-to-result and energy manipulation skills and spends long "days" in a library of universal knowledge researching all manner of topics.

When Richard meets Jennifer, his twin flame, the two become inseparable, sharing a love so profound that it has no earthly equivalent and defies description. In his travels, he meets inventors who perfect new devices before telepathically sending the details to their Earth plane counterparts during dreams and as intuitive flashes. He meets his guide, David, who reveals the full scope of guidance that Richard received during his Earth plane lifetime. He visits classrooms where souls are being taught political science and review recent Earth history to prepare them for lives as world leaders, and metaphysics classes intended to prepare other souls for lives as spiritual teachers and leaders to guide humanity after upcoming Earth changes.

He attends a lecture in which a huge three-dimensional model of the solar system (as in the movie *Mission to Mars*) shows the effects of the planets on us at our moment of birth. It is followed by a "discussion period" in which he sees showers of "sparks" rapidly leaping among attendees as they exchange thoughts about the subject. The hologram resumes showing the combined effects of astrology and numerology (based on name and time of birth) on a newborn and then factoring in free will. This display is followed by an even more frenzied exchange of sparks. Richard's mind is boggled by the complex interactions of all the forces guiding each of our lives, and his guide explains that the attendees were mathematicians while on Earth and are now studying to become counselors to those planning to reincarnate. One of the counselor's tasks will be to compute all possible outcomes for each lifetime.

Because their next incarnation will be the last for Richard and Jennifer, they visit the Hall of Records where they review their entire incarnational history. During this visit, a semi-transparent apparition appears who, the librarian says, is an Earth plane psychic medium seeking information on behalf of a client. The request is deemed in the client's interest and is allowed.

At one point, David asks Richard if he wants to attend his father's "birth." Apparently, Richard's father is approaching earthly death and is about to be "born" into their world. Together with a number of other relatives, Richard gathers to greet his father for a joyful reunion. On a sobering note, his father tells Richard how painful his WWII death had been for his parents, especially when they had no body to bury.

Richard visits David at one point and finds him in meditation with a number of others. They are all guides in deep communication with their earthy charges, who are having what they think are dreams. David explains that, if someone is really straying from the agreed life path and not following guidance, a guide will arrange for an NDE in order to temporarily free the spirit from the body for a conscious encounter. The benefit of this extreme measure is that when the NDE is over, the person has full memory of the encounter and cannot dismiss it as imagination.

Richard is told that the time is approaching when he must prepare to return to the Earth plane for his lifetime as Martin. The fact that during his soul plane activities, 20 Earth years have passed (1942 – 1962) takes him by surprise. He is deeply saddened at the thought of leaving Jennifer for, although they will later meet and marry, their Earth plane relationship will have only a fraction of the depth and intensity of their soul plane relationship.

In great detail, Richard previews his life-to-be as Martin, and the wake-up calls he will receive from David, his chief guide. He watches his parents-to-be growing up and how each will help and hinder his mission, how his psychic gifts will open up, how members of his soul group will incarnate with him as sister and friends, and how Jennifer will join him as his second wife.

Following a tearful goodbye with Jennifer, he is told that he will remember little of the interlife but that, unlike most people, he will be reminded of this *during* his next incarnation rather than afterwards. He lies down, closes his eyes, and is suddenly hurtling through a tunnel. Welcome to planet Earth and 28 years of relative sleep until he returns to the soul plane to bring this story back with him. The interlife appears so busy that it mocks the old saying "Laid to rest."

After-Death Communication in the Electronic Age

Throughout history, those on the soul plane have had to rely on psychic mediums to contact those on the Earth plane. With the advent of the electronic age, that's changing rapidly. As soon as wireless transmission was invented, forward thinking inventors such as Nikola Tesla and Thomas Edison reasoned that, since the spirit world is electromagnetic, those on the other side should be able to use the technology to contact us.

True research began after WWII and took a major step forward in the fifties when Swedish movie-maker Jurgenson was recording birdsong and picked up voices. He was followed by Latvian researcher, Konstantin Raudive who began leaving a tape recorder running in his lab. Over the years, he captured more than 75,000 voice messages. Apparently, soul plane senders used their thoughts to modulate white noise (the static hiss when a radio is tuned between stations).

A group of soul plane scientists, including Nikola Tesla, Thomas Edison, Albert Einstein, Wernher von Braun and Madame Curie have formed the "Timestream" project to use our technology to contact us, and, on his death in 1974, Raudive, too, joined Timestream.

Instrumental Transcommunication (ITC), or Electronic Voice Phenomena (EVP), received another boost in 1977 when researcher George Meek introduced the Spiricom device to a lukewarm reception by the British media. However, research flourished in the rest of Europe. In 1982, a German researcher hooked a receiver up to the European superstation, Radio Luxembourg. During the live broadcast, to everyone's surprise, voices came through clearly, making believers out of millions of Europeans.

Over the years, Timestream scientists worked from their end to improve the Earth side receivers, and today's images show dramatic improvement over early attempts.

The Timestream project operates from Level Three of Tom Woods' soul plane model and in turn receives guidance from higher levels. EVP/ITC literature documents many messages from the project members who tell us that many such groups of souls form who share common views and interests, and live and work together in harmony on the soul plane. They inspire many Earth inventions by working in telepathic contact with Earth plane researchers.

Myths of the Afterlife

In my lectures and workshops, I often encounter misleading beliefs about the afterlife, and close this chapter with some of the most common, hopefully laying these myths to rest once and for all.

Myth: The afterlife is an undirected state of aimlessness.
Nothing could be further from the truth. Yes, new arrivals may undergo a period of R & R, usually to heal any Earth plane trauma and get used to being in a new dimension. (Older souls who cross over in full knowledge of what to expect may skip the formalities and rush to rejoin their soul group and renew old relationships.) The soul plane is extremely well organized, with schools, universities, science labs, meeting rooms, residential areas, etc. However, new arrivals may not comprehend the vast organization, much as first-graders on their first day of school may be confused and awed because everyone else seems to know what they're doing and where they're going.

Myth: You will be judged, and punished or rewarded accordingly.
True, you will conduct your own life review, either of your own voli-
tion or prompted by your guide. In this, you will experience every one
of your actions as others experienced it. Admittedly, if you have just
come from a lifetime where you were cruel to others, you will experience what you put them through, which could *feel* like punishment,
but the real purpose is insight and understanding. The only theme of
the soul plane is growth, and the best way to grow after a sojourn on
Earth is to hash over every detail of that life: what you did, why, and
how it contributed or not to the amount of love on the Earth plane.

The material for the review comes from the Akashic Record, a
huge multi-dimensional databank. You can either review life events
from the outside, or enter the replay and become part of it, receiving
physical, emotional and mental input to do with everyone concerned.

Your review may involve a meeting with wise counselors who ask
you pointed questions to further the depth of your review and hence
your growth. After the review, you are free to resume whatever activities occupied you before you left for your Earth life (to those on the
soul plane, no time would have passed since you left).

Myth: The afterlife is either heaven or hell.
The soul plane is a "mental plane" so what you experience follows
directly and instantly from your thoughts. Devoutly religious people
may initially experience whatever reality their religion taught, and be
delighted to find that heaven is Presbyterian, Baptist, Catholic, Hindu
or whatever. At some point, however, a guide will appear and begin to
reorient the new arrival to the true nature of the afterlife.

The soul plane spans countless levels and dimensions, and the level
you find yourself on depends on the frequency of your energy. Just as
water finds its own level, the new arrival is inexorably drawn to the
level with which it resonates. This means, of course, that those with
dark, cruel energy will find themselves in like company, possibly targets of the cruelty of those already there. Guides and angels monitor
these lower levels closely for any sign of penitence in the denizens,
and whisk them away for reorientation.

Myth: The soul plane doesn't exist; "dead is dead."
Dyed-in-the-wool skeptics may initially be confused when they slip
out their physical body and still feel very much alive, except that they
can't get the attention of those still on the Earth plane. A guide or

deceased relative may show up to break the news gently. Really tough cases may wake up in a hospital-like setting, where they rest for a while before being visited by counselors. To such skeptics, I would say, "A little open-mindedness on this side can save you much time and confusion when you get to the other side."

Myth: The Interlife is just a holding pattern between incarnations.
While the interlife period may be as short as just a few months, this seems to be the exception. More likely, it spans many years, centuries even, during which we actively pursue our passions, be they scientific, artistic, philosophical, or whatever.

At some point, however, you or a guide will see the need for a "field trip" to the Earth plane as an adjunct to your soul plane studies. This may be to test your understanding of some aspect of human inter-action, or even to serve as a receiver for information to be transmitted to the physical plane by those still in the interlife. (Many of the great scientific discoveries on Earth stem from the infusion of ideas from the soul plane.)

Earth plane lives are strictly side-trips and not the reason for the soul plane's existence. In fact, many souls, such as the Kryon entity, choose not to incarnate at all, preferring to work strictly from the higher realms to effect changes on Earth, free of the distractions of incarnation.

Myth: God is intimately involved in day-to-day running heaven.
Of the countless regression cases that Tony and I have reviewed, not one mentions anything directly about God or any other deity, except in terms of a vast impersonal force so far up the dimensional structure as not to be relevant to life on the soul plane. Even ascended masters and archangels occupy such lofty dimensions that they rarely interact with most souls. Just meeting with the councils of wise elders who are no longer on the wheel of reincarnation is as close to divinity as most souls deem necessary for their growth.

Myth: We have one lifetime and are judged on the basis of that.
It seems highly unlikely that the vast, eternal soul which we are would have one shot on Earth and hope to experience all we need in order to achieve perfect understanding of our own nature. The Michael entity talks in terms of a cycle of up to 400 lifetimes, at the end of which, you can sign up for another Earth cycle or move on to other realms or realities.

Myth: A young life cut short is a tragedy.
On the Earth plane, the death of a child is perceived as tragic, but not from the soul plane, where it is known that the soul plans every detail of life and death. A young life may be cut short for many reasons; for example, the soul needed just the birth experience, it changed its mind, or the parents needed to experience grief for some reason. Or the child's death may make a statement that changes the world, as with Nicholas, the American boy who was killed by gunfire while on vacation in Italy with his parents and sister. The publicity surrounding his parents' decision to donate his organs created a tremendous boost in organ donation in Europe.

Myth: We reincarnate as punishment for the sins of a previous lifetime.
Karma is never punishment; the word translates simply as "action." For full understanding, the soul volunteers to experience the *results* of its actions in the same or different lifetime. This may be a direct "eye for an eye" or indirect in some other way that fosters understanding.

We on the physical plane should avoid judging the situations that spirit sets up for its own learning. Nor should we turn from a brother or sister in need of our help with: "You set it up, so deal with it."

Compassion requires that we help those whose souls have set up challenging lifetimes; it may be our turn next lifetime to need help.

Conclusion

Anyone still afraid of death? I should hope not. In fact, my greatest worry is that we have painted such a rosy picture of the interlife that people will try to hasten their arrival there. We also know what a mistake that would be.

One of the greatest eye-openers is that death is not something that just "happens" to us but the final step of our Earth plane journey event that we ourselves carefully orchestrate for maximum growth, for we *are* Divine Architects.

Chapter 12

The Divine Architect: Living the Spiritual Life

THIS BOOK IS ABOUT YOU as body, mind, spirit and soul, and hopefully helps you to better integrate all your component parts. They were never separate to begin with, nor could they ever be. Although this book has dwelled on the psychic abilities of professional mediums, we are *all* moving towards greater psychic powers as our frequency rises, for this affects everything, especially our interaction with each other and with spirit.

Telepathy and psychic abilities are nothing new to our species. At one point, they were the *only* way we communicated. However, we let those powers go in order to study separation, but now we are reclaiming them as we heal the perception of separation from each other and from spirit. In our relationships, we strive to reconnect with other human beings as a way of healing the *perceived* separation from spirit, even though we were the ones who created that perception in the first place.

This book is about being an architect, not of a building but of reality, and we have explored many "tools of the trade." Over countless lifetimes, you have honed your skills and fashioned your beliefs. As a much younger soul, you may have lived lifetimes based on simplistic beliefs or traditional religions and, as a maturing soul, you may have evolved to a more inclusive view of God. But now, as an old soul, you are letting go of the "God-as-separate" mindset and are seeing each of us as part of the Creator, indivisible and equal. Once you take this step, you are ready to begin your career as a reality architect.

There are many facets to honing your skills. New Age and self-help bookstores offer feasts of information on such topics as reclaiming your power and letting go of attachments. These are all aimed at moving us beyond conventional, limited belief systems. But, we've seen how, as souls, we incarnate on Earth with a specific mission plan and, although our guides do their best to help us follow it, it's really up to the ego to listen to spirit's subtle urgings and hopefully trust and execute them.

At the ego level, we cannot know the time and manner that we as soul propose to return to the soul plane. All we can do is lead our lives to the fullest, knowing that when the transition happens, it's perfect for our soul growth. There are no accidents. If two passengers are in a car wreck and one walks away while the other doesn't, then that is exactly as their souls intended.

When it *is* time to go, what are you going to take with you? All the wealth and power you've amassed at the expense of love and compassion? Of course not. But if you eschewed wealth and power, and you have practiced unconditional love and compassion, you will take that straight to the celestial bank!

Part of being a Divine Architect is living in conscious awareness of how you're spending your days—growing or stagnating. If the latter, you're actually slipping backwards because of the inexorable rise in frequency of the world around you. In 1998, I attended a sweat lodge led by Native American Walking Eagle, and he prefaced the experience with, "Many people sit on their couches watching their TVs so that they do not have to face themselves, but that's not happening here. Here you will face your pain and fear, and put them into the fire."

We are not here to escape into our TV sets but to live and love and grow. It's up to us to use our time wisely. All my promotional literature bears the words, "Personal Growth Activist." The word "activist" connotes purpose, mission, direction, action and, above all, *passion*. In my lectures, I am delighted to see so many people who are passionate about growth, pursuing it with great zeal.

Once, Tony Robbins was broke, overweight and felt powerless. Today he is a dynamic, successful motivational speaker, the perfect example of one who walks his talk. And why is he on stage and the rest of us are in the audience? Because he took the one little step that the rest of us have yet to take. He committed to his own growth, and what he did, we can do. So why not commit today, here and now, to being the best Divine Architect you can be?

We have read much in this book about creation skills, so why not begin by applying them to yourself? Why not create the best Divine Architect you can? Why not maximize the love, joy, compassion and bliss in your life? And how do you receive these things? You know! By first giving them, of course. In the movie *Holy Man*, Eddie Murphy's character tells the story of a young girl walking on a beach littered with dying starfish washed up by the waves. She picked one up and threw it back into the water. When asked, "So many starfish are dying that what does it matter to throw back just one?" she replied, "It matters to *that* one." So many people live in pain and fear that you cannot help them all, but if you do something loving for just *one* person a day, it matters to that person.

There is much talk today about the Zero Point Effect, the increase in Earth's resonant frequency and the speeding up of time. Whatever is happening, one thing is certainly changing—our level of consciousness. As it rises, we come closer to the frequency at which soul operates, and we can tune into it more readily. We can then access our soul's memories of other lifetimes where we knew and practiced so much—Lemuria, Atlantis, ancient Egypt, other planets, even.

As our frequency rises, we can invite more of our soul to come in and infuse with the body which further increases our frequency and so on. We will find that skills, experience, and understanding begin to bleed through from our co-incarnations, spontaneously, in dreams, and during hypnosis.

Ascension

Let us begin with the phenomenon of ascension. According to Tony, my co-author, ascension is basically a change in frequency of the Earth's electromagnetic field, of our very cells, and in the focus of our consciousness. This change heralds a new influx of love on to the planet.

He talks a lot about energy as the "stuff" behind everything that combines in indescribably complex ways to form everything everywhere on every dimension. Energy has two main qualities: amplitude (with sound, this equates to loudness), and frequency, the rate at which it vibrates (with sound, its pitch).

We each possess four bodies: the physical body with which we are most familiar, plus our emotional, mental, and spiritual bodies. Each of these bodies is made up of energy of different frequencies. This energy, plus the energy behind what we call matter, is an even higher frequency energy. It's not detectable by scientific instruments because they, too, are made of matter, and no instrument can detect frequencies higher than the frequency from which it's made. (This, incidentally, is the challenge of EVP/ITC and why those on the other side of the veil must step down the frequency of their communications.)

This higher frequency energy is the energy of Source, the ultimate origin of *everything*. It is the energy from which third-dimensional energy such as light is derived and the energy that congregates as sub-atomic particles that make up atoms. The most amazing thing about this energy is that it is *conscious*. It voluntarily agrees to participate in things like the cells of your body. We repay the debt to this energy by providing a means by which it can express itself and its creativity. Yes, the universe is creative at all levels.

Our physical bodies, emotions, thoughts, and spirits (or souls, if you prefer) are all made of this Light, blended in ways that make us each unique in the universe. Because the energy making up our physical bodies has frequency, we can change it. As we do, our physical bodies become less dense. Eventually, we will be vibrating above the level of the physical plane and be free of its limitations. In fact, we are on our way to becoming fifth-dimensional beings. Once there, low frequency energies such as fear and limitation cannot exist and we'll be one with spirit. At this point, we will also be one with Christ Consciousness and with the spirit of everyone else. That is ascension.

Once we have ascended, anyone left on the physical plane would no longer see you, for your energy would be too high a frequency for physical eyes to see. However, no one will be left.

Ascension is not just a personal thing. The entire physical plane is ascending, along with the planet, too. This is what I was shown by my nocturnal visitors in the summer of 1992, and this is what all the fuss is about. It's the most exciting thing to have ever happened on this planet, and it will happen within the lifetime of most of us.

Catch the Wave

People are waking up to the world of spiritual growth in three waves:
1. Numbering a few thousand, those in the *first wave* were already in place by the time of the Harmonic Convergence in 1987, living, eating, and breathing their spirituality. They're likely to be found in high-energy locations. They wrote the books and gave the workshops that woke the second wave up in the early 1990s.

2. Numbering a few million, those in the *second wave* came online in the 1990s, and reworked the "out there" teachings of the first wave into something digestible by the third wave. They are communicators and can be found in such jobs as metaphysical publishing houses, possibly having switched careers often in their unconscious quest for their niche. Flexible and adaptable, they are equally comfortable with the "far out" first wavers and the more conservative third wavers, building a bridge between them.

3. Numbering maybe 50 million, those in the *third wave* are coming online right now as we enter the new millennium, ready to serve the bulk of humanity. But unlike first and second wavers, they operate from within mainstream (shops, offices, factories) but bring a spiritual element to their work and lives. Dubbed "cultural creatives" by Madison Avenue, they are active in causes such as rainforest survival, dolphin-safe tuna nets, and animal rights, but are not overtly "out there" in their spirituality.

In the words of Sherlock Holmes, "The game is afoot," and you are probably already in position on the field or doing some last minute jostling. You're now a fully trained lightworker, engaged in play, whatever that looks like for you.

As you move about the world around you, seek out opportunities to carry out random acts of senseless kindness. Smile at strangers. Let other drivers out into the traffic flow. Let another motorist complete a turn. And look for ways of reducing the stress level of those around you.

If you encounter a pocket of negativity, do what you can to dispel it or at least do not add to it. If someone you know stands at a fear/joy choice point, help them choose joy. Due to the ripple effect, their joy will spread out and infect many more people. So could their fear.

The next decade will bring us choice points at ever faster rates, and people will need help, including you. Do not be afraid to reach out and ask.

The New Human

A new group of individuals has been coming into the world since the mid-1970's, according to authors Jan Tober and Lee Caroll (of Kryon fame) in their book, *Indigo Children*.

These children began arriving in great numbers in the 1990s, are highly intelligent, technically competent and, in the main, spiritually advanced, often expressing, at an early age, knowledge of past lives.

These Indigo Children are no fools and do not suffer fools gladly. They need their space, although they are gregarious. They don't tolerate being talked down to and have a problem with authority. They know who they are and are not afraid to say so. Tragically, many of them are wrongly diagnosed with Attention Deficit Disorder and live their lives under heavy sedation.

Drunvalo Melchizedek tells of another group of children with super-psychic powers in China. He recounts that when *OMNI* magazine went to China to do a story on a super-psychic child, reporters found many more such children. Assuming it was a hoax, they conducted their own experiments, such as putting 100 kids in a room, randomly tearing a page out of a book and crumpling it up. Those kids could recite every word on the page.

He also talks about yet another group that emerged about 1990 with the birth of a baby born with AIDS who tested HIV-positive at 6 months but, by the age of 6, was completely HIV-negative with no trace whatsoever. According to Drunvalo, tests revealed that the child did not have normal human DNA.

Human DNA is built from four nucleic acids that combine in sets of three, producing 64 possible combinations called codons—the letters making up the alphabet that DNA is written in. Normal human DNA uses only 20 of these codons, and scientists have always assumed that the unused 44 combinations were old "letters" from our past. But the boy's DNA uses 24 codons, four more than any other human being.

Suspecting that the four extra codons involved his immune system, researchers mixed a highly lethal dose of the HIV virus in a petri dish with some of his cells, which remained completely unaffected. The researchers kept raising the lethal level of the composition, but even at 3,000 times more than would infect a human being, the boy's cells stayed completely disease free. Further tests revealed that the boy was, in fact, immune to everything!

According to Drunvalo, worldwide testing turned up more children with the extra codons in their DNA. So far, 20 million worldwide are *known* to have this new DNA and are therefore not human by the old criteria. The new codons are beginning to appear in adults, too, and it appears to be spreading quickly, just like the outbreak of a disease.

Drunvalo speculates that one child somehow changed spontaneously, and the blueprint got into the grids around the planet, and that it is now in the mass consciousness and therefore accessible to anyone. Once that happened, people have tapped into it on a subconscious level in deep meditation or prayer and made the change.

This new DNA leads researchers to believe that a new human race is currently emerging on the planet, and they speculate that it is being spread by specific emotional and mental waveforms coming off the body that cause human DNA to mutate in a certain way. Whatever they are doing within themselves is producing a distinctive waveform that looks almost identical to the DNA molecule itself. Researchers think that, by the very expression of their life, these people are remapping their DNA and introducing the four new codons. In so doing, they become immune to disease.

As adults, we can choose to emulate these children, and benefit from immunity to disease. Increased longevity and lower death rates would bring their own challenges, but Drunvalo claims that immunity to disease shows that one is definitely in harmony with life.

"Can you do this yourself? I believe so," Drunvalo asserts. "If you know about your lightbody, how psychic energy works, and how all life on this planet is connected at the level of the subconscious mind, then you can ask your subconscious to make the changes I talk about. Your subconscious knows exactly which new codons those kids have manifested and, if you ask for those things to happen through your lightbody and in the presence of God, it should occur. It also requires dropping polarity—no longer thinking in terms of good or bad—and seeing the wholeness, completion and perfection of life.

"The emergence of a new race of human being is, to me, one of the most remarkable phenomena that has happened on the planet and that no one seemed to know about it until now is incredible! I have been tracking this for about two years and waited to say anything until recently because I wanted to make sure it was real. But suddenly, books are being published and websites are springing up with the results of research on these children. Parents can now visit websites to report what is going on with their gifted child and get advice on how best to deal with them. Parenting an Indigo Child is especially challenging because these kids know exactly what you are feeling and thinking. You can't hide anything from them."

My friend Robert Gerard, author of *Change Your DNA; Change Your Life!* concurs that, along with love, *intent* is the most potent force in the universe and, the purer the intent, the more precise its manifestation.

"The DNA within a cell is an electrically charged system," he explains, "that can be affected by intent, which after all is an electromagnetic thoughtform. So, if you want to feel better, from your heart, create the intent of better health, visualizing that with as much emphasis as you can muster. The cells of your body will respond to that image. So look to your inner resources and become accountable for your own health. Your intuition and heart-driven impulses contain answers to life's concerns. The more you listen, the more you will trust yourself and your feelings, until you build a high state of confidence in yourself and the things you do. Allowing your body to become a partner in your decision-making enables the body consciousness to fully express itself physically, emotionally, intellectually, and spiritually.

"As our faculties become more balanced, our awareness of mind over matter becomes clearer. We will no longer wait for others to do our deeds; we are empowered to do them ourselves. The real miracle lies within. It is trust. It is divine. It is ours."

The Spiritual Life

Most readers of this book will be second and third wavers, and part of your life mission is to take this information and pass it on to others in your wave and out to the masses. The best way to do this is by example, and there are many components to living the spiritual life, two of which weave together interactively:

1. Focus on your divinity, your soul. Stay mindful all day; live in gratitude for your blessings. (Until this focus is second nature, you could wear a colored thread around your wrist to help remind you.) In every situation, respond with the unconditional love of your soul.

2. Control your ego's judgment, pride, envy, jealousy, and any other response except unconditional love. The first step is to stop denying them in yourself. They are there even if you wish they were not. Acknowledge these parts and embrace them. Make friends with them. Do not criticize yourself, for having them is human and one of the reasons you incarnated. These traits simply do not exist on the soul plane for they are simply ways of getting love, which is unnecessary over there. You learned them as a child as ways of manipulating the world to feel safe. By healing them and removing them from your repertoire of responses, you allow more of the light of soul to shine out.

This two-pronged process shifts us from valuing "what we *have*" to "what we *are*." Many people define themselves by their house, car, bank balance, social position, etc., but this can be dangerous because you can lose these things in a heartbeat. People affected by tornados or earthquakes often say, "I've lost everything," but that's just not true. Of course, our possessions make us feel good, but it's bad positioning. Instead, fall back on your true identity—soul—for you can never lose that.

Switch your focus to those things you value on the soul plane, such as loving relationships, working with truth, and creating and enjoying beauty. Here is a little routine for the start of your day. Begin by asking yourself, "In what ways can I express my soul today? What loving and kind acts can I perform?"

Invoke awareness of your soul as you go about your day, with "I invite you fully into my life so that I feel you constantly." Enjoy the feeling of having your soul fully present during the day, and look for and encourage the presence of soul in others. As always, live in gratitude for the blessings your soul manifests.

If you make the above into a habit, over time, you will find your life begin to shift in wonderful ways:

- You begin to live in openness, vulnerability, and humility. The presence of your soul burns away your personality's sense of self-importance.
- You begin to view the world and your life from the perspective of your soul's immortality rather than your personality's focus on "just one life to live." You generate no karma, because you know that *you* will be the one to have to deal with it, and not some other incarnation.
- You deal with life *as it is* rather than how you think *it should be*. Realism accepts what is; idealism pouts if life doesn't conform to how you want things to be.
- You live with gusto, fully embracing the moment.
- You know yourself, you love yourself, and you live life on your own terms.
- You trust and surrender to your own soul, knowing that it is always operating in your highest and best interest.
- You live selflessly in service to others, with no thought of return.

We must continue to grow, and we can do that in two ways. We can either grow in reaction to fear, limitation and contraction, i.e., we can *run away* from the things that cause pain, or we can grow in response to love and expansion, i.e., we can *run towards* the things that bring us joy.

One of these hurts, the other does not—it's your choice. Your soul wants joy-based growth but, if your ego chooses the pain, know that there is another way. The painful approach works—slowly—if you can quickly identify the behavioral and emotional patterns in your life that bring pain and then dump them as fast as you can. This frees you up to focus on following your joy.

For example, if your job doesn't bring you joy, then find one that does, for then it ceases to be work. Every day brings you joy, which increases your frequency. Easy to say, of course, but Chapter 10 gave you a variety of tools to create change in your life.

Personal growth aside, your primary task is to dispel the fear brought on by humanity's separation from our soul identity. You can do this by spreading knowledge such as in this and other books, through conversation, your own writing, and other outreaches, such as posting to spiritual websites (many of them have bulletin boards).

It is also important to spread love in your everyday interactions, simply by virtue of being the loving person you are (remember the girl and the starfish).

One thing is inescapable—as a Divine Architect, you are a lightworker, and you must do your light work to feel fulfilled. So get out there and spread your light. Wherever you encounter fear, swamp it with love and light. Challenge those who spread fear of earth changes or social collapse, and tell them to expect smooth sailing. Challenge the conspiracy buffs, those afraid of ET encounters, and those who expect to be simply "beamed up" one day. It's just a cop out to avoid taking responsibility for your own growth and doing the work.

Join together with other lightworkers. This decade calls for teamwork. There are events to organize, seminars to put on, and they all require volunteer helpers. You have spent hundreds of lifetimes perfecting your skills for what is happening, so find your part in the Divine Blueprint and engage in the play. Look for the roles that other people are playing and for ways you can work together. Treat your fellow lightworkers as you would if they were family members. They are. Your soul family. Seek them out and ask how you can help them, first making sure that they are "on target" and not chasing some ego-driven agenda.

Is there something you have always wanted to do, such as teach, work in the media, or with books? Maybe that's telling you something. Or you could ask your spirit or guides to arrange an unmistakable synchronous event to show you your way.

Remember that you have probably signed up for a series of assignments, so when one feels complete, let it go rather than hang on out of habit. If a metaphysical study group you belong to begins to unravel, maybe you should let it, for it may already have served its purpose and it's time to move on.

Whatever your actual tasks in life, the most important part of your light work is to love yourself and others unconditionally, and let your example shine forth.

The Divine Architect's Toolkit

Deepak Chopra defines success as the enjoyment of happiness, the realization of worthy goals and the abundant flow of good things to you. It also involves enjoying miracles in your life and the unfolding of your own divinity.

None of this happens accidentally but follows inexorably if we live by certain spiritual laws, which he identifies in his delightful little book, *The Seven Spiritual Laws of Success.* These laws govern how the world we experience manifests from the realm of all unmanifested possibilities. If you know how to work in harmony with these laws, you can influence and guide the reality you experience. (Of course, the laws still operate if you don't know about them, delivering a wonderful life full of loving abundance or fearful monsters, depending on your disposition.) Each of Chopra's seven laws is a wonderful tool in the Divine Architect's toolkit if you know how to use them. Here, we only scratch the surface of the wisdom in his book, and I heartily recommend it as a "must read."

The Law of Pure Potentiality

As spirit, you are infinitely creative, and through silence and non-judgment, can you tap into that. Take time to simply *be*, remaining silent and still for maybe an hour a day. After a little practice, you'll begin to sense the underlying unifying field of creation. An important part of maintaining silence is to stem the flow of inner dialogue that is constantly analyzing, comparing and judging.

The Law of Giving

An essential characteristic of the matrix of Creation is that it's in constant motion, with its components harmoniously exchanging energy and information. One obvious form of energy that flows through the

3-D matrix is money. We talk of "currency in circulation," implying flows and loops of energy. Fear or greed will stop the flow by clogging the channels with stuck, dead energy. The give-and-take within all your relationships is akin to the ebb-and-flow of the tides. You cannot have one without the other. To work with this law, give something in every encounter, be it a kind act or just a prayer. And be open to receive from others, expressing your deepest gratitude for all the blessings in your life.

The Law of Cause and Effect

If you live by the biblical admonition, "As ye sow, so shall ye reap," then every thought, word and deed becomes a conscious act of sowing, performed in full knowledge of what will grow from it. Our lives today are the direct result of yesterday's choices. So what choices are you making *today* out of which will grow tomorrow's reality?

Your personality is simply a bundle of conditioned reflexes, often as unconscious and automatic as dropping something that's hot, and most of us let those reflexes determine how we react to events and other people. The more conscious of this you become, the better you can program for a reality that brings you the most fulfillment.

The Law of Least Effort

A tree doesn't try to grow. It just grows. Vedic wisdom tells us that the slightest intention manifests effortlessly when you are in harmony with the laws of creation and motivated by love. But if you're driven by greed, fear or the ego's need to control, life is an uphill struggle.

So *accept* that things are the way they're *supposed* to be. Second, take *responsibility* for "what is" because you put it there. Thirdly, stop defending yourself and your point of view. When you resist "what is" or blame others for it, you only get more of "what is." Instead, embrace it and merge with it, and you will discover the joyful freedom of effortless ease.

The Law of Intention and Desire

The constant flow of energy and information in the matrix is influenced by your intention and desire. As a sentient species, our advantage is that we can *know* this and apply it consciously. As a vital node in creation's web, you can use the so-called "ripple effect" to influence the local web around you.

It's simple. Whatever you focus on will grow in strength, and what you ignore will wither and die. (This law is totally impartial. If you focus on the pile of unpaid bills, guess what? You'll get more, of course.) If you superimpose your *intention* on the object of your *attention*, you unleash an awesome force to manifest your intent, assuming, of course, that it is in humanity's best interest.

The Law of Detachment

Under this law, you balance detachment to an outcome with focused intent. Attachment is a fear-based need for security. Detachment is a love-based trust in your own spirit's ability to manifest whatever you truly need in your life at that moment.

Attachment to a given outcome denies the universe's infinite power to deliver an even better outcome, just so that you can feel a little more secure. But security is an illusion, for no one really knows what will happen next. However, the search for security is an attachment to the known, and where's the growth in that? A state of uncertainty opens you up to the freedom to create anew, to manifest what was not there before.

The Law of "Dharma," or Purpose in Life

We incarnate here with a specific soul purpose and assemble the needed skills and qualities along the way. When you discover that purpose and apply your unique talents, the resulting creative spark sets the world ablaze and creates great abundance in your life.

Finding your mission is the first part of working with the seventh law. The second part involves expressing your unique talent, which leads to the third part, service to humanity. When you fold in your connection to the field of Pure Potentiality, success is inevitable. And when you discover your divinity, develop your unique talent, and use it to serve humanity, you are in your Dharma.

The foundation of Chopra's principles is the knowledge that we live within a conscious, loving matrix that will support and nurture us if only we let it. So try to sense it all around you, and feel its ebb-and-flow of energy. Try not to block this flow but become an effortless part of it. Then you can imprint your own loving intent on it to guide your interaction with it and with other people. Try also so sense the role in the matrix your soul intends you to play, and move towards that role, for doing so will bring you unparalled joy.

Onward and Upward

Our journey together is almost over. We have seen how we, as pure spirit, need to make periodic field trips to the physical plane for experiences that we cannot get on the soul plane because there, we know we are part of the Divine energy we call God. So we carefully select the circumstances that will best serve those experiences, take up residence in a soon-to-be-born body, and forgot that we are God.

Some souls may just need the birth experience itself. That life will be brief but meaningful to the soul and those other people involved. Or the soul may come in with an extensive "to do" list and live a long, healthy, productive and fulfilling life. Only one thing is sure—no one can or should judge the outcome of anyone else's life, for *only* the soul knows what it meant to accomplish.

We also saw how we can become better game-players by following the advice and example of coaches such as Tony Robbins, until the soul "feels done" down here and readies to return home. Of course, one or more of our loved ones may beat us to it, and we can deal with that either by plunging into grief at our loss or by soaring into celebration at their gain.

When our time comes, we can approach the threshold either fearing the unknown or embracing the uncertainty of the final growth opportunity of the human cycle.

And between birth and death, what have we accomplished? Have we scattered love and light along the path like so much fairy dust, or have we spread darkness and fear? One thing is certain, during your life review on the other side, you *will* be asked how you have helped your fellow man. It's never too late to step up and become the Divine Architect you already are.

"Me? Divine? And an Architect?" some may protest. "Of course you are!" I tell them. "You're here on Earth, aren't you? So it must be true. As a soul, you are a Divine Spark, a vital piece of God, and together we make up what God is. So, of course, you're Divine."

You are also an Architect because you designed your life. You didn't "just happen," because that's not how things work. You came here with a purpose, a mission, and a plan. If you're not on your "sweet spot," as the Kryon energy calls it, it's time you were.

Learn everything you can about who you are, why you are and how you are. But forge out on your own, urging you-the-soul to enter into full partnership with you-the-human, so that you're fully conscious of your relationship.

Finally, relish your Divine Architecture—the good works that you do and the service you perform for the rest of us—and constantly seek new ways to serve Source, giving gratitude for the opportunity to do so. For it is a wondrous opportunity.

You are among the most valiant souls in all Creation. You bravely tackled the most difficult assignment imaginable. You are Divine, yet you volunteered to come to the densest planet *anywhere* and forget your Divinity. Why? For the sheer exhilaration of the Source rediscovering Itself. What a grand game!

You are a Divine Architect and all other souls in Creation salute and honor your bravery and courage. To be human is the greatest challenge there is, but also the greatest gift. Use that gift wisely, dear reader, and let your light blaze brightly as a beacon to the rest of the Cosmos. Celebrate your Divinity, for you are truly a Divine Architect.

Suggested Reading List

Anderson, George, *Lessons from the Light: Extraordinary Messages of Comfort and Hope from the Other Side*, Berkley, 2000

Bernstein, Morey, *The Search for Bridey Murphy*, Doubleday, 1989

Braden, Gregg, *Walking Between the Worlds: The Science of Compassion*, Radio Bookstore Press, 1997

————, *The Isaiah Effect: Decoding the Lost Science of Prayer and Prophecy*, Harmony Books, 2000

Brinkley, Dannion, *Saved by the Light: The True Story of a Man who Died Twice and the Profound Revelations He Received*, Harper, 1995

Carroll, Lee & Tober, Jan, *The Indigo Children: The New Kids Have Arrived*, The Kryon Writings, Inc., 2000

Chopra, Deepak, *The Seven Spiritual Laws of Success*, Amber-Allen/ New World Library, 1993

Cuddeback, Marge, *Vanishing Veil*, Empowering Light, 2001

Dalai Lama & Cutler, Howard, *The Art of Happiness: A Handbook for Living* Riverhead Books, 1998

Dunn, Chris, *The Giza Power Plant*, Bear & Co., 1998

Edward, John, *One Last Time: A Psychic Medium Speaks to Those We Have Loved and Lost*, Berkley Books, 1998

Gerard, Robert, *Change Your DNA, Change Your Life!* Oughten House Foundation, 2000

Goldberg, Bruce, *Past Lives, Future Lives: Accounts of Regressions and Progressions Through Hypnosis*, Newcastle, 1982

Guggenheim, Judy & Bill, *Hello From Heaven*, Bantam Books, 1995

Heald, Martin, *Destiny: The True Story of One Man's Journey Through Life, Death, and Rebirth*, Element, 1997

Kubis, Pat, *Conversations Beyond the Light: With Departed Friends and Colleagues by Electronic Means*, Bridgeport Books, 1996

Kübler-Ross, Elisabeth, *On Life After Death*, Celestial Arts, 1991

MacLaine, Shirley, *The Camino: A Journey of the Spirit*, Pocket Books, 2000

Melchizedek, Drunvalo, *The Ancient Secrets of the Flower of Life, Volumes 1 & 2*, Light Technology Press, 1999 & 2000

Puryear, Anne, *Stephen Lives: My Son–His Life, Suicide, and Afterlife*, Pocket Books, 1996

Perala, Robert, *The Divine Blueprint: Roadmap for the New Millennium*, United Light Publishing, 1998

Rieder, Marge, *Mission to Millboro: A Study in Group Communication*, Blue Dolphin Press, 1993

———, *Return to Millboro: The Reincarnation Drama Continues*, Blue Dolphin Press, 1996

Sitchin, Zecharia, *The 12ᵗʰ Planet*, Bear & Co., 1991

Stubbs, Tony, *An Ascension Handbook*, New Leaf, 1999

Whitton, Dr. Joel & Fisher, Joe, *Life Between Lives*, Warner Books, 1986

Woods, Walda, *Conversations with Tom: An Adventure in After-Death Communication*, White Rose Publishing, 2000

RESOURCES

Anderson, George < http://www.georgeanderson.com>
Boylan, Dr. Richard
       Official website: <http://www.jps.net/drboylan>
       News group: <http://UFOTruth.listbot.com>
Braden, Gregg <http://www.greggbraden.net>
Carroll, Lee <http://www.kryon.com>
Cayce, Edgar < http://www.are-cayce.com>
Chopra, Deepak <http://www.randomhouse.com/features/chopra>
Edward, John
       Official website: <http://www.johnedward.net>
       Crossing Over show: <http://www.scifi.comjohnedward>
Guggenheim, Judy ADC site: <http://www.after-death.com>
MacLaine, Shirley <http://www.shirleymaclaine.com>
Melchizedek, Drunvalo
       Official website: <http://www.drunvalo.net>
       Flower of Life Teachings: <http://www.floweroflife.com>
Michael Teachings:
       <http://www.itstime.com/michael.htm>
       <http://www.summerjoy.com>
       <http://www.pivres.com>
       <http://www.mef.com>
       <http://www.michaelteaching.com>
       <http://www.themichaelteaching.com>
       <http://www.kayheatherly.com>
Oughten House Foundation < http://www.oughtenhouse.com>
Robbins, Tony <http://www.anthonyrobbins.com/trhome.html>
Stubbs, Tony <http://www.tjpublish.com>
Twilight Brigade
       Official website: <http://www.twilightbrigade.org>
United Light Publishing <http://www.unitedlight.com>
Winfrey, Oprah <http://www.oprah.com>
Woods, Walda <http://www.whiterosepublishing.net>
Wright, Serena <http://www.vimana.org>

TONY STUBBS

Tony was born in England in 1947, and after graduating in electronics, worked in the British telecommunications industry. He emigrated to the U.S. in 1979 to continue working with computers. In 1980, he woke up to the world of spirit and immersed himself in metaphysics while continuing a career in computers and desktop publishing.

Tony began channeling and in 1989, the Ascended Master Serapis announced that they were to write a book together: *An Ascension Handbook*, published by Oughten House Publications. Providing a clear and concise explanation of the ascension process, it has enjoyed five printings and is a metaphysical best-seller.

After a period of living in Mexico where he was the editor of an English daily newspaper, Tony moved to Denver, Colorado and started a computer school. He continued with his desktop publishing business while teaching at universities and computer schools in Denver.

Tony then moved to California to join Oughten House Publications as Editor-in-Chief and Director of Operations and is now an independent consultant to authors and small publishers on writing, editing, self-publishing and book production. He can be reached at <tjpublish@aol.com>.

ROBERT PERALA

Robert is an internationally acclaimed speaker, and author of *The Divine Blueprint: Roadmap for the New Millennium*. He originally hails from Saratoga, California, and is considered by many to be one of the most unique clairvoyants in North America. His background includes 23 years of research into the metaphysics, spirituality, the paranormal, past lives, extraterrestrial science, and earth-based anomalies.

He has led expeditions to the sacred sites of Egypt, England, France, and the Far East. While the media has dubbed him "a messenger," he prefers to think of himself as a "spiritual reporter" and motivational speaker. His message? That remarkable changes in consciousness and the world are upon us as we enter a new age of enlightenment.

Robert is a recent graduate of "Mastery University" from The Robbins Research Institute and is the founder of United Light Publishing. He is a sought-after guest on national and international television and radio shows. In honor of Robert's contribution to society, the American Biographical Institute bestowed on him their prestigious Distinguished Leadership Award.

The Divine Blueprint and now *The Divine Architect* are the next logical outlets for this spiritual reporter and his enthralling message. He can be reached at <www.unitedlight.com>.

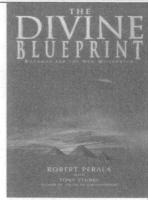

LECTURES AND LIVE ENGAGEMENTS

Robert Perala is an internationally acclaimed author and motivational speaker. Countless audiences have enjoyed his charming and witty style of spiritual teaching throughout the United States, Canada, and abroad. His personal growth results-oriented programs weave together many empowerment techniques and include lectures, full day workshops and the popular weekend "Spirit Bootcamps."

Robert's speaking engagements create an atmosphere of motivation, excitement, and a belief in one's life purpose, creating an experience and a life-changing moment. These are the elements of positive and dynamic change that people hunger for today. As the house lights go down, music fills the room, accompanied by wondrous projected images of world leaders, spiritual shamans, current events, and mystical phenomena.

Presented as highly motivational and visual experiences, Robert's lectures are a magical blend of spirituality, metaphysics, personal growth, and anecdotes for living that take the audience to a place of love, hope, and wonder.

For more information and reservations in Robert's lectures, workshops, and weekend Spirit Bootcamps, visit us online at www.unitedlight.com.